JOHN BOGLE AND THE VANGUARD EXPERIMENT

JOHN BOGLE AND THE VANGUARD EXPERIMENT

One Man's Quest to Transform the Mutual Fund Industry

Robert Slater

IRWIN
Professional Publishing®
Chicago • London • Singapore

This publication is designed to provide accurate and
authoritative information in regard to the subject matter
covered. It is sold with the understanding that neither the
author or the publisher is engaged in rendering legal, accounting,
or other professional service. If legal advice or other expert
assistance is required, the services of a competent professional
person should be sought.

From a Declaration of Principles jointly adopted by a Committee
of the American Bar Association and a Committee of Publishers.

Times Mirror
Higher Education Group

Library of Congress Cataloging-in-Publication Data

Slater, Robert, 1943–
    John Bogle and the Vanguard experiment : one man's quest to transform the
mutual fund industry / Robert Slater.
        p.   cm.
    Includes bibliographical references and index.
    ISBN 0-7863-0559-2
    1. Vanguard Group of Investment Companies—History.   2. Mutual
funds—United States—History.   3. Bogle, John C.   I. Title.
    HG4930.S47   1996
    332.63'27—dc20   95-52838

Printed in the United States of America
1 2 3 4 5 6 7 8 9 DO 3 2 1 0 9 8 7 6

Acknowledgments

THE IDEA for *John Bogle and the Vanguard Experiment: One Man's Quest to Transform the Mutual Fund Industry* came from John C. (Jack) Bogle, the founder of the Vanguard Group of Investment Companies. He favored such a project as a way of pulling together the corporate history of this remarkable enterprise and providing an orderly road map of his own philosophy and values for future generations. Bogle relishes his role as "conscience of the mutual fund industry" and prides himself on founding Vanguard and developing it into one of the nation's most remarkable business enterprises. As he neared retirement, he was ready to cooperate with a book that would delve into the unique, compelling, and controversial world of Vanguard. Bogle put the idea to the publisher of his mutual fund guide, *Bogle on Mutual Funds,* Irwin Professional Publishing, which happened to be my publisher as well. Happily for me, Irwin asked me to take on the assignment.

I was pleased to immerse myself in this subject for a number of reasons.

While working on previous business book projects, I had come to appreciate the fact that during the 1980s and 90s millions of Americans had become "players," however large or small, in the mutual fund industry. And yet while the industry was the fastest-growing segment of American business, it was also one of the least scrutinized. Investors had a pretty good idea of the various kinds of mutual funds, but few had much insight into the large mutual fund companies, how they operate, what challenges they face, and what their philosophies and strategies are.

The more that Americans began to put their trust in mutual fund companies, the more crucial it became to take a close look at their operations.

A book on Jack Bogle and Vanguard, therefore, made a lot of sense to me. That few others had written about mutual fund personalities struck me as one more reason to write *John Bogle and the Vanguard Experiment.* Books on the mutual fund field exist, of course, but they have focused almost exclusively on the advice-giving side, explaining what mutual funds are and giving suggestions about the best strategies when investing in mutual funds. What sets this book apart is that it is the first authorized inside look at a major mutual fund company.

When I met Jack Bogle for the first time in his office at Vanguard's headquarters in Malvern, Pennsylvania, we agreed that the project would be mine, and not Vanguard's; that is to say, that I would enjoy a free hand in writing whatever I saw fit to write, by including whatever material I deemed important and omitting whatever I thought irrelevant or uninteresting. As if to underline the independence I would enjoy in researching the book, Bogle permitted me to peruse a box-load of confidential documents dating back to the founding of the company in 1975, documents that portrayed a whole array of Vanguard personalities, including Bogle, sometimes in a negative light. I was also able to interview Bogle at length about the most unpleasant period of his career, his dismissal as head of Wellington Management Company in early 1974, an event he has never spoken about in public until now. I was able to interview other participants in that event as well. In allowing me full rein, Bogle arranged for me to interview the heart specialist, Dr. Bernard Lown, who treated his heart ailment for a number of years. Lown's candor in discussing the precise details of Bogle's heart condition helped me to report on one of the most private parts of Bogle's life.

Most important, Jack Bogle promised that I would have access to him. We did not discuss at our first meeting how much time he would give me; as it turned out, I conducted 30 hours of interviews with him spread over a nine-month period (February to November 1995). In addition, Bogle made sure that I had access to as many of Vanguard's employees as I wished to interview, including his top executives. I was also able to talk to Vanguard board members, past and present. And, to gauge Vanguard's reputation within the mutual fund industry, I spoke with a number of industry leaders as well as academic experts.

■ ■ ■

I am indebted to a number of people, both at Vanguard and elsewhere, for giving of their time generously for the research of this book.

First and foremost, to Jack Bogle. We met in different places, sometimes at his office at Vanguard headquarters; sometimes at his summer home in Lake Placid, New York. We had long phone conversations as well, some of them while he was in a Philadelphia hospital awaiting a heart transplant.

My research spanned one of the busiest and most challenging periods for Bogle—including the announcement of his retirement in May 1995, turning over the leadership to Jack Brennan, and subsequently, Bogle's stay in a heart transplant ward. Though Bogle's time was limited, he treated this book as a top priority. In my previous book projects, I have rarely been able to sense how important my project was to the person about whom I was writing; in the case of this book, I could feel and see how large a priority it was for Bogle. That knowledge gave me an even greater sense of responsibility to do the best job possible.

I want to give special thanks to Jack Brennan, who in early 1996 became Vanguard's new chief executive officer. For a number of years Bogle's heir-apparent, Brennan granted me a number of lengthy interviews; his insights have been particularly useful to me and have helped to shape this book in many ways. And I want to express my gratitude to Walter L. Morgan, who founded the Wellington organization, Vanguard's forerunner, in the late 1920s, and who continues to work at his office at Vanguard headquarters at the age of 97. I met with Morgan on a number of occasions and learned a good deal about the early days of Wellington as well as of the entire mutual fund industry.

Jim Norris, Jack Bogle's assistant, played an important role in this book, adding to my understanding of Vanguard considerably and providing me with a continuing stream of facts and figures. I am very grateful to him.

I also want to express my gratitude to the other people I interviewed both inside and outside of Vanguard. They are: Peter Bernstein, John C. Bogle, Jr., Mike Brascetta, Robert W. Doran, Jeremy G. Duffield, Matthew Fink, Richard Fentin, Philip J. Fina, Jon S. Fossel, James French, James H. Gately, Nick Giangulio, T. Chandler Hardwick, Barbara B. Hauptfuher, John T. Jackson, Raymond J. Klapinsky, A. Michael Lipper, Deborah Lockwood, Bernard Lown, Peter Lynch, Ian A. MacKinnon, Burton G. Malkiel, Kenneth G. Martin, Brian S. Mattes, F. William McNabb III, Duncan M. McFarland, Daniel C. Maclean, Sid Mendelsohn, Paul F. Miller, Jr., John B. Neff, George Putnam, James S. Riepe, Charles D. Root, Jr., Paul Samuelson, George U. "Gus" Sauter, Barbara Scudder,

John J. F. Sherrerd, David Silver, Stan Swalla, Jan Twardowski, Karen E. West, Arthur Zeikel, Daniel P. Wiener, and Dena G. Willmore. I also wish to thank the countless others who helped to explain Vanguard to me during my visits to its headquarters, especially Vickie Leinhauser, Emily Snyder, and Leanor Silver.

Various friends and family members provided me with moral and other support during the writing of this book. They are: Jack and Bea Slater, Roslyn and Judd Winick, Michael and Bobbi Winick, Mitchell Slater and Leslie Dickstein, Mel and Anat Laytner, and Jean Max. A warm thank you.

I was blessed with a wonderful editor for this book: Amy Gaber, the Executive Editor at Irwin Professional Publishing. She not only brought her considerable knowledge of Vanguard and the mutual fund industry to our project, but also engaged in an ongoing dialogue with me about the subject matter as part of the process of improving the manuscript. Her editing talents are in great evidence throughout the book and I thank her very much. I also want to thank Jeffrey Krames, Editor-in-Chief at Irwin Professional Publishing, who urged to me write this book and who made it possible.

To my family, a very warm thank you. To my wife Elinor, my children Miriam, Shimi, Adam, and Rachel; and to my grandson Edo, I am grateful for all the help and support I received while writing this book.

Robert Slater

Introduction

J OHN C. BOGLE, a lover of military, naval, and aviation history, has taken part in many battles of his own throughout his life. Some have been personal, particularly a series of debilitating heart attacks; others have been on the field of business, including the ill-fated merger he engineered between his mutual fund firm, Wellington Management Company—which Bogle had been selected to lead by its founder, Walter L. Morgan—and a high-achieving Boston investment-counseling firm, whose partners eventually would mount a successful campaign to fire him from his post as Wellington's president and CEO.

For Jack Bogle, the battles in which he has engaged have, more often than not, ended triumphantly. Despite the gloomy prognoses of the many cardiologists who treated him throughout his life, Bogle was still thriving 35 years after his first heart failure. Following his ouster from Wellington Management Company, Bogle moved on to found The Vanguard Group of Investment Companies and build it into a powerhouse with few equals in the mutual fund industry. Most important of all, Bogle led numerous efforts, many of them successful, to end what he saw as the overall greed of the mutual fund industry, its excessive claims of investment management success, and its lack of candor in advertising and marketing.

On May 8, 1995, when Bogle turned 66, he decided it was time to turn Vanguard's reins over to the next generation. Medically speaking, Bogle was a walking miracle. When he suffered his first heart attack at the age of 31, his cardiologists believed he would not live to see 40; Bogle, a bit more optimistic, told friends that he doubted he would make 50. Not surprisingly, at least to those who know him, he defied the odds, blessed by what doctors called the Jack Bogle Factor—an incredibly strong will to survive. Nonetheless, Bogle had long considered the day when his business career would end and he would no longer report to the office to command the crew, as he liked to call Vanguard's employees. At the same time, it saddened him to think that he would no longer be able to challenge his colleagues at other mutual fund companies so fervently in his quest to transform the mutual fund industry.

As Bogle considered his decision over the next few days, he knew he wanted to assume a greatly diminished role in Vanguard's leadership only when Vanguard was in as strong a position as possible, and the time was right. As Vanguard approached its 20th anniversary, it was enjoying its best year ever. Assets under management—a mere $1.4 billion at the firm's inception—surpassed $150 billion on May 16, 1995, making Vanguard the second largest mutual fund company in the United States, behind Fidelity Investments. Index funds, long scorned by the industry, had finally begun to gain acceptance, and the media were praising Bogle for introducing index funds into the industry and championing their cause. Finally, the company's conservative investment strategies, as well as its mutual funds, were being applauded for their high performance rankings, and the firm was winning legions of new clients, now some 5 million in all.

For the past two decades, Bogle had been the dominant influence in building one of the largest and most successful mutual fund companies in the world. He was an intimidating presence in the company, and while he sought counsel and listened to the advice of his associates, the company was no democracy. In the end, it was usually his vote that counted. If he seemed difficult to work for and if his ego made him seem self-righteous, his crew members gave him their full support—not simply out of loyalty, but because he was right about so many things so much of the time. And being right, in a climate of unprecedented bull markets in stocks and bonds, he presided over a long period of prosperity at Vanguard. While all of the mutual fund leaders in the industry made strident declarations about caring for their shareholders and employees, none was as zealous as Bogle.

Thus, as Bogle prepared to leave the arena he loved so much, the moment was bittersweet. Eleven days after his 66th birthday, he walked into the boardroom at Vanguard's new headquarters in Malvern, Pennsylvania, and announced to the company's nine other board members that he wished to step down as chief executive officer effective January 31, 1996, but with the board's consent would like to remain as chairman. Bogle further announced that he planned to nominate his heir apparent, John J. Brennan, to succeed him as CEO. It obviously gave him no pleasure to give up the command of Vanguard, and he insisted that he would "still be around as chairman, watching over the interests of shareholders and the crew, remaining involved in investment policy, writing annual reports, and speaking out in public on shareholder issues."

When Bogle founded Vanguard in 1974, he often referred to it as the Vanguard experiment. His goal was to establish a mutual fund company that was like no other in the industry. Until Bogle came along, the conventional mutual fund company employed a management company to direct the activities of its mutual funds, including administration, distribution, and investment counseling services. Bogle, on the other hand, came to believe that shareholders were being shortchanged under such a system, and that they would be treated fairly only if power were taken from the management company and placed directly in the hands of the independent directors and shareholders of the funds.

By seeking to have Wellington Management Company—Vanguard's predecessor—relinquish its near-total control over its mutual funds, Bogle embarked on an experiment that at first seemed to have little chance of success. He got his chance to put his plan into action when Wellington fired him in 1974. In the wake of the skirmishes and bad blood that surrounded his dismissal from Wellington Management Company, Bogle built a new mutual fund company based on his unconventional model. It would be the first time anyone in charge of a mutual fund company had challenged the status quo, that is, the belief that management companies deserved to reap enormous profits at the expense of their fund investors. But controversial as it was, Bogle's conception of the perfect mutual fund company became a reality.

As he prepared to step down as chief executive officer of Vanguard, Bogle was proud that the Vanguard experiment had come so far: Vanguard was the largest pure no-load mutual fund organization in the world and a dominant player in what had become a $2.8 trillion industry. Quite literally, mutual funds had revolutionized the way many Americans provided for their future and the way in which they thought about investing and the financial markets. Bogle, however, felt a lingering sense of disappointment and frustration that his larger dream—to transform the mutual fund industry into Vanguard's image—had yet to be realized.

While the industry had changed somewhat as a result of his preachings—becoming aware of cost competition, considering some sharing with fund shareholders of the economies of scale that were generating enormous profits for fund management companies, and beginning to exhibit a new sense of candor and responsibility—Bogle still was not satisfied.

After all, Vanguard remained, for the most part, a leader without followers. Bogle believed that only when mutual fund companies liberated themselves from their management companies would the interests of all mutual fund shareholders truly come first. He optimistically predicted that this restructuring would occur within the next 25 years.

Had Bogle been a minor player in the industry, his colleagues at other firms, who were earning huge profits from the status quo, could have dismissed his jeremiads. To their regret, however, Vanguard was too much of a presence in the industry for Bogle to be easily dismissed. His company had become a benchmark, an industry standard on many different levels, from its minuscule expense ratios, to the candor of the descriptions of its funds' returns and risks in annual reports, to the investment accomplishments of its mutual funds. Indeed, in mid-1995, Vanguard was increasingly regarded as the number one mutual fund family in the industry. In short, Bogle's quest to remake the mutual fund industry was showing signs of success, but only when the first Vanguard clones appeared would Bogle acknowledge that the Vanguard experiment had truly succeeded.

This book is the story of Jack Bogle—a man both revered and reviled—and the Vanguard experiment, his quest to transform the mutual fund industry.

Contents

1

"I THOUGHT I WAS IN HEAVEN"

WILLIAM YATES BOGLE, JR., WAS BORN in Montclair, New Jersey, in 1896. In 1924 he married Josephine Lorraine Hipkins, born in Brooklyn also in 1896. In the early years of their marriage, the Bogles lived a well-to-do existence in a spacious home in Verona, New Jersey, a bedroom community not far from New York City. Their first son, William Yates Bogle III, was born in 1927. Then, on May 8, 1929, Josephine gave birth to twins—John Clifton ("Jack") and David Caldwell—named after their maternal grandfather and great-grandfather.

Jack Bogle remembers his mother as a beautiful woman with a sparkling personality and her own special charm; his father, above all else, was a dashing aviator, having served as a pilot in the British Royal Flying Corps during World War I. He recounted that his father was often called the Prince of Wales by his friends, in part because of his strong physical resemblance to the prince, and in part because of his high living style. No matter what else Jack would learn about his father, his war service was enough for Jack to put him on a pedestal. Jack's first model of a successful businessman, however, was his grandfather, William Yates Bogle, Sr., who had founded the American Brick Corporation and cofounded the American Can Company (later Primerica). When Jack's father returned from the war, he worked first for American Brick, then for American Can. In both of these jobs he prospered, and the family enjoyed a genteel life.

Then came the 1929 stock market crash, which had a nearly disastrous effect on the Bogles, wiping out the family's inheritance. The harsh new economic realities of the ensuing depression forced the family to sell their home. As the depression wore on, and Jack entered childhood, he came to realize that he was the son of no-longer-wealthy parents, and he developed a sense that life was precarious—especially financially.

As a result of the family's setbacks, Jack came to equate financial insecurity with weakness and having money with success. He became determined to help his family restore the Bogle legacy and to help his parents regain their financial security. All three boys held down time-consuming jobs at early ages. By age 10, Jack was delivering newspapers and magazines (*The Ladies' Home Journal, Collier's,* and *The Saturday Evening Post*) and working at an ice cream parlor. Although the jobs suggested only modest responsibility, Jack was relentless about them: "I wouldn't slacken. I didn't just get the job done. I was super-responsible." By the time they were 16 (and Bill had joined the U.S. Marine Corps), Jack and David were working summers in Bay Head, New Jersey, dropping mail into the U.S. Post Office's interior mailboxes for summer residents. Paid $1.04 an hour, Jack recalled his delight at crossing his "first wage milestone: more than $1.00 an hour!"

Like many Americans who drew lessons from the depression, Bogle had plenty of reasons to avoid recklessness with money, to resist get-rich-quick offers, and to protect whatever money he had saved. Having watched his parents and many of their friends sink into a financial abyss, he vowed that he would take the conservative path in whatever career he pursued. More important, his parents' financial losses turned him into a driven young man.

■ ■ ■

Jack and David spent their freshman and sophomore years at Manasquan High School on the New Jersey shore, as had their older brother Bill before he went on to spend a year attending Blair Academy, a prestigious boarding school located in Blairstown, New Jersey. Jack's academic record during his sophomore year was excellent: A's in English, the sciences, and math; B's in mechanical drawing, typing, and physical education. His character was described as excellent; his personality as pleasing; his industry and ability as above average.

Beneath the surface, though, Jack's home life was turbulent. His father had become a heavy drinker and early in the 1940s lost his job at American Can. A few years later he separated from Josephine. (Both died in 1952 at the age of 56.) At least on the surface, Jack forgave his father, whom he considered a wonderful man who had done his best to take care of his family. Josephine, however, became the dominant figure in Jack's life as she struggled to keep the family together and functioning.

Even as a teenager, Jack yearned for an environment that would allow him to create his own identity and succeed on his own merits. His mother helped to provide him with such an environment when she decided that the twins, like their older brother, should transfer to Blair Academy. Josephine's brother, investment banker Clifton Armstrong Hipkins, arranged for both Jack and David to obtain work scholarships at Blair.

Founded in 1848, Blair Academy was an all-boys school with an enrollment of 300 during Jack's junior and senior years. Although Blair was no boot camp in Jack's day, it had some of the ambience of a military school. Students rose at 6:00, attended classes, worked at part-time jobs on campus, and hurried to complete their homework before lights out at 10:00. Pampered students would have found Blair stifling, but Jack thrived in the atmosphere. Attending Blair, he said later, was the signal event of his life.

Jack must have found it a relief to get away from his tenuous life at home. At Blair, he got his first chance to show what he could do—in academics, athletics, and the jobs he took to maintain his scholarship—and he was determined to make the most of the experience. He was driven to make his mark at Blair, to attain good grades, to please his parents, and to attend college.

Both in the classroom and on the athletic field, Jack's self-confidence grew as he found that he could not only compete with his fellow students but also outshine them in many endeavors. He showed competitiveness and ambition, qualities he would exhibit throughout his life. He had to excel at anything in which he participated. Even when waiting on tables, Jack wanted to be the best, and soon became captain of the student waiters. He came to hate the idea of defeat; winning, no matter what the obstacles, became a part of his makeup.

Jack had a particular aptitude for math. Numbers fascinated him; he could look at a stack of figures and point out an error in the computation before anyone else had started to work on the problem. He could analyze mathematical problems in his head and arrive at answers long before other students, using pencil and paper, could. His ability to use a slide rule became his trademark.

In 1947 Jack graduated from Blair *cum laude*. Although his senior classmates voted him most likely to succeed as well as best student, he failed by a fraction of a percentage point to be named class valedictorian. Jack was so determined to succeed that he regarded number two (he was named class salutatorian) as a stinging defeat. He visited several of his teachers and urged them to reconsider his grades so that he could graduate number one. None would. (Even now, he does not think number two is good enough, often citing the crossword-puzzle definition of "came in second," which is "lost.")

Bogle came to believe that he owed his greatest debt to Blair Academy. His success there enabled him to attend a top-ranking college, without which he may not have accomplished as much as he did in later life. As a result, repaying Blair became of great importance to him, and the bulk of his charitable contributions would be directed to Blair, eventually making him the largest single contributor in Blair's 148-year history. In 1972 he joined the board of trustees of Blair and has served as its chairman since 1986.

Because of the family's limited finances, only one of the Bogle boys could attend college; the two other brothers would have to work to help support the family. With little discussion, it was understood that Jack would be the one to attend college while David and Bill would help the Bogle family keep above water financially. Against this backdrop of responsibility and guilt, Jack became even more motivated, more determined that nothing should interfere with his success.

Jack's academic achievements at Blair qualified him to apply to top colleges, including Williams College and Haverford College, but he ultimately decided on Princeton University, which offered a generous scholarship and student jobs that together would cover all of his expenses. In his determined frame of mind, he sifted through the Princeton curriculum, majoring in economics but discovering Shakespeare, English history, and, for the first time, art history. A few courses gave him trouble. Despite his aptitude for mathematics, he found calculus a challenge, and a course in international trade was no snap. (In later years, he quipped that perhaps he owed his skepticism about investing in foreign markets to the troubles he encountered in that course.)

THE TWINS

Throughout their adult lives, the Bogle twins remained close. They engaged in friendly competition over who could complete the Sunday *New York Times* crossword puzzle first, one often phoning on Monday morning to help the other finish. Long after he graduated from college, Jack felt grateful for David's sacrifice, even mentioning it when he eulogized David, who died suddenly in December 1994. In the eulogy, Jack described himself as "the more competitive, determined, egocentric, introverted twin" and David as "the warmer, more caring, outgoing soul who seemed to place everyone else's concerns ahead of his own." Bogle went on to say, "By reason of family circumstances, David did not go on to college. But let me make it clear to you, as I always did to him, that he was more intelligent and, finally, better educated— a self-taught scholar, a voracious reader, a competent writer—than most of us who had the advantages of a Princeton education." He went on to muse about success, implicitly comparing himself with his twin: "Success is an elusive concept. David was wise enough to realize that success has little to do with money, with starting a business that grows . . . or even with writing a book. What success has to do with, I think, is personal integrity, good citizenship, giving joy and comfort and support to others . . . On all counts, David was an extraordinary success. I know that he was proud of me; you should know that I was even more proud of him."

In the economics department, Bogle particularly enjoyed the introductory course in economics, a course on money and banking, and a course on the history of economics. Paul Samuelson's now-classic textbook *Economics: An Introductory Analysis,* published in 1948 when Bogle was a sophomore, affected him more than any other textbook. He recalled, "It opened my eyes to the world of economics, a world I never knew existed. I knew what earning and saving money was, but I never thought about economics as a body of lore, quasi-scientific or scientific." As it happened, in 1993 Professor Samuelson would write the foreword to Bogle's best-selling book, *Bogle on Mutual Funds: New Perspectives for the Intelligent Investor.*

During his early years at Princeton, Bogle had difficulty getting top grades. Though he ended his freshman year with a B average, by the end of the first semester of his sophomore year he had only a C average, the minimum he needed to keep his scholarship. Pulling himself together, he achieved a B average by the end of his sophomore year, then a B+ average a year later. In addition to classes and studying, he waited tables and later worked at the university athletic ticket office, becoming manager for his junior and senior years, when he sometimes worked 30 hours a week to fulfill the requirements of his work scholarship.

It was during his college years that Bogle initially became fascinated with the written word—and learned an enduring lesson. To boost his income, Bogle asked a college acquaintance to arrange an interview for a summer job with the managing editor of the *Philadelphia Bulletin*. Paid the then-princely sum of $40 a week, he covered the police beat out of the 10th and Jefferson Streets precinct as a stringer. To cover the news in person, he had to take the trolley around the city. Early one Sunday morning, he learned that word of a house fire had reached the police station. Tired from the previous night's reporting, he called the story in to the newspaper from the police station without going to the actual site. Unfortunately, the only fact he had correct was the address. A perceptive rewrite man caught on and asked Bogle the color of the house. Of course the embarrassed stringer had no idea. The experience provided Bogle a lesson that would last a lifetime: "Not just to tell the whole truth and nothing but the truth. More than that, the lesson was to skip the shortcuts." In later years, he would treat the pursuit of truth and integrity with a kind of religious zeal.

By his junior year, Bogle had stepped up his search for something that would set him on a path to success. The search bore fruit when he began thinking about a topic for his senior thesis in fulfillment of his economics major. He was determined to tackle a subject that had not been analyzed to death by hundreds of other economics majors. One day he was browsing through magazines in the university library when he came upon an article headlined "Big Money in Boston" in the December 1949 issue of *Fortune*. The article examined Massachusetts Investors Trust, which, with assets of $100 million, was then the largest mutual fund in the United States.

Few people at that time had heard of the mutual fund industry; small and centered in Boston, it had only $2 billion in assets under management. Noting that the industry represented only about 1 percent of the total savings of American families, the article acknowledged that "mutual funds may look like pretty small change." But *Fortune* concluded that the mutual fund industry was "a rapidly expanding and somewhat contentious indus-try of great potential significance to U.S. business." Bogle was intrigued by the combination of a bland present ("small change") and a bright future ("great potential significance"); he decided that he had found his thesis topic. The thesis would give him the opportunity to conduct original research, apply his writing skills, and learn in depth about an emerging industry. In retrospect, he later said about his fortuitous finding of such a provocative topic: "I thought I was in heaven."

Bogle spent his junior and senior years working on the project. During his senior year he had an A average, and in June 1951 he graduated from Princeton *magna cum laude,* in large part because his 123-page thesis, "The Economic Role of the Investment Company," received a grade of A+. In later years, what most impressed readers of Bogle's thesis were his prescience and his understanding of this infant industry. Not only did he demonstrate a grasp of how the industry worked, he knew enough of its strengths and weaknesses to offer prescriptions for its future. It was as if the thesis had been drafted not by a college student but by the head of a mutual fund company.

The thesis provided an early glimpse of the principles that would serve as the intellectual contours for The Vanguard Group. Bogle predicted that the then-nascent industry was set for a giant leap forward. "The investment company," Bogle concluded, "can realize its optimum economic role by the exercise of its dual function: to contribute to the growth of the economy, and to enable individual as well as institutional investors to have a share in this growth."

The thesis argued in favor of many concepts that were to become pivotal many years later at Vanguard, including (1) serving investors with efficiency, honesty, and candor; (2) being innovative in developing new funds and opening institutional markets; (3) curtailing advertising abuses, "since investors who are misled will not buy more mutual fund shares"; and, finally, (4) focusing on costs as a crucial factor in the choice of an investment. (Bogle anticipated his later interest in low costs when he wrote: "The investment company has grown up to now by concentrating it sales power on the prospering stratum of the economy; perhaps its future growth can be maximized by a concentration on a reduction of sales loads and management fees.")

Bogle went on in his thesis to chastise mutual fund companies for concentrating their efforts on marketing their funds rather than on serving the interests of investors. He noted that investment companies should avoid creating "the expectation of miracles from management . . . and make no claim for superiority over the market averages" (a precursor to his later interest in matching the market with an index fund). He further noted that "to minimize investors' misconceptions, the mutual fund industry must state fund objectives explicitly." He finished this argument, as if anticipating his later concern that the industry's interest in asset gathering was supplanting its focus on its responsibility of trusteeship, with this citation: "the principal function of investment companies is the management of their portfolios. Everything else is incidental to the performance of this function."

The Bogle philosophy was in place, etched by a 21-year old who was preaching to an industry he knew only as an outsider.

C H A P T E R

THE MUTUAL
FUND PIONEER

WALTER L. MORGAN BEGAN HIS LEGENDARY CAREER in
the mutual fund business in the 1920s when he founded
the Wellington organization, the forerunner of Vanguard.
By the time he stepped down as chairman of Wellington
Management Company in 1967, then three years later as
chairman of Wellington Fund, he had become one of the longest-serving
leaders in the mutual fund industry and one of the longest-serving presi-
dents of any American corporation. He still appears two times a week at
the Wellington Management Company offices, part of the Vanguard
complex in Malvern, Pennsylvania. The only mutual fund pioneer who has
been alive longer is Philip L. Carret, founder of the Pioneer Fund in 1928,
who turned 99 in November 1995.

Born in Wilkes-Barre, Pennsylvania, on July 23, 1898, Morgan learned
at an early age what a miserable experience it was to lose money, when
he borrowed money from a family member to buy some oil stock that
proved worthless. Adding salt to the wound were his father's losses in the
stock market and his grandfather's losses in a Montana gold-mining
company and a trolley line. Morgan promised himself that whatever he
did later in life, he would do his best to protect his earnings. He would
never veer from that conservative philosophy.

9

In 1920, Morgan graduated from Princeton University, where he majored in money and banking. But even a Princeton education did not impress his uncle, Charles Loxley, who worked in a brokerage office. "You're not worth a damn to anybody," Loxley told his nephew. "I want you to go out and learn something." Morgan obliged, but only because his uncle found him work at the Philadelphia office of the accounting firm of Peat, Marwick, and Mitchell. There, for $28 a week, Morgan learned as much as he could about how financial statements were produced.

A few years later, Morgan asked for a raise. When he was turned down, he began his own accounting firm, giving investment advice to its numerous clients. Morgan came to believe that he could provide investment guidance more efficiently and profitably by combining accounts into a single large fund. Through such a fund he could offer potential investors a wider range of securities than they could otherwise afford to hold. With the mutual fund industry still in its infancy, Morgan had few colleagues with whom he could converse about his ideas. One was W. Wallace Alexander, the Philadelphia investment counselor who, in 1907, began the Alexander Fund, the progenitor of the mutual fund in the United States.

■ ■ ■

In the late 1920s, most investment companies were closed-end funds. They pooled money from a group of investors and issued a fixed number of shares at an initial offering. Once the initial offering was completed, investors could neither purchase additional shares nor sell their existing shares through the fund company. Instead, they had to buy or sell shares in the stock market through a stockbroker.

The founding of Massachusetts Investors Trust (MIT) in March 1924 marked a radical departure from the closed-end concept. As an "open-end" fund—later called a mutual fund—it continuously offered new shares to investors and redeemed existing shares at their net asset value. This open-end feature gave investors daily liquidity to convert their investments into cash. More important, it gave smaller investors, with little money and expertise, the ability to enjoy the same returns as larger investors by pooling their money and investing it under the watchful eye of a professional investment adviser.

Investors were slow to accept Massachusetts Investors Trust; only some 200 people invested in MIT during its first year of operations. But as other funds appeared, including Incorporated Investors and State Street Investment Trust (all now operate under slightly different names), Walter Morgan began to get the itch to join this new industry by starting his own mutual fund firm. With encouragement from his grandfather, who told him he was better off starting his own business "even if it was a peanut stand," Morgan raised $100,000 to form a mutual fund by pooling his own savings of $25,000 with funds from friends and family. He incorporated his new mutual fund on December 28, 1928, and opened for business the following July.

Morgan was helped in those early days by investment banker A. Moyer Kulp and by Brandon Barringer, head of the investment management division of First Pennsylvania Bank in Philadelphia. Morgan first called his fund the Industrial & Power Securities Corporation, but it was known almost from its inception as Wellington Fund, a designation reflecting Morgan's love of British history and his admiration for the "Iron Duke" of Wellington, who had defeated the French at Waterloo in 1815.

Thus, the three existing funds—MIT, State Street, and Incorporated Investors, all equity funds—were now joined by Morgan's Wellington Fund. Morgan's fund, though, was unique among the open-end funds in that, for safety's sake, it provided substantial allocations (30 percent at the outset) to high-quality corporate and government bonds, rather than investing primarily in common stocks. Hence, it was known as a "balanced" fund, at the time, the only one of its kind offered to the public. By committing a portion of its portfolio to bonds, which were less risky than equities, the balanced fund was meant to appeal to the cautious investor. Adding to the conservative hue of Wellington Fund was Morgan's policy— in contrast with that of the closed-end funds—of avoiding leverage (borrowing against fund assets to magnify its gains or losses), a move aimed at discouraging speculation and risk taking.

In early 1929, hundreds of closed-end investment firms were managing most of the investing public's assets—roughly $7 billion. In contrast, there were only 19 open-end funds like Morgan's, managing a mere $140 million in assets. Many of the closed-end funds, however, were time bombs. Directed by professional managers who were expected to produce miraculous returns, most closed-end funds traded at premiums of 100 percent or even 200 percent over the actual market value of their investments. When the stock market collapsed, many of the funds' premiums quickly turned into discounts, as the funds' shares sold for less than the market value of the investments they held. By 1933, the share prices of closed-end investment firms had plummeted, on average, by 90 percent. Many went bankrupt.

In retrospect, Morgan had chosen the worst time in U.S. financial history to launch a new investment firm. However, because Wellington

Fund's investment policies entailed less risk than those of its competitors, to say nothing of the closed-end funds, it mitigated the effects of the crash on investors. Three factors in particular benefited Wellington Fund: (1) as an unleveraged fund, it did not rely on borrowed money; (2) as an open-end fund, it could redeem shares on demand, eliminating speculative swings from premium to discount; and (3) as a balanced fund, it had a large position in bonds and cash reserves, which cushioned the fund from the steep stock market drop. In fact, during the summer of 1929, Kulp and Barringer, who were the principal investment consultants to the Wellington Fund, had urged Morgan to reduce the company's common stock allocation from 75 percent of its assets to 33 percent. Taking their advice, Morgan sold, for example, Curtis Publishing at $124; three years later the stock was worth $5 a share.

While other investment firms fared miserably in the three-year stock market crash—MIT, for instance, lost more than 60 percent of its asset value—Wellington Fund lost far less and attracted modest public attention. Its assets grew from $100,000 in July 1929 to $500,000 at the end of 1933. Never doubting that his mutual fund was a wise investment choice, Morgan exuded self-confidence: "I knew we could do a better job of investment management for most people than they could do for themselves," he said. Because of the success of funds like Wellington in combating the worst effects of the Great Crash of 1929, most new investment companies founded after that debacle were open-end.

The growth of Wellington Fund led to some changes at Morgan's firm. Its management, which had been handled by W. L. Morgan & Co. from 1929 to 1933, was now in the hands of the newly created Wellington Management Company. Morgan also hired a distribution and management team. As investment dealers in Philadelphia, and then on the rest of the East Coast, began to learn about Wellington Fund and its impressive performance record, its assets started to grow. By December 1934, the fund's assets had reached $600,000; a year later they passed $1 million; four years later, they topped $5 million.

World War II brought new investment opportunities. When Hitler moved into Poland in 1939, Morgan purchased a number of stocks that he correctly predicted would benefit from the fighting. By the end of the war, Wellington Fund's assets had grown to $25 million. With this impressive growth, Morgan needed new staff. He hired Kulp to head the investment management division full-time, and Alvin J. Wilkins, whose firm since 1935 had been the leading seller of Wellington Fund shares, to head the national sales and distribution team. Joseph E. Welch, who had been associated with Wellington Management Company since 1937, became executive vice president. (He would become president in 1959.) Under the leadership of this team of senior executives, the fund's growth continued. In 1949 the fund's assets reached $100 million; within two years assets had nearly doubled, reaching $190 million.

By mid-1951, Wellington Fund was the fourth largest mutual fund in America, and Walter Morgan was clearly established as a pioneer and an industry leader. While Morgan could not have known it at the time, the young fellow Princetonian he was about to hire would, in time, step into his shoes as an industry leader and become a pioneer of a very different sort.

"HE KNOWS MORE ABOUT THE FUND BUSINESS THAN WE DO"

AFTER GRADUATING FROM PRINCETON IN 1951, Jack Bogle narrowed his career options to banking and investments. He was finding it difficult to choose between offers from the Philadelphia National Bank and Boenning & Company, an old-line Philadelphia brokerage firm, when a third offer arose. During Bogle's senior year at Princeton, Walter M. Geisler, the manager of Elm Club, Bogle's campus dining club, encountered Princeton graduate Walter Morgan and suggested that he hire Bogle, referencing Bogle's thesis on the mutual fund industry. Initially, Morgan resisted, believing that Princeton students were spoiled, but eventually he agreed to have his staff interview Bogle—still with no intention of hiring him.

The interview was conducted by two senior Wellington executives, A. Moyer Kulp and Joseph Welch. They were impressed enough by

Bogle's thesis to suggest that Morgan read it as well. Morgan was fascinated by Bogle's astute observations on the industry, still a tiny one with just 100 funds and roughly $2.5 billion in assets. Morgan observed to his associates, "He knows more about the fund business than we do." Morgan marked the thesis with notations and sent it to Wellington's 50 employees, urging them to pay attention to Bogle's views.

Bogle was coy during the interview process, letting the firm know that others were courting him and that he had a solid offer from a bank. Morgan, in turn, toyed with Bogle, saying, "I don't know what we're going to do with you. We don't need anybody." But he had already decided to hire Bogle, so at last he pulled out all the stops: "Jack, you'll never get anywhere in a bank. Join us. We're a growing company. You'll be one of the top guys eventually."

Bogle was in a quandary. He was flattered by Morgan's interest, but he knew that banks offered a great deal of stability—in 5 or 10 years the bank would still be there and so would his job, important considerations for someone who valued stability as much as Bogle did. The little-known mutual fund industry was somewhat disreputable at the time, a holdover from the days of those risky, highly leveraged closed-end funds that had collapsed with the stock market in 1929. But Bogle also had some reservations about taking the bank job. The bank seemed old-fashioned, and although he had conservative instincts dating back to his childhood experiences in the depression era, Bogle had an adventuresome streak as well. He longed for the chance to be creative, to be entrepreneurial, and a bank was unlikely to give him that chance.

Hoping for clarity, he talked to his cousin, Edward L. Winpenny, who worked as a research analyst and broker, but instead he got the ambiguity he deserved: "You wrote a thesis about the mutual fund business," his cousin reminded him, "so you ought to be able to figure out if you want to be in the business or not. You should be able to figure out better than anyone else how to deal with the risk." The more Bogle contemplated his options, the less concerned he became about the risks of accepting Morgan's offer. Bogle began to see the mutual fund industry as brimming with opportunity, and although Wellington was a small company, it seemed poised to expand and diversify. He decided to accept the Wellington offer.

In mid-1951, the entire mutual fund industry had only 1 million shareholder accounts and managed just $3 billion in assets. The industry was small in comparison with the $54 billion in life insurance reserves, $74 billion in savings deposits, and $50 billion in U.S. savings bonds. Put differently, mutual funds managed only about 1.5 percent of the $178

billion total of these savings programs. Just two top funds at the time—
Massachusetts Investors Trust and Investors Mutual—accounted for 25
percent of the industry's assets.

The mutual fund industry in the 1950s was not only small but witness
to a great shakeout as well. By mid-1955, the combined market value of
Massachusetts Investors Trust and Investors Mutual families fell to 3
percent of the industry. As companies came and went, investors often
never had a chance to learn their names. Of the top 20 firms in the industry
in 1951, 7 ceased to exist by the 1990s, including some of the early giants.
Others not only survived but prospered, and are today household names.
In 1951, for instance, Fidelity Investments, with assets of $64 million and
a market share of 2 percent, ranked number 16 in the industry; today
Fidelity, with a market share of 12 percent, is the largest fund complex
in the nation. Fund assets under management at Franklin Resources were
$2.5 million; at T. Rowe Price, $1.2 million; and at Dreyfus, a paltry
$800,000—a total of $4.5 million and an aggregate market share of one-
tenth of 1 percent. By mid-1995 these three companies' combined assets
had soared to $210 billion, a 9 percent share of market.

Bogle went to work for Wellington on July 5, 1951. At the time, the
company managed only Wellington Fund, with net assets of $194 million
and a 6.2 percent share of the industry's assets. Years later, Walter Morgan
would call hiring Bogle "the best thing I ever did in my life in connection
with Wellington Fund." Besides being impressed with Bogle's academic
credentials, Morgan liked the fact that he was young and inexperienced,
for he enjoyed hiring young people and letting them prove themselves on
the job—a trademark he would pass on to Bogle. Bogle always remembered the chance Morgan gave him when Morgan, "a loyal Princetonian,
took on a shy, crew-cut, boyish-looking, insecure, energetic, serious, and
terribly ambitious young man and gave him his first break." Bogle always
stayed in close touch with Morgan over the years, and in May 1995
personally delivered to Morgan the news that Wellington Fund had surpassed the $10 billion mark—just one in a series of milestones the two
had celebrated together.

Bogle initially began work at the Wellington organization's office on
Walnut Street in Philadelphia. Still not quite sure what to do with him,
Morgan stuck him, in Morgan's words, over in the corner. Bogle needed
little time, though, to get Wellington's senior management to take notice
of him. He was intelligent, he understood the functions of each of the
departments, and he showed no hesitation about busying himself in the
work of those departments.

James C. French, who would later rise to senior vice president for equity trading, joined Wellington just days before Bogle did. When Bogle arrived, he took an empty desk in French's office. Joseph Welch, Wellington's executive vice president, gave the two some clerical work to do. At the time, in an effort to boost fund sales, Wellington Fund had just begun to offer a program that permitted shareholders to automatically reinvest their dividends at the fund's net asset value. Welch assigned to Bogle and French the task of demonstrating the plan's benefits by showing, for example, what a $10,000 investment made 15 years earlier would have been worth in 1951 with all dividends reinvested. As they went through the calculations, Bogle made a bet that he could perform the calculations more quickly with his slide rule than "Frenchy" could with his state-of-the-art rotary calculator. Bogle won the bet.

Bogle and French were responsible as well for calculating the average cost of each investment held by Wellington Fund. To calculate the fund's net asset value, brokers phoned twice a day—once at midday and again when the markets closed—and gave the prices of each of the fund's investments to the accounting department. At the end of each week, French, using his calculator, would calculate the average costs, while Bogle checked the calculations with his slide rule. After a few months of this kind of clerical work, Bogle was promoted, given the task of assisting Morgan with writing fund reports, corresponding with shareholders, and carrying out a variety of administrative chores.

Intelligent, charming, and fun to be with, Bogle got on well with everybody. He and French played "basketball" in their office with rolled-up pieces of newspaper and a wastebasket. If he became excited about something, everyone else at Wellington became excited, too, even if it had nothing to do with mutual funds. For instance, by that October, baseball's New York Giants had come from 13 games back to tie the National League–leading Brooklyn Dodgers. In their best-of-three play-off series to determine who would go on to the World Series, the two teams split the first two games; the third and decisive play-off game came on the afternoon of October 3. When Bogle, an avid Giants fan, listened on a radio in Morgan's office, the rest of the office felt compelled to do so as well, and when the Giants' Bobby Thomson hit the home run ("the shot heard round the world") that won the game, everyone in the office cheered wildly.

The excitement that Bogle generated in the office about baseball was an early example of his leadership ability. Even though he had no title, he reached for the top with hard work and a feeling of responsibility for the company. "I was clearly the kind of person who wanted to run whatever I had anything to do with," he said later. "I may not have been innately bright, but I was very determined."

By 1953, Bogle was becoming more of a public-relations voice for the company, speaking to sales representatives and industry groups, often in defense of balanced funds. One of his favorite ways of explaining their virtues was to compare stock funds to a 70-mile-an-hour driver and balanced funds to a 50-mile-an-hour driver. The first driver, he said, would arrive at his destination first *almost* every time, the notable exceptions being those times when the driver crashed his car and completely destroyed it. Thus, Bogle noted, stock funds earned higher returns over the long term, but they were riskier and more volatile. Balanced funds, on the other hand, helped protect investors during periods when stocks were dropping. While their growth was slower, they were more dependable.

Morgan knew that slotting Bogle as the head of a department would prove too limiting for someone of his wide-ranging abilities. In 1955, therefore, he formally made Bogle his assistant, a position he held for the next seven years, using the post to learn all aspects of the business. Morgan gave his protégé a long leash, and Bogle thrived on the independence. He ranged throughout the company, dabbling in analyzing stocks and bonds alongside the investment department staff, number-crunching with the accounting department, writing letters for Morgan, and preparing annual reports and memos to the sales department. He knew how to wander through the thicket of charts and graphs and put together statistics that shed the best light on the company. Morgan and Welch were sometimes harsh taskmasters, scrutinizing Bogle's work until they felt it was perfect, making him correct letters as many as five times. With these role models, it is little wonder that, when he ran the company in later years, Bogle was the same kind of tough boss.

THE SUMMER OF 1956

In the summer of 1956, Bogle invited friends to join him and his brothers at their Bay Head, New Jersey, summer cottage. The play *My Fair Lady* had opened that spring and taken Broadway by storm, and Bogle sat glued to the hi-fi listening to the show's tunes. When he was not listening to music or Giants baseball games, he generally was out on the basketball court, tossing a ball around with his brothers or playing a "vicious" game of Ping-Pong with his Princeton schoolmate and good friend John J. F. (Jay) Sherrerd. Bogle was also around the Sherrerd home in Merion,

Pennsylvania, a good deal of the time then, and was captivated by Sherrerd's sister, Eve. (They had met when he was 20 and she was 15; he was especially impressed that she shined her brother's saddle shoes.) Eve had graduated from Shipley School in 1951 and Smith College in 1955. Shortly after her college graduation, Bogle began courting her. They became engaged in July 1956 and were married on September 22. They built a solid family life with six children: Barbara, born in 1957; Jean, 1958; John Jr., 1959; Nancy, 1961; Sandra, 1967; and Andrew, 1971.

■ ■ ■

By the late 1950s, Bogle had enough self-confidence to try to persuade Morgan to adopt a new investment strategy. For years, the Wellington formula had been a success; its conservative strategy had helped it survive the 1929 crash and the depression of the 1930s. The distribution system Morgan built up after World War II, combined with the rapid expansion in the mutual fund industry, enabled Wellington Fund's assets to grow to $280 million by December 1953 and to $600 million by December 1957. By the late 1950s, however, the Wellington Fund formula was being questioned. Bogle believed that balanced funds were losing their attraction and that Wellington Management Company should branch out by introducing new funds. Rival funds were riding the bull market in stocks and making much more money for their shareholders than was Wellington Fund.

It would not be easy to persuade Morgan to change. He had always considered it an advantage to focus the business on a single fund—and a balanced fund at that—and he had always been able to convince brokers that balanced funds minimized the risks of investing. Morgan's associates, too, genuinely believed that selling a fund comprising only stocks was too risky and therefore might breach their fiduciary duty to shareholders. As evidence, they pointed to the lackluster performance of firms that ran common stock funds, noting that their share of mutual fund assets was not rising. Morgan's team also argued that running more than one fund would increase the firm's expenses. Because few firms had experience operating a fund family, the conventional wisdom was that if the management company doubled the number of funds it ran, its expenses would automatically double. A second fund, for example, might require a second portfolio management team, and so on.

Bogle, though, looked into the future and saw risks for Wellington Management Company if it clung to a one-fund strategy. He believed that the firm should have not only a balanced fund but a growth fund, an income fund, and several bond funds as well. But it was still too early for him to have much of an impact on Morgan and the other senior executives at Wellington; to them, the balanced fund was gospel and the idea of starting new funds was heresy. (Later, Vanguard officials liked to say that Morgan's strategy of concentrating all resources on a single product was similar to Henry Ford's market approach: "You can have any color car you want, just so long as it is black.")

Wellington Management Company was not alone in its resistance to new funds; few other fund companies at that time were prepared to branch out and start additional funds. Even those that did, did so cautiously. Bogle laughed when he recalled Massachusetts Investors Trust's early decision to start a second fund. Typical of the industry's lack of creativity in those days, it chose the name Massachusetts Investors Second Fund. (Later it was renamed Massachusetts Investors Growth Stock Fund.)

Bogle was determined to get his point across: If in later years the industry was to innovate to attract new customers, Bogle reasoned, a single-fund strategy represented burying its collective head in the sand. In his Princeton thesis, he had identified many potential new funds, including "funds composed of tax-exempt securities, funds with the securities of industries in given geographical areas, and special investment companies to serve the specialized demands of pension and trust funds." Picking up on this theme, he wrote a rudimentary business plan for his company, envisioning the day when Wellington would sponsor a range of funds—becoming a sort of fund supermarket.

Even as Bogle was trying to make his case for expanding Wellington Management Company's operations, it was becoming clear that Morgan was grooming Bogle as his successor. The promotion would have to be earned, though, and Bogle would have to demonstrate initiative and creativity. Despite his own reluctance to change, Morgan wanted his replacement to be an activist. In seeking to transform Wellington's corporate strategy, Bogle was meeting the activist test.

Bogle repeatedly heard all the arguments against change, but he also listened to investors and dealers urge Morgan to develop a stock fund. By 1958 Bogle was convinced that it was time to act, so he suggested to Morgan that Wellington sponsor a pure equity fund.

By this time Morgan was ready for a change as well, sensing that balanced funds were indeed losing popularity, that the public had become enticed by higher-risk equity funds, and that risk was no longer the ugly word it had been in the postdepression era. Making such a fund more appealing to him was the fact that a few recent Wall Street underwritings of new mutual funds had succeeded in raising substantial initial capital. An initial public offering for the new mutual fund would help it to quickly accumulate "seed capital" to achieve economies of scale, the better to enhance Wellington Management Company's profits.

Concluding that there was money to be made in managing equity funds—by shareholders and by sponsors—Morgan gave his blessing to Bogle, who labored with great urgency on the prospectus for the Wellington Equity Fund. (Bogle and Morgan were hardly more imaginative than their rivals at MIT when it came to choosing the name for their new fund; it would be renamed Windsor Fund in 1963.) To Morgan's credit, when Bogle proposed taking the company down this revolutionary path in 1958, Morgan agreed that changes were necessary, although he portrayed the new fund in less-than-revolutionary terms, noting that its purpose was simply to provide a managed common stock program for those investors who believed they had enough fixed-income investments.

The creation of the new fund was a turning point in Bogle's career at Wellington Management Company. He had gone out on a limb and succeeded, and now Morgan was telling others that Jack was on the fast track to lead the company someday. Meanwhile, the birth of the new fund meant that Bogle was given his first fund officer title: Secretary of Wellington Equity Fund. Along with the title came some mundane tasks, such as keeping minutes, helping with correspondence, and hanging pictures. Leading a revolution was not all fame and glory.

A MARRIAGE MADE IN HEAVEN

LTHOUGH MANY OBSERVERS HAD THEIR DOUBTS as to whether Wellington Equity Fund would be successful, it got off to a very good start. Buoyed by a sharply rising stock market, the fund's original underwriting was to prove one of the three largest mutual fund underwritings up to that time, raising initial assets of more than $33 million, a sum that Wellington Fund had taken 17 years to reach, and totaling $44 million by the end of 1959. This favorable beginning established Wellington Equity Fund as a major new entrant to the industry, and carried Wellington Management Company's total assets under management across the $1 billion threshold at year-end, helping to maintain the Wellington organization's standing as one of the largest mutual fund firms in the nation.

In January 1960, just after the assets of the company's funds had reached the magic $1 billion level, Walter Morgan took Wellington Management Company public by selling stock to investors. He created two classes of shares—867,800 A shares, entitled to one vote per share, and 10,000 B shares, entitled to 250 votes per share. Morgan gave a number of Wellington executives the right to buy the one-vote shares and helped them finance their purchases; Bogle, for instance, purchased 10,000 A shares, repaying the company with regular annual payments. The owners of the B shares—principally Morgan and Welch—controlled 2.5 million out of roughly 3.4 million votes, maintaining their firm control over the company.

AN AFFAIR OF THE HEART

Just as his career was switching into high gear, Jack Bogle suffered a major personal setback. For most of his life he had enjoyed good health; in 1956, he took a physical examination and the physician described his heart as normal—undoubtedly the last time such an assertion about his heart was made. On a cool Labor Day weekend in 1960, Bogle was playing tennis with his brother-in-law, Jay Sherrerd. Bogle was 31, Sherrerd 30, so there was no reason to believe that a simple tennis game might cause either of them physical harm.

Yet as Bogle was starting to serve in the middle of the first set, he suddenly felt pain and saw a large flash of light before him.

"Are you all right?" Sherrerd asked his brother-in-law, who looked dazed.

Bogle whispered, "Jay, I have to stop a minute." After he caught his breath, he said, "You're not going to believe me, but I think I just had a heart attack." Both men laughed, for the idea seemed preposterous.

Incredibly, the two men resumed play. Bogle even won the set, the first time that summer he had beaten Sherrerd. But he began to feel ill again, so they retired from the court chatting about business, as Bogle leaned against a tree. Bogle improved enough to drive home, but once there, he again began to feel worse, so his wife, Eve, took him to a doctor, who diagnosed the problem as a heart attack and put him in the hospital, where he remained for six weeks. "I was in a decent amount of trouble," Bogle recalled.

Bogle would later suffer five more serious heart attacks. Once while he was playing squash, his heart suddenly stopped. His opponent, Philadelphia brokerage executive Raymond H. Welsh, revived him by pounding on his chest. Another time he collapsed in a Philadelphia train station after leaving a meeting, leading to another stay in the hospital. He also had a cardiac arrest in a school auditorium; two doctors were present and used CPR to get his heart beating again. Living on borrowed time became routine, for the doctors had gloomily predicted in private that his chances of long-run survival were small.

Although his colleagues were worried about him, Bogle continued to function at full throttle. He had always been a driven, determined man, but now he had something to be truly driven about. He now knew that his life was precarious, but he was not prepared to retire from business and sit at home. "It's something that has made life . . . rather difficult for me, although I've always plunged into everything I had to do with great enthusiasm and concentration, and that probably ain't bad if you've got a malady." (He whispered the last phrase as if he didn't want anyone to hear.) "It's certainly better than doing absolutely nothing, waiting for the Grim Reaper to come."

■ ■ ■

Despite Wellington Equity Fund's auspicious beginning, the early 1960s were not kind to the Wellington organization. A new generation of investors was emerging, with more money at its disposal and a greater inclination to take risks with that money. Wellington Management Company, though, was still heavily dependent on the conservative Wellington Fund—regarded as following an increasingly archaic style of investing—which produced 95 percent of the company's revenue. If balanced funds, with their heavy bond component, made sense to a generation for whom the 1929 crash was still a vivid memory, the new generation thumbed its nose at bonds. Less concerned about preserving its hard-earned money than the previous generation, new investors looked at the hot new "high-performance" funds and dreamed of making a killing despite the risks. Out of step with the new, aggressive style of investing, Wellington Fund's share of industry assets declined, as the market share of balanced funds in the aggregate fell from 30 percent in 1955 to 20 percent in 1964.

The addition of Wellington Equity Fund in 1958 had not improved the company's bottom line very much. Although it had done well in its first three years, the new fund met with disaster in 1962. The portfolio manager was replaced in June 1964 by John B. Neff (who would serve in that capacity until his retirement 32 years later, all the while building a reputation as a true investment guru, along with Peter Lynch and Warren Buffett). About the only passion Wellington Equity Fund aroused came from several Wellington Fund shareholders who sued the fund, claiming it had capitalized unfairly on the Wellington name and insisting that

Wellington Fund had exclusive rights to the name. The suit was settled in 1963, when Wellington Equity Fund agreed to change its name to Windsor Fund. The practice of starting the name of a fund with the letter W and giving the name a British flavor continued, as new funds were given such names as Westminster and Wellesley. Even after Vanguard was founded, the practice endured with the introduction of Warwick Fund and Whitehall Fund.

Although Wellington Management Company crossed the $2 billion mark in assets under management in 1965, sales of its funds shares continued to decline in 1965 and 1966. To remedy this situation, the company enlisted one portfolio manager after another, but investment performance continued to lag, purchases of fund shares continued to fall, and share redemptions remained dangerously high. Bogle believed that the company needed something new to boost its assets—and there was no question in his mind what that something was. High-performance ("go-go") funds had taken hold in the industry, climbing from 21 percent of new sales in 1955 to more than 40 percent in 1964 and 64 percent in 1966. Bogle knew, however, that growing a performance fund in-house would not be easy, as the experience in building Windsor Fund had proved.

"THE LIFE BLOOD"

New cash flow is the life blood of a mutual fund organization, since mutual fund companies get the bulk of their revenue by extracting management fees and other expenses from the assets of the funds they manage. For each $1,000 invested in its funds in 1970, the typical mutual fund company received $10 to cover the operating expenses of the funds, their investment advisory expenses, the costs of advertising and marketing, and profits for the management company.

In short, funds must constantly be infused with new cash flow in the form of share purchases by investors; first, to grow to an efficient size, which facilitates adequate portfolio diversification; second, to achieve a size at which fee revenues cover operating expenses; third, to cover share redemptions, which increase as assets grow; and finally, to leverage the profits of the management company. On this basis, a fund company with $1 billion of assets would earn revenues of roughly $10 million, largely in the form of investment advisory fees. If new cash flow were to increase assets under management to $2 billion, revenues would double to $20 million, often without a major increase in management expenses.

From Bogle's vantage point, one viable alternative was to buy the adviser to an already existing fund and merge it into Wellington Management Company. At the time it seemed like a revolutionary idea, but Wellington Management Company was trapped in its past, and revolutionary thoughts were what it needed. Bogle had already tried to liberate the company when he helped to develop Windsor Fund, but his latest idea—a merger—would represent a far more sweeping change. As a result of a series of promotions, Bogle wielded a big enough stick to hope to pull it off. In 1962, Morgan had promoted him to the position of administrative vice president; then, in 1965, Bogle was named executive vice president and was told by Morgan and Welch to do whatever it took to turn the company around.

Bogle was excited at the prospect of a merger. A merger could provide what Wellington was sorely lacking—investment management talent. By getting the company out of its conservative rut, a merger could boost sales and assets and quickly turn the company around. It might even help move the company beyond mutual funds, allowing Wellington Management Company to break into the institutional investment counsel business. Bogle saw no downside to the idea. "If you're stupid as well as impatient," he said later with a touch of bitterness in his voice, "you say 'Let's merge, we'll solve all the problems at once. It will be a marriage made in heaven.' It actually isn't that simple. Basically, mergers are always bad for one side or the other."

Unfortunately, Bogle arrived at this conclusion only with the benefit of hindsight. In late 1965, he was looking for that proverbial marriage made in heaven. One day over lunch with John C. Jansing, the national fund sales manager for Bache & Co., one of the largest brokerage firms of the day and Wellington's major distributor, Bogle casually mentioned that Wellington Management Company was having difficulties and that he wanted to acquire a firm with investment talent and a high-powered performance fund. Jansing knew of a group of investment advisers who might fit the bill. "If you are really thinking of doing a merger with a 'hot' fund, there's a group in Boston," Jansing said. "They also have a good counseling business run by four people you'll be very comfortable with."

The phrase *hot fund* was one that Bogle would grow to detest, running counter as it did to his conservative, stay-the-course philosophy. His ears perked up, however, when he realized that Jansing was talking about the Ivest Fund, the hottest fund in the business, the number one performing fund for the previous five years, but still relatively unknown to most investors. The fund had been enormously successful almost from the very start, accumulating $1 million in assets by the end of its first year of operations in 1959. Over the next six years it enjoyed a total return of 389 percent—as its assets under management grew to $17 million—while the Standard & Poor's 500 index rose only 94 percent during the same period. Ivest's investment strategies were decidedly more aggressive than either Wellington Fund's or Windsor Fund's, but that might be the key to a turnaround for the Wellington organization.

Managing Ivest Fund was a counseling firm called Thorndike, Doran, Paine & Lewis, Inc. (TDP&L). Its four partners were all under the age of 35, but the firm's total assets under management had already reached $200 million. In addition to Ivest Fund, TDP&L had built a thriving counseling business, including among its clients corporate pension funds, college endowments, religious institutions, and labor unions. Wellington Management Company had not been in the booming pension fund management business, but Bogle thought that its synergies with the mutual fund industry might benefit the firm. The partners of TDP&L were soon to be featured in a book by Martin Mayer, *The New Breed on Wall Street,* which was subtitled, ironically (as later events would prove), *The Men Who Make the Money Go.*

A courtship of TDP&L began in late 1965. Bogle negotiated the details of the merger opposite Robert W. Doran and W. Nicholas Thorndike, who represented the four partners of TDP&L. If matching personalities mattered, the merger negotiations should have failed before they even started. Bogle was outgoing, exuberant, brimming with self-confidence; Doran, on the other hand, was quiet to the point of shyness, not given to emotion, reluctant to stand in the spotlight. Unlike Bogle, he was not inclined to insist that only he knew what was right. As someone who preferred to paint a problem in broad strokes and leave the detail to others, Thorndike was also very different from Bogle, a hands-on man who made sure he grasped every detail.

Oddly enough, however, Bogle and Doran instantly felt a good chemistry. "I liked him," Doran said nearly 30 years later. "I found him very bright, very enthusiastic. He was vital, alive. Those initial conversations were very, very positive." Doran had a huge stake in getting along with Bogle because, despite the high-performing Ivest Fund, TDP&L was relatively small and lacked a powerful distribution system for marketing its fund. Wellington Management Company, in contrast, was strong in distribution, offering administrative and marketing capabilities that would mesh with the Boston firm's investment management skills. A merger between Wellington Management Company and TDP&L could produce a powerful new force in the mutual fund industry.

The Boston partners were flattered to be courted by a giant in the field, and they enjoyed the prestige of being in the same room with the legendary Walter Morgan. Then aged 67, Morgan acknowledged that Wellington had to become a more aggressive enterprise. Nearing retirement and proud of Bogle's achievements, Morgan made a point of attending cocktail parties with the Boston group, regaling them with tales of the mutual fund industry from the 1920s and 1930s. With his shock of wavy white hair, Morgan exuded a mixture of self-confidence and stability, of conservatism and maturity, that put the Boston partners' minds at ease about the merger. Yet the Bostonians had their own confidence that they could provide the ailing Wellington and Windsor Funds with a shot in the arm. Robert Doran, for one, told Bogle, "I can't wait to get my hands on Wellington Fund." At least for the time being, those words were music to Bogle's ears.

Nearly 30 years later, there was a certain dismay in Bogle's voice when he recalled an event that might have scuttled the proposed merger with TDP&L—the tempting opportunity to bring his good friend Paul F. Miller, Jr., a partner in the Philadelphia investment banking firm of Drexel Harriman Ripley, into Wellington Management Company in early 1966. Miller and his partner, Jay Sherrerd, Bogle's brother-in-law, had gained solid reputations running an institutional research department at Drexel Harriman Ripley. Miller, though, had become increasingly frustrated because he was devoting less time to research and more time to managing people, so he decided it was time to make a move. Miller visited Bogle at his home one night and proposed that the two of them join forces and work together. Bogle would run the administrative and marketing side of Wellington Management Company, while Miller would take charge of the investment management side.

Bogle was overwhelmed at his good fortune. In the middle of negotiations that offered the opportunity to diversify Wellington Management Company's asset base and perhaps improve the investment performance of its funds, Paul Miller, one of the brightest stars in the investment advisory field, was interested in joining the Wellington team and becoming one of its leaders. Given the ongoing merger discussions with TDP&L, however, Bogle cautioned Miller that the Boston group's investment strategies could clash with Wellington's more conservative philosophy. A dilemma for Bogle arose when Miller expressed serious reservations about whether he would be interested if Wellington joined forces with the Boston group. Bogle would have to choose.

While Bogle was intrigued by the possibility of working with Miller, the idea had its flaws. A partnership between Bogle and Miller without the Boston group meant no hot fund. Moreover, the merger talks with

TDP&L had progressed too far to be halted. Bogle, however, did not want to lose the talents of his friend, so he tried to convince Miller to join Wellington even if the merger went through. He proposed that he and Miller could run the Philadelphia-based funds while the Boston partners would do the same with the Ivest Fund and the TDP&L counseling business.

Miller finally agreed to Bogle's proposal, and expected that the deal would be done by the time he and his family were to visit Bogle at his summer home in Lake Placid, New York, in July. Joseph E. Welch, president of Wellington Management Company since 1963, felt confident enough to draft a press release announcing that Miller would be joining the firm. Jay Sherrerd, however, had little desire to lose his partner's talents, so he labored to keep Miller at Drexel by convincing Miller that he and Bogle could never work together.

"You both have to be the boss," Sherrerd told him. "Jack's a detailed, hands-on manager. You hate details, you're a policy guy. I can't imagine Jack telling you what to do, or you telling Jack what to do."

Before the press release was issued, Drexel made Miller an offer he could not refuse, including a huge pay hike and the chance to run his own personal investment fund. Although Bogle was crushed, years later both he and Miller agreed that a partnership between the two men probably would not have succeeded. "We're both pretty reasonable people," Miller suggested, "but I'm more compromising and reasonable than Jack is. I think we'd ultimately have had some real clashes. At the time, we both thought we were indispensable."

■ ■ ■

In the spring of 1966, following nine months of negotiations, the merger with TDP&L was moving toward a positive conclusion. In response to a comment that the merger seemed out of character for him, Bogle simply said, "Everyone likes a deal." Bogle was so confident that the merger would be free of conflict that he agreed, in the division of the 10,000 Wellington Management Company Class B voting shares that would be relinquished by Morgan and Welch, to have 1,250 shares granted to each of the four Boston partners, representing roughly 33 percent ownership of the company's voting power. Together with the 148,000 A shares that they would receive in the merger (then valued at about $4 million), the four TDP&L partners would control 40 percent of the company. Bogle, however, would own 4,000 B shares, which, with his own A shares, would give him control of 28 percent of the vote. In his eagerness to complete the merger, Bogle had underestimated the peril he had placed himself in by relinquishing so much voting power. "I had this naive idea that I could always persuade one of them to my position and that would give me 38 percent to the three others' 30 percent," Bogle later said. "Naive? Stupid might be more like it."

The merger agreement was reached on June 6, 1966. Nearly 30 years later, Bogle remembered the date as clearly as if it had been yesterday. It was a time for celebration on both sides, for the merger did not appear to have a downside. As *Institutional Investor* magazine wrote, "Putting together Wellington's vast assets, elegant reputation, and marketing ability, and the Ivest group's research and investment management talents and the winning reputation of its fund seemed like an extremely felicitous combination." To mark the occasion, Bogle had small silver trays made and presented them to the four Boston partners. Soldered on the middle of each oval tray was a silver dollar on which was inscribed the word *Peace*.

Even though all seemed well, the merger had its skeptics. The flamboyant and controversial Bernard Cornfeld, whose overseas Fund of Funds, managed in Switzerland, owned 10 percent of Wellington Management Company's A shares, had little faith in TDP&L and believed that the Ivest Fund's spectacular results were a fluke. He suggested to Bogle that Bogle had placed himself in a difficult position, for he was stuck with the Boston firm even if Ivest Fund began to falter. Even worse, Cornfeld thought that if things went badly, the Boston group would probably try to fire Bogle. Cornfeld was so opposed to the merger that he let it be known that he planned to sue Wellington Management Company to stop it. When Bogle learned of the potential suit, he immediately flew to Geneva for a meeting with Cornfeld, hoping to change his mind.

"Look," said Cornfeld to Bogle, "this merger is ridiculous. Those people from Boston think they have all the advantages, that they know how to get a fund to perform. The problem is not that they are SOBs. You'll find that out. The problem is that, in terms of investment wisdom, they're *no good* SOBs. If they fail to measure up to your expectations, you won't get rid of them, they'll get rid of you. And you'll find that out, too."

Bogle is not sure how, but despite Cornfeld's strong opposition to the merger he ultimately persuaded Cornfeld to drop the threatened suit.

5

THE STORM
BREWS

S THE MERGER TALKS between Wellington Management Company and TDP&L proceeded, Walter Morgan arranged it so that he would retain control of Wellington Management Company, at least for the time being. As of January 1, 1966, Morgan's holding company owned 7,600 of the company's 10,000 B shares; the remaining 2,400 were owned by Joseph Welch, then Wellington's president and CEO. Morgan knew that eventually he would have to cede partial ownership of the new company to the Boston partners, but he was reluctant to relinquish too soon the control of the company he had founded and built up.

He therefore devised an ingenious plan. Rather than give Bogle and the Boston partners part ownership immediately, he arranged that they be given such ownership only after the merger was five years old. During that five-year period, the voting shares that would give them partial ownership were to be placed in what Morgan described as a voting trust. This arrangement would give the directors a chance to determine whether or not the merger was working. When the voting trust was terminated on April 1, 1971, the 10,000 B shares—the ones that determined how much real ownership anyone had in Wellington—would be redistributed, with 4,000 going to Bogle; 1,250 each to Thorndike, Doran, Paine, and Lewis;

and 500 to Walter M. Cabot, whom Doran had tapped to run the funds on a day-to-day basis. The remaining 500 shares would be reserved for future issuance. Thus, five years after the merger, the principals would own the amounts originally agreed upon, giving Bogle a 28 percent voting interest in the company and the four Boston partners 10 percent each. The remaining 32 percent would be held largely by public shareholders.

A CORPORATE SHELL

Like an ordinary corporation, a mutual fund has a board of directors (including outside independent directors); however, the mutual fund does not in any real sense have officers or employees. It is, in the eyes of many observers, merely a corporate shell. The mutual fund traditionally enters into a "management agreement" with a separate entity (in this case, Wellington Management Company), which provides a set of services, including employing and compensating the individuals who will serve as the officers and employees of the fund. In short, except for the one-day-a-month directors, there are no human beings to act on behalf of the funds.

The management company establishes the fund and its board of directors, and the directors authorize the management company by contract to provide all of the services required by the fund. If the management company determines to make changes in the officers who serve the fund, the fund as a practical matter has no real option other than to simply accept the designated individual. The only recourse the fund has is to terminate the contract with the management company. Unfortunately, this is an impractical remedy since, without the management company, there would be no one to run the fund's daily operations.

Within the Wellington Management Company organization, each fund had its own board of directors, the majority of whom were unaffiliated with the company. The same individuals constituted the board for each fund. This one group came to be known as the fund board.

After the merger was completed, it was agreed that Bogle would become president and CEO of the merged firm. From the standpoint of his health, however, 1967 was not a very good year for Bogle. He was frequently hospitalized, and at one point he was away from his desk for six weeks, one of the longest periods of time he had ever missed work.

Suffering from a condition known as heart arrhythmia, Bogle traveled to the Cleveland Clinic that spring to have a pacemaker installed. The clinic was the leader in cardiac catheterization and at the time was one of but a few hospitals in the country that installed pacemakers. Bogle was in such poor condition that a senior cardiologist in the Cleveland heart program gloomily predicted to him that he would never work again.

Bogle has retained a vivid, nightmarish image of the surgery required to implant the pacemaker: "They put the pacemaker in with a saw. They spread [my] ribs and cut a great big hole in my chest. Then they dropped the damn thing in. It almost killed me. Up to then, that was the closest I'd ever been to death. I went into cardiac arrest. I got through that very luckily."

Bogle continued to suffer heart problems through the summer. Adding to his discomfort, though, was the feeling that Bob Doran and Nick Thorndike, the men who ran the Boston operation on a day-to-day basis, were afraid to announce his appointment as president and CEO of the new firm until his heart condition stabilized and improved. One day during the summer, for example, Doran came to the hospital and told Bogle of their plans to delay the appointment until his health improved. Bogle kept to himself his anger at their insensitivity.

Shortly after the pacemaker was installed, it became clear that his heart problems were not improving, so Bogle asked around for the names of the best cardiologists in the United States. The consensus was that he should turn to Dr. Bernard Lown at the Brigham & Women's Hospital in Boston. Lown was a pioneer in the emerging treatment of heart arrhythmia, and had invented the defibrillator, which shocks irregular hearts into normal rhythm. (In 1981, Lown would cofound the International Physicians for the Prevention of Nuclear War, which in 1985 was awarded the Nobel Peace Prize. Lown accepted the award on behalf of the organization along with the other cofounder, Soviet cardiologist Eugene Chazov.)

Lown recalled that a senior member of Wellington Management Company's board phoned him just before Lown examined Bogle, explaining that the board was about to appoint Bogle president of the firm and wanted some clarification on his health. Specifically, they wanted to know his life expectancy; if it was only a few years, they said, they did not want to burden him with the position. Lown promised to get back to the board member after he had completed the examination.

When Bogle suffered his first heart attack in 1960, the diagnosis was that he had suffered a myocardial infarction, what Lown later described as a garden-variety heart attack caused by the closure of a coronary artery that results in the death of heart muscles. When Lown examined Bogle in 1967, however, he made a different assessment—that in 1960 Bogle had suffered a massive heart rhythm disturbance. "It was clear that his survival was limited. He would have had maybe 5, at the most 10 years to live," Lown said. "I was troubled by how well he had met his health challenges from 1960 to 1967. There should have been a trajectory down, there should have been deterioration. But here was this vigorous young fellow who wasn't any worse for the wear of a massive heart disability."

Putting Bogle through a motorized treadmill test, Lown expected that, like other heart attack victims, Bogle would fail the test after 7 minutes or so, but Bogle lasted 18 minutes. One explanation was that the remaining heart muscle was still strong. But the other, less scientific, explanation was what Lown called the Jack Bogle Factor: "the will for somebody to overcome, to persevere, that mystical quality that medicine has been very uncomfortable with." After the examination, Lown contacted the Wellington board member who had asked about Bogle's life expectancy. He apparently calmed the board's concerns, for in November 1967 the board announced Bogle's appointment as president and CEO of the new firm.

A CHANCE ENCOUNTER

The year of the merger, 1966, was notable for another event in Bogle's life. A young man who had graduated from Boston College in 1965 and had embarked on an MBA from the Wharton School at the University of Pennsylvania was writing a thesis, "The Marketing of the Mutual Fund Industry." Someone at Fidelity, where the man had been working that summer, suggested he see Bogle for help, so the man paid Bogle a visit that fall. Bogle was the only person he interviewed for the thesis other than Fidelity employees. Had Bogle known that his guest would one day become an industry legend, he might have asked him to stay and work at Wellington Management Company. But this was the fall of 1966, and Peter Lynch's brilliant career as the manager of Fidelity's Magellan Fund was far off in the future.

In the meantime, Lown told Bogle that he had serious reservations about the wisdom of the pacemaker implant. Additionally, he identified an immediate, urgent problem—a potentially lethal condition in which the heart beats rapidly and becomes ineffective to function as a pump. Fortunately, Lown found that Bogle could identify the circumstances under which this was most apt to happen: when he arose early in the morning, and when he engaged in vigorous exercise. Knowing that enabled Lown to put Bogle on a regimen calling for high dosages of medication at those times. "The reason Jack Bogle would have these attacks," he said, "is because he is tightly wound up, and there is a lot of adrenaline released when he awakes or when he competes. He's like a prizefighter when he goes into the ring."

During the next month, Bogle remained in the Boston hospital, where he was given a series of stress tests. On later visits there, Bogle broke a hospital record by performing 50 separate exercise tests, so the nurses gave him a party, even getting out their cameras to preserve the occasion for posterity. Bogle followed the doctor's instructions regarding the drug treatment, which generally worked effectively for the next eight years. As far as Bogle was concerned, Lown's greatest accomplishment was to improve his health enough so that he could return to the tennis and squash courts again.

■ ■ ■

After the merger, Wellington Management Company became more aggressive in its investment management strategies. By 1968, the bulk (70 percent) of its new sales came from Ivest Fund. From an asset level of about $1 million at the end of 1961, its first year of operations, Ivest had accumulated assets of almost $50 million by the end of 1966, and $340 million two years later. During the five-year period ending in 1966, Ivest Fund was the top-ranking fund in the country, ahead even of Edward Johnson III's Fidelity Trend Fund and Fidelity Capital Fund, managed by the legendary Gerald Tsai. (Tsai left Fidelity in 1970 to start the Manhattan Fund and his own fund organization. Manhattan Fund, like Ivest Fund, was to plummet in value as the go-go era ended in 1969.)

Reflecting Wellington Management Company's new aggressiveness, Wellington Fund's annual report dated November 30, 1967, had a different tone. In that report, Chairman Walter Morgan suggested that, while Wellington Fund's investment objectives of "conservation of principal, reasonable current income, and profits without undue risk" still made sense, change was needed to bring the portfolio into line with modern concepts and opportunities. "We have chosen 'dynamic conservatism' as our philosophy," Morgan wrote. *Dynamic conservatism* was an odd phrase for the conservative Walter Morgan to use. Believing in a slow, steady, cautious approach to investing, he had always avoided go-go adjectives like *dynamic*. The new Walter Morgan was undoubtedly the product of a changing industry and the influence of Bob Doran, Nick Thorndike, and Walter Cabot; the words may have been attributed to Morgan, but the people behind the Ivest Fund seemed to have dictated those words.

Following the merger, the climate at Wellington Management Company had changed, seemingly for the good. Ivest Fund continued to fly high, its assets reaching $340 million by the end of 1968, a two-year record of growth that was remarkable in the burgeoning mutual fund industry, even among the go-go funds that had so attracted investors' attention. Trying to capitalize on the public's love affair with aggressive funds, Wellington Management added more funds. Explorer Fund (investing in stocks of emerging companies) was introduced in December 1967, followed in 1968 by Technivest Fund (investing on the basis of technical stock market indicators), and in 1969 by Trustees' Equity Fund (despite its name, trading on the basis of short-term trends in stock prices and engaging in rapid portfolio turnover). All of these new funds were highly aggressive and risk oriented; all were run out of Boston; and all were greeted with enthusiasm by brokers and investors. Ultimately, all of them would fail to provide competitive returns and all would tumble sharply in the ensuing bear market in 1972–74. By 1977, only Explorer Fund survived.

One new aggressive fund, formed in 1968, served a unique purpose at its formation. W. L. Morgan Growth Fund, named, ironically, after Wellington's conservative founder, was formed to solve a growing problem related to the Wellington and Ivest funds. In earlier years, investors had done little shifting of their assets back and forth between funds, preferring to keep their money in one fund for the long haul. More recently, however, investment dealers had been coming under pressure from their clients to arrange for them to move their money from the so-so Wellington Fund to the go-go Ivest Fund, without payment of additional sales charges. The dealers, in turn, pressured Wellington Management Company to allow investors to make such a free exchange.

Bogle, however, resisted the idea, fearing that conservative Wellington Fund shareholders would be enticed by the record of the more aggressive Ivest Fund without recognizing the substantially higher risk involved. He offered an alternative solution: the creation of a brand-new fund, W. L. Morgan Growth Fund, which would be aggressive enough to appeal to investors who wanted a performance fund like Ivest, but would not be so aggressive that conservative investors who switched over from Wellington Fund would suffer severe losses if the new fund fared poorly. (Bogle's original intention to use the name Morgan drew a challenge from Morgan, Stanley & Co. and the Morgan Guaranty Trust Company, but Wellington

Management agreed to add its founder's initials, and the dispute was quickly resolved.) After some bad years in the 1970s, W. L. Morgan Growth Fund went on to develop a successful long-term performance record. The fund's early growth was slow, but by 1995 its assets would total $1.2 billion.

Although conservative funds were anathema to the Boston group, in 1970 Bogle recommended that the firm launch a bond fund. Bogle had always had contrarian instincts, and he was inspired by an *Institutional Investor* cover illustration that depicted bonds as dinosaurs. Here was a chance for him to test his instincts by creating a bond fund, then almost universally considered an endangered species in the industry. (In 1970, there were but 10 bond funds; today there are 3,000.) The Boston group was shocked by the recommendation, and the Wellington Management Company directors would have none of it.

"The stupidest idea I've ever heard of," argued Stephen Paine, one of the four Boston partners and a particular thorn in Bogle's side. "Bonds are yesterday."

"No," replied an irate Jack Bogle. "Bonds are tomorrow."

Bogle pressed on with the idea to the fund directors, who were more sympathetic. When Bogle offered a compromise by recommending an income fund comprising 60 percent bonds and 40 percent high-yielding stocks, both the Wellington Management Company directors and the fund directors approved it, and Wellesley Income Fund began operations in mid-1970. Nonetheless, Bogle persevered in his belief that an all-bond fund would be successful, and, early in 1973, both boards approved the formation of Westminster Bond Fund.

As 1973 began, Wellington Management was running 10 funds and had aggregate assets under management of $2.6 billion. Only three of the funds, however, were of any notable size. Although its assets were declining, Wellington Fund's $1.3 billion was one-half of the company's entire asset base. Windsor and Ivest, the other sizable funds, had grown to an aggregate of $900 million in assets.

With his health restored—at least for the time being—Bogle was hitting his stride, overcoming a sometimes cantankerous Wellington Management Company board, adding new funds, and building the company's narrow base into a broad-ranging fund family.

"MY GOOD RIGHT ARM"

James S. Riepe had graduated in 1965 from the Wharton School at the University of Pennsylvania, where he had been an outstanding linebacker on the school's football team. He received his Wharton

MBA in 1967. Two years later, the 25-year-old Riepe was working for the public accounting firm of Lybrand Ross Brothers & Montgomery (later, Coopers & Lybrand) in Philadelphia.

During National Guard duty, he became friendly with Duncan M. McFarland, who worked as Bogle's assistant at Wellington Management Company, and the two often talked about business. After returning to civilian life, Riepe received a phone call from someone at Wellington, asking him whether he would be interested in interviewing for the job of assistant controller. Though flattered to be asked, Riepe was not thrilled at the prospect of remaining an accountant for the rest of his life. He went for the interview but showed little interest in being hired.

Then came another phone call, this time inviting him to meet the president of the company, Jack Bogle. Trying to sound as uninterested as possible, Riepe told Bogle's secretary, "My schedule is awfully tight right now. I'm not sure I can make it."

"Well, Mr. Riepe," the secretary replied acidly, "Mr. Bogle is a busy man. I'm sure he won't take too much of your time." Humbled, Riepe agreed to see Bogle.

Bogle was looking for a new assistant and had heard about Riepe from McFarland. After meeting Bogle, Riepe landed the $13,500-a-year job, beating out a Xerox salesman. He began working in March 1969, just a few months after Bogle had been elected chairman of the Investment Company Institute. (Riepe was himself to become the Institute's chairman in 1990–92.) Riepe would advance rapidly and prove to be Bogle's "good right arm," instrumental in the formation of Vanguard in 1974. "He stood by me and gave me the business and personal support without which I could not have survived the crisis of 1974 and the changes that followed," Bogle said of Riepe.

Riepe was named Vanguard's executive vice president in 1976, and in 1979 was appointed a Vanguard board director. Bogle made it clear that Riepe would have become president of The Vanguard Group, but Riepe instead accepted a senior management position at T. Rowe Price & Associates in 1982, where he is now a managing director and president of its mutual fund unit.

■ ■ ■

Throughout the late 1960s, Bogle was saying publicly that the merger was working better than anyone had expected and that it would be a boon to the company's stockholders, "even though," Bogle acknowledged later, "I was . . . very skeptical that the merger would be good for me."

Indeed, the merger slowly began to trouble Bogle, who started to question the rhetoric of the Boston partners and to doubt they were as good at the investment management business as they claimed to be. He noticed, for example, that Ivest Fund's long-term performance record had been inflated by attaching to it the results of a predecessor private fund called Professional Investors, which was a private investment pool and not a mutual fund at all. He also questioned personnel decisions, including Doran's choice of Walter Cabot to handle the day-to-day management of the funds. Although Cabot was dubbed "Moses" because he was supposed to lead Wellington Fund to salvation, just as the biblical Moses was to lead the Children of Israel to the Promised Land, his performance left a great deal to be desired relative to that of his biblical namesake. In fact, the fund's returns deteriorated alarmingly during the 1967–74 period.

Later, Bogle was critical of himself for believing too fervently that the Boston group would always perform miracles and for not grasping quickly enough that the go-go bubble could burst. He grew contemptuous of the Boston team for being, in the words of John Jackson (since 1971 a member of the Wellington Fund board), "people who didn't work very hard, or at least not nearly as hard as Jack Bogle, mostly dilettantes." Said Charles D. Root, Jr., also a member of the fund's board, "Bogle was right on top of the investment performance. Nick Thorndike might have looked at it every quarter. Jack Bogle looked at it every day." In a confidential memo he wrote in 1970, Root contemptuously referred to George Lewis as a Boston blue blood who had no interest in the business and to Stephen Paine as "a disappointment as a portfolio manager."

Raymond J. Klapinsky, an associate counsel for Wellington Management at the time, sensed the friction between Bogle and the Boston partners. "While the Boston group's intention was to be more aggressive in investing than Bogle's instincts, they were less interested in strategic issues. Jack was always looking for new ideas and new things. The Boston group was more apt to take what they had to try to get new customers. They managed . . . in a more relaxed way than Jack wanted to."

Bogle began to sense that the merger was fragile and vulnerable. Worse than that, he began to fear that the Boston partners' true intention was to seize control of Wellington Management Company, a fear which proved to be accurate. The Boston partners were troubled by Bogle's dominant personality. Doran and Thorndike claimed to believe in participative management, in which decisions are made only after all the pros and cons are debated. The only participant Bogle thought worthy of sharing decision-making power with was himself. Asserted Barbara B. Hauptfuhrer, a member of the Wellington Fund board, "[Jack's] way is *the* way. Bob Doran was much more of a consensus taker, a very thoughtful man, low-key in his approach."

Unfortunately for the partnership, Bogle had little interest in changing. He had gotten to the top of Wellington Management with brains, hard work, and in-your-face zeal, and he did not care if others found him brash or arrogant. He thought of his nonparticipative management style as a badge of honor: "I knew I wasn't tactful or diplomatic. I am the kind of person who is either going to run something or not. I don't want committees; I don't want a lot of people to be involved. I don't want to be in an argument about the final decision, once it is made."

In stark contrast, the Boston group, particularly Thorndike, dealt in generalities. To Bogle, a detail man, dealing in generalities was tantamount to being asleep at the wheel. "I don't mind knowing things from the ground up when I'm going to make a decision. I don't like a committee to come in and say, 'Thumbs-up on this one,' because how am I going to know whether it should be thumbs-up or not if I don't get into the process as early as possible?" To the participative group in Boston, such talk amounted to a declaration of war.

Bob Doran recently spoke about those trouble-filled days with great reluctance. He acknowledged in general terms that there had been differences of management and leadership styles between the Boston group and the Philadelphia contingent. He described the situation as follows: The Boston group was "private, independent, with a nonhierarchical structure, collegial, participative in its management style with shared decision making, dialogue and debate among peers, while the management style in Philadelphia was more . . . autocratic, hierarchical, and those traits tended to clash." The Boston group might have admitted that Bogle was better equipped to run the company than they were; they simply did not want him bossing them around.

Geography played a role in the feud as well. Boston focused its labors on investment counseling and the pension management business, a world driven by a select group of professionals who sold their wares to institutions. Philadelphia, in contrast, was actually running mutual funds, then a retail business aimed at brokers, wholesalers, and consumers. Carrying out such different responsibilities, the Boston and Philadelphia executives had little empathy for one another. "At the time, the investment counsel side was a bit more fast paced and perhaps a little bit more glib and more investment oriented," observed Jim Riepe, "whereas the mutual fund business was much longer term; things didn't happen quickly. You had to build relationships."

Compounding the problem of geography was that responsibility for the funds was divided between the two cities. Wellington Fund and Windsor Fund were managed out of Philadelphia; the Boston-based funds included Ivest, Explorer, Morgan, Technivest, and Trustees' Equity. Turf became an issue. TDP&L questioned the logic of having the company based in both Boston and Philadelphia, and wanted the entire operation based in Boston to end the company's bifurcated existence. "The logic was history, practicality, and sentiment," retorted an irate Jack Bogle.

Differences in investment policies added further fuel to the feud, particularly the issue of how to run Wellington Fund. As a balanced fund, it had typically invested about 60 to 65 percent of its assets in equities, with the remainder in fixed-income securities. The Boston group, which had the ultimate investment responsibility for Wellington Fund, wanted the fund to invest more heavily in equities—but with lower representation in traditional blue-chip stocks—and less heavily in fixed-income securities. The Philadelphia contingent, loyal to the fund's original objectives, thought that it should remain a conservative balanced fund, emphasizing high-grade securities. There were other differences in investment strategy. The Boston group adhered to a market-timing strategy, hoping to ride the stocks currently favored by the market, while shunning whichever stocks were out of favor. In Philadelphia sat John Neff, manager of the Windsor Fund and the closed-end Gemini Fund (established in 1967), a confirmed contrarian who seemed to want to buy any stock the Boston group wanted to sell.

Bogle admitted that the feud was not one-sided, that the Boston group was not solely at fault, and that he had been too intolerant of other people's opinions. Morgan took some of the blame, too, acknowledging that he had influenced Bogle's management style. "I taught Jack to be pretty tough—like I had been, because I owned all the stock and could do any damn thing I wanted. But you can't quite do that when you have four or five guys who are virtually equal to you."

■　■　■

As time went on, Bogle lost respect for the Boston group, believing they knew less than he did about the business. He could have tolerated their aggressive investment strategies if those strategies had worked, but soon there was no disguising that the feud had evolved into open, bitter hostilities.

As the bitterness among the partners progressed, it began to spill over into Wellington Management's board of directors, heavily represented by the Boston group. As Bogle noted, "Wellington Management's board and I were in a real power struggle. I wanted to control everything, and so did they."

The hostilities grew so heated that junior employees at Wellington began to worry that they would have to take sides—a precarious position, since choosing the wrong side might have cost them their jobs. Jan M. Twardowski, then Bogle's assistant, went to Paris in 1969 to work on an international joint venture for Wellington Management. When he returned to Philadelphia three years later, the situation had deteriorated. "The elephants were fighting and the mice were worried; I was one of the mice." Twardowski said, "As the battle started, I was afraid for my job and for the company. Who knew what could happen?" Twardowski faced a major dilemma: Did he side with Bogle, his old boss, or with the Boston team? "I had a terrible time, but I trusted Jack," he said. "I trusted him to be straight with me."

6

THROWING DOWN
THE GAUNTLET

B
Y THE LATE SUMMER OF 1970, the friction between Bogle and the Boston group had intensified, despite an improvement in the company's financial showing. In 1969, the funds experienced a net cash outflow of $50 million, the first year of negative cash flow in Wellington Management Company's history. In 1970, the trend reversed, and cash inflow totaled more than $100 million. But a sharp decline in the stock market in 1969 fueled an overall decline in the assets of the company's mutual funds during the two-year period, from $2.7 billion to $2.2 billion. However, with the growth of the private counseling business, total assets managed by Wellington Management Company at the end of 1970 held firm at about $3 billion.

Against this background, Walter Morgan, at the age of 72, decided to step down as chairman of the funds. The logical choice to succeed him was former Wellington Management Company president Joseph Welch, a fund director and a veteran Wellington executive. Yet Welch, also advanced in years, stepped aside quietly when Morgan suggested that Bogle was the better choice.

Even as he assumed this position of leadership in the organization, Bogle's relationship with the Boston group continued to deteriorate. Feeling that his back was against the wall in the feud, he thought about resigning. He even considered mounting a proxy fight against the Boston group, but it was by no means certain that he would win, and he was not sure he'd have the heart to put the company, in his words, through the wringer.

The board of directors of the mutual funds, nervous about the worsening situation, proposed that two of its members, Charles Root and Robert E. Worden, try to get the parties to make peace. (Root would again play a key role at a time of crisis four years later, in 1974. Worden would die suddenly in December 1970.) The board of directors of the mutual funds was responsible for overseeing fund management policies, while the Wellington Management Company board had the direct responsibility for managing the activities of the company. Accordingly, Root and Worden set up a series of meetings with Bogle and his adversaries.

In their meeting with Bogle, Root and Worden learned that he was eager to find allies among the board members of the funds. "Jack has decided," Root wrote in a confidential memo, "that the only chance he has of remaining in power . . . is to have the independent fund directors want him to remain so. He seems to feel that whatever we as independent directors want we will get because our power is great." The power to which Bogle referred was the legal right of each fund's board of directors to terminate the fund's investment management and distribution contracts with Wellington Management Company at any time with 60-days' notice. The fund boards needed no explicit reason for taking such action, but, as a practical matter, no board would dare sever ties with a management company without extraordinary cause. Although a change in the management of the management company itself could be considered a valid reason, no major fund group had ever taken such action against a management company.

In late August 1970, Bogle was ready to resign. He was so serious about this step that he had even mentally drawn up a list of names of those he hoped would join him in starting a new company. But Andrew Young, counsel to Wellington Management Company, persuaded Bogle to make one last effort to resolve his differences with the Boston Four.

The feud was put on hold until mid-September, when Root and Worden met with Thorndike, who was highly critical of Bogle. In a memo after the meeting, Root recorded Thorndike's complaints: "JCB apparently finds difficulty in relying on others, doesn't like meetings to share ideas, gives directions by order rather than discussion." They met with Doran the same day, and in another memo, Root noted Doran's opinion of Bogle: "CEO out of touch with the ugly realities of his company, and with his lieutenants. CEO makes no effort to understand the deep-rooted feelings of his peers . . . no forum for honest exchange." One month later, Root and Worden reported to the Wellington Management Company board members that the rift was serious enough to blow the whole thing apart.

In the meantime, the Boston group had concluded that Bogle had to go. In yet another memo, Root noted: "Bogle acknowledged . . . to be one of the most knowledgeable mutual fund experts extant. Bogle also acknowledged by TDP&L to be a good deal smarter than any of them. Trouble is Bogle has a dim view of [Thorndike's] management abilities and [Doran's] investment abilities, and has been less than diplomatic in his handling of and communications with these two men—accentuated by geographic separation . . . Thorndike and Doran have decided they can't work with Bogle and would like to . . . heave him out."

Root, however, achieved some temporary success in healing the rift. When he met with Doran and Thorndike on December 1, Doran informed him that, since there was no chance of the three working together harmoniously, the only solution was for Bogle to resign. Root was incensed: "I in effect threw down the gauntlet. I said 'You've got a great thing going for you and don't mess it up. We've got to stop it.' . . . Then things kind of leveled off." Later in December, Bogle expressed some willingness to improve his relationship with Doran and Thorndike. In a memo to Root he wrote: "JCB, WNT and RWD all agreed to forget past problems and make a Herculean effort to make the new arrangements work and to put aside personal differences for the good of the organization."

DINNER AT THE WHITE HOUSE

On May 27, 1970, Jack Bogle dined at the White House for the first and only time in his life. His encounter with President Richard M. Nixon that evening remained a highlight of his career.

It was a time of great national turbulence. The National Guard killings at Kent State University had occurred earlier in the month. The financial markets were in turmoil. The Pennsylvania Railroad had filed for bankruptcy, and questions were being raised about whether the Federal Reserve Board would pump enough money into the American economy to avoid a liquidity crisis. With so much negative financial news, the announcement that Nixon planned to meet with a group of financial leaders at the White House sent the Dow Jones Industrial Average of stock prices up 32 points (equivalent to some 250 points at the Dow's current level)—a 5.1 percent increase that remains one of the largest one-day increases in market history. As one of the 35 business leaders invited to the dinner, Bogle felt he was of great importance.

At 2:00 in the afternoon he joined several other invited guests for a meeting with Arthur Burns, the chairman of the Federal Reserve Board, who sought their advice about the financial situation. According to Bogle, after a wide-ranging discussion, Bernard M. Lasker, head of the New York Stock Exchange and a friend of Nixon's, observed out of the blue, "You should know that the Securities and Exchange Commission is riddled with Communists, and until we root them out of the SEC, this industry is going to be in deep trouble. You know, they've gotten right off the boat and infiltrated the SEC." Their goal, Lasker concluded, was to destroy the capitalist system.

Bogle had no idea what to make of these outlandish statements. He found Lasker's comments insulting and no doubt fabricated, and when he got in the car later, he told Lasker how uncomfortable he had been. Lasker was disturbed by Bogle's reaction, and asked that the comments remain confidential. Although Bogle agreed never to discuss their conversation with anyone, years later he discovered a reference to the episode in a magazine article, and felt free to divulge their "secret."

Dinner began at 8:30 in the State dining room, and Bogle said he got quite a kick out of the chosen entree: filet of beef Wellington. After dessert, served at 10:00, several high government officials addressed the group, after which Nixon offered to answer questions. The room remained quiet until Bogle stood up.

"I don't think that what's troubling the nation are the things we've been talking about tonight," Bogle began, alluding to Vietnam and the economy. "I think the trouble that America is facing, which underlies the problems in the stock market and the deterioration in the business outlook, is the deep division between two generations, the younger and the older. People are just not seeing eye to eye on the state of the nation. In view of your campaign pledge to 'bring us all together,' what are you going to do about it?"

Confronted by such an unlikely question from an audience of conservative financiers, Nixon looked like he had been struck. After a long pause, he observed that Bogle had asked a good question and that, while his administration had given a lot of thought to these issues, more was required. He noted that he had appointed a presidential commission to investigate Kent State and related matters.

After the dinner, Bogle noted that he happened to walk out of the room at the president's side. "You know," Nixon began casually, "I really appreciated that question of yours. It was right on the money. We all ought to be doing something about it. Perhaps we haven't done enough." When he returned to his hotel, Bogle found six phone messages from the media. Eileen Shanahan of the *New York Times* reached him at 2:00 in the morning. "We heard there was one questioner who really shocked the president." When Bogle didn't respond, Shanahan hazarded, "I'll bet it was you."

Bogle was hesitant about discussing his exchange with the president. Before the dinner, he asked Nixon aide Charles M. Colson and Press Secretary Ronald L. Ziegler whether the dinner with the president was on or off the record. "Both," Ziegler said ambiguously, with a laugh. Even when Ziegler said, "Yeah, I think that's fine," Bogle remained uncertain about White House policy regarding the dinner discussion. Despite his uncertainty, he decided to answer the questions raised with him about the dinner. When a reporter from *The Wall Street Journal* telephoned him in his office the next morning, Bogle later learned that some of his dinner colleagues were annoyed that he had violated an unstated rule that White House dinners were off the record, but in his defense he pointed out Ziegler's ambiguity. Secretly, though, he was pleased that his encounter with the president had made the papers. He was in his favorite place: the center of attention.

■ ■ ■

Morgan's voting trust terminated as planned on April 1, 1971, without notable event. The B shares were transferred to Bogle and the Boston principals, and relative peace between the warring partners reigned for a time. But by early 1973 the merger was unraveling before Bogle's eyes. He had underestimated the Boston Four, interpreting their complaints as mere carping, never believing they were serious about getting rid of him. On February 28, however, trouble began to brew again when Nick Thorndike requested a meeting with Bogle in Boston. During the meeting, Thorndike said that he planned to reassert his leadership of Wellington Management Company, which might mean crossing swords with Bogle.

The company's worsening financial prospects were not helping matters. The returns on the once-hot Ivest Fund had slumped severely, and even Windsor Fund was beginning to show signs of weakness in the stock market decline. With the sharp stock market drop in 1973, total assets of the funds, which had reached a peak of $2.6 billion in late 1972, tumbled to $2 billion at the end of 1973, a one-year plunge in assets of nearly 25 percent.

Wellington Fund was also faring badly. Its performance relative to that of its peers not only failed to improve—a key objective of the merger—but, under dynamic conservatism, which called for greater equity exposure and the use of lower-quality stocks, severely deteriorated as the go-go era came to an end and the overall market tumbled. The company tried valiantly to stem the fund's fall from grace, first under the investment direction of Doran, then Walter Cabot, then Daniel S. Ahearn, the company's economist, and finally with all three serving as a committee. Nothing worked, and the merger that was supposed to be Wellington Fund's dream was turning into a nightmare. The fund's assets, which had fallen from $2.1 billion in 1964 to $1.2 billion in 1972, would drop another $300 million, to $900 million, by the end of 1973. (Little could Bogle have known that the decline would continue for eight more years, with Wellington Fund's assets hitting a low in 1982 of $470 million, where they had been back in 1955.)

At $2 billion by the end of 1973, mutual fund assets managed by Wellington Management Company had fallen below their $2.4 billion level at the time of the merger some seven years earlier. While revenues from management fees and sales commissions had risen from $10.4 million in 1967 to $16.4 million in 1972, that proved to be the high-water mark; revenues declined to $15.3 million in 1973, the beginning of a steep descent. Wellington Management Company's earnings, at $2.3 million in 1967 and $2.7 million in 1972, tumbled to $1.9 million in 1973. Reflecting these reversals, in an increasingly bearish stock market environment, was the market price of the company's stock: $40 per share at the time of the merger in 1967, it fell to $8 per share early in 1974—hardly the expected result at the time of the merger.

A FRONTLINE PERSPECTIVE

In the late 1960s, Wellington Management Company had grown into a far larger organization than either Morgan or Bogle had ever imagined. At about that time, Karen West, who had spent four years working as a commercial paper specialist for Sears Roebuck Acceptance Corporation, joined Wellington as a staff accountant. Her first assignment was to bring order to the huge paper flow in the company by automating much of its operations.

Karen recalled that Wellington's staffers were still using giant, antiquated calculators, twice the size of today's desktop computers. Armed with these lumbering machines, as many as four people were needed to supply the price of Wellington Fund each day to the public. Staffers relied on punch-card computations, and if someone dropped a stack of cards or stepped on the tape and tore it, horrific delays were the consequence.

On occasion, West came into contact with Bogle, who often showed up just to chat with employees to make them feel good about their work. Sometimes, as someone worked out a problem on a calculator, Bogle would duck back into his office, grab his slide rule, and arrive at an answer first. But to West, Bogle's best characteristic was his ability to get beyond the numbers. While he crunched them swiftly, he seemed more concerned that Wellington protect the value of its clients' money.

Against this backdrop, and alarmed by Thorndike's threatening rhetoric, Bogle sought out Bob Doran to let him know that such talk made him a little nervous. Doran tried to reassure Bogle that Thorndike's comments were nothing more than those of a dissatisfied executive who wanted a larger role in the firm. Doran, though, knew otherwise, for he and Thorndike were plotting behind Bogle's back.

By the fall of 1973, Bogle was again feeling the heat from the Boston Four. They were careful to behave in a low-key fashion, so it was difficult to know what motivated them, but Bogle had two theories. One concerned James F. Mitchell, Jr., a veteran Wellington Fund director whom the Boston Four believed was about to retire. The Boston Four hoped that Mitchell's departure from the fund boards would help swing the boards in Wellington Management's favor, assuring the partners that they would be able to sweep Bogle out as head of the fund boards after firing him as president and CEO of Wellington Management. With Mitchell gone, the composition of the fund boards would be such that the Boston group seemingly would only have to persuade Richard Corroon to side with them, since Corroon was in neither the Boston nor the Philadelphia camp.

For his part, Bogle assumed that the Boston Four would move against him in April 1974, at which time Mitchell would be required to retire because of a fund board resolution from several years earlier that mandated retirement at the age of 70 for fund directors. With the Bogle–Boston feud in full force, the members of the fund boards who were sympathetic to Bogle wanted to keep Mitchell around so they would have his vote. As a result, when Mitchell turned 70 during the spring of '73, Charles Root submitted a resolution to the fund boards recommending that Mitchell be permitted to temporarily remain on the fund boards until the turmoil was resolved. Thus the Boston group suffered a major setback.

Another motive, in Bogle's mind, may have been the Boston partners' anger at Bogle's earlier decision to replace Stephen Paine as the manager of Explorer Fund because of its poor performance. The fund began successfully in 1967, ending the year with $17 million in assets; one year later, assets stood at $58 million. During its first years of operations, the fund earned a respectable return; however, during 1969–70, the fund's adjusted asset value declined 35 percent in a market off just 5 percent. Assets, in turn, fell by one-half, to $29 million.

Given this sorry performance, Bogle decided to turn the portfolio over to a new portfolio manager. Bogle believed that Doran, Thorndike, and Lewis were secretly pleased that he had carried out the dirty work. But the Boston Four maintained that Bogle was simply trying to undermine their standing in the company.

On September 26, 1973, one month after Wellington Management Company moved from Center City in Philadelphia to suburban Chesterbrook, near Valley Forge, the Boston Four met with Bogle. At the meeting, Doran informed Bogle that the four wanted more control over mutual fund activities. The dialogue was ominous, and Bogle felt that the die had been cast. Then, on November 14, 1973, Doran visited Bogle. "Things are just not working out," Doran said with more emotion in his voice than he usually betrayed. "I've talked to the others, and we think it would be best if you left the company." He added that there would be a financial settlement, suggesting a $20,000 annuity over 15 years; in return, Bogle would be required to relinquish his 4,000 shares of management company B stock at the current market value of the publicly traded A shares ($6.00). Doran, however, must have been aware that the real value of the B shares, which constituted a controlling block, was far higher.

Although Bogle's heart stayed steady, his voice did not. "I've heard of few stupider things than that," he sneered. "I've done an effective job. I've gone the extra mile to assure communications and harmony with all of you. I am just tired and annoyed enough by all of this to say, 'Make me an offer in writing and have it signed by all four participants.' " Bogle's proposal, however, was little more than idle talk, for he had no interest in taking the money from the company as part of a deal that required his resignation and ceded control to the Boston partners, his opponents, who would pay nothing for the privilege.

The Boston Four apparently believed that Bogle's offer was a serious one, for they began to put the word out that Bogle was about to be fired. The first to be informed was Walter Morgan, Bogle's mentor, who was crushed at what they were saying. "You can't fire him," said Morgan "He knows more about this business than all the people in Wellington Management Company put together." Then Doran met with Charles Root, who was "thunderstruck" at the news. He knew that the fund boards had neither the time, inclination, nor expertise to challenge the manner in which the company functioned, but he also knew that Jack Bogle was head and shoulders above the Boston group and that dismissing him could have serious consequences for the future performance of the funds. Root said he made it clear to Doran that if Wellington Management Company proceeded with its plan to fire Bogle, he would recommend to the fund boards that Wellington Management Company be removed as the investment adviser for the funds. At this point, Root recommended that the independent directors of the fund boards would be wise to seek their own counsel, so they hired Richard B. Smith, former commissioner of the Securities and Exchange Commission and a partner at the New York law firm Davis, Polk & Wardwell.

Despite how far the situation had deteriorated, Bogle still had trouble taking Doran and Thorndike seriously. In his mind, he was right, they were wrong, and in the end they would back down. Root explained to Bogle that such thinking was not grounded in reality, for he believed that the Boston group would not back down. He assured Bogle, however, that the fund boards would support him and that, if forced, they would move against Wellington Management Company. Bogle should have felt relieved, but he simply felt numb.

Fifteen days later, Bogle and Doran met again. When Bogle made it clear that he had no intention of resigning, Doran presented Bogle with two options. One was to leave the Wellington organization completely; the other was to leave the management company but to stay on at the funds solely in an administrative capacity, in essence as a chief clerk.

Bogle had to decide whether to cave in or fight.

FIRED WITH
ENTHUSIASM

JACK BOGLE DID NOT INTEND TO LEAVE the firm quietly. He intended to fight. He believed that the financial settlement offered to him was insulting. First, it was too small. Second, the money would be paid out of the pockets of Wellington Management Company, not those of the Boston partners. In the end, though, the nature of the financial offer did not matter, for Bogle had no intention of settling with the Boston Four on their terms.

In an effort to discover whether there was a way to save the situation for himself, Bogle talked with some of the Wellington Management Company directors. He knew it was pointless to seek out board members Thorndike, Paine, and Lewis, who clearly would vote with Doran, so he concentrated his efforts on the other Wellington Management board members. Doran, for his part, was not worried; he knew Bogle's efforts would be fruitless because he already had enough votes on the management company board to assure Bogle's dismissal.

One Wellington Management Company board member who belonged to neither camp was William G. Gallagher, hired after the merger to run the firm's national sales department. Knowing that Gallagher's vote would make no difference in the outcome, Bogle urged him to vote with the Boston group without regard to who he thought was right. "You probably will want to vote to get rid of me," he began one conversation with

Gallagher. "If you feel you ought to do it for your career, I'll understand." Bogle had read Gallagher correctly, for Gallagher felt that he could not afford to harm himself by alienating the Boston group.

When the round of calls to the board members was over, Bogle knew that the cause was lost. Doran had the votes. Bogle was going to be fired.

■ ■ ■

Although the Wellington Management Company board had all but made its decision, Bob Doran and the other members of the Boston group wanted to keep the matter from going before the fund boards, so they pressured Bogle to agree to a financial settlement. They asked Colman Mockler, who was an executive vice president of Gillette, a former member of the Ivest Fund board, and a friend of Thorndike's, to negotiate the terms of the settlement with Bogle.

On December 12, 1973, Bogle met with Mockler, whose mission was to persuade him to accept Doran's financial offer in return for resigning all his posts and relinquishing, without a "control premium," his management company B stock to the Boston group—the same deal the Boston group had offered on November 14. Enraged, Bogle called the offer blackmail. "If they want control of the company," he told Mockler, "they'll have to pay me out of their own pockets." The funds' board members were beginning to sense that the feud was getting out of hand. Barbara Hauptfuhrer wrote to Charles Root on January 3, 1974: "I am concerned about the possibility of reports of Wellington dissension causing damage to the shareholders. For example, such reports could conceivably trigger panic redemptions which would not permit orderly liquidations and therefore would be very harmful to the shareholders. Can this be avoided?" Apparently the answer was no, for four days later Bogle informed Doran that he would not accept the request for his resignation, "in part because of my belief that it was simply unfair for [Doran's] group to expect me to give up my control block of B stock to them without appropriate compensation." In light of Bogle's repeated insistence that he would not accept a financial settlement, it is unclear why the matter remained on the table.

The formal effort to relieve Bogle of his posts as president and CEO would undoubtedly come at the next meetings of the Wellington Management Company board, scheduled for January 23, 1974, and the fund boards, scheduled for the following day. Bogle knew that the only weapon left in his arsenal was his brainpower, so he planned to use the board meetings to talk about what he had done for the company and to propose creative ideas for the future. To prepare for these meetings, he wrote a 20-page memo that he distributed to the independent directors of the fund boards.

In his memo, Bogle touched on an idea that had been in his mind for several years, an idea he called mutualization. To appreciate how far-reaching this idea was, it is important to bear in mind how the conventional mutual fund company was (and still is) structured. The board of directors of a mutual fund routinely employed a management company that carried out all the functions that the fund required, from account administration, to distribution, to investment management. Because it invested the time and money to create and run the fund (or set of funds)—that is, because it assumed the entrepreneurial risk—the management company argued that it deserved to be compensated generously through the advisory fees it charged. Thus, a common contractual arrangement called for the management company to take an annual fee equal to, say, 1 percent of every dollar of fund assets under management. No one had ever questioned the benefits to fund shareholders of having an external management company, in part because the chief executive officer of the management company routinely chose his friends to serve on each fund's board, resulting in a cozy relationship between the management company and the fund board of directors.

In 1966, there seemed to be some momentum behind efforts to reform this traditional arrangement between the funds and the management company. When the Securities and Exchange Commission published a 300-page report entitled "Policy Implications of Investment Company Growth"—the first comprehensive review of mutual fund regulation since the 1930s—it commented favorably on two mutual fund groups that had, since their inception in the 1920s, operated on an "internalized" basis. By internalization, the SEC was referring to funds that had taken on for themselves the responsibility of handling the administration and investment-counseling functions rather than relying on an "external" management company. Referring to the two internalized fund groups, the SEC cited the many benefits they created for fund shareholders; however, for various policy reasons the SEC stated that it was not prepared at that time to recommend that the Investment Company Act of 1940 be amended to require mutual fund companies to internalize the management function. (As it happened, by 1981 both groups had abandoned their internalized structure in favor of the conventional external structure.)

Starting in the early 1970s, Bogle began to believe that Wellington's financial difficulties were partly the result of the company's organizational structure: The management company had all the power; the funds had none. In his view, the organizational structure was wrong because it permitted the management company to base its decisions on what was good for the company's executives and its shareholders (typically, then, they were the same individuals; the public offering of Wellington Management Company in 1960, which brought in outside public investors as shareholders, had made it an early and notable exception to the rule), rather than what was necessarily good for the fund shareholders. He believed that control and decision-making authority should be taken from the management company and turned over to the fund shareholders. Accordingly, he began to champion his proposed mutualized structure, which would transform Wellington Management Company from a publicly owned company into one that looked more like a mutual life insurance company. In essence, the fund boards would take over the management company, internalizing the various functions it originally handled. Not surprisingly, none of Bogle's early discussions about this idea had met with much enthusiasm, particularly on the part of the Boston group.

Still, in his January 1974 memo, Bogle proposed that the Wellington group of mutual funds acquire Wellington Management Company and its business assets. Wellington Management would then become a wholly owned subsidiary of the funds and would serve as their investment adviser and distributor on an "at-cost" basis. Bogle wrote: "Thus, the funds would become 'mutualized' and have an internal management structure. This conversion from the traditional industry pattern in which the mutual funds are served by an external investment advisor is, I believe, unprecedented in the mutual fund industry."

His idea certainly would have been unprecedented, which was why Bogle had little chance of getting it adopted. What's more, although Bogle was proposing that the funds buy out Wellington Management Company, he was not suggesting that the funds acquire TDP&L, which was itself managing $1.6 billion in assets. Under his plan, the private counseling firm would become a separate and independent entity; the funds would pay $6 million to acquire Wellington Management Company and its mutual fund activities, and in return would receive liquid and fixed assets valued at about $4 million. The remaining $2 million would represent payment for the "going concern" value of the enterprise. Bogle, of course, would be CEO of the newly acquired Wellington Management Company.

Bogle submitted his memo to the boards of directors of the funds and Wellington Management Company on January 15 and 17, offering four reasons that mutualization made sense:

1. It would be consistent with the broad changes in American life, including consumerism and a lessened public tolerance for conflicts of interest.

2. It would be consistent with specific changes in the mutual fund industry: "It would put to rest the nagging question of the appropriateness of a 'publicly held management company,' which has become a profound problem; it would help to relieve the marketing dilemma that a separate underwriter faces; it would do away with the perverse relationship in which the management company revenues inevitably decline when markets decline, requiring expense control when increased expenditures might be more appropriate. It would increase the role of the independent directors of the funds, placing them in the traditional posture of the directors of an ordinary corporation."

3. The cost savings to the funds would be, as Bogle put it, awesome. Costs to the funds could be reduced by 40 percent, equal to the annual profits of $2 million then being earned by Wellington Management Company on its fund activities. (Thus, the funds' net cost of $2 million for the acquisition would be repaid in a single year.)

4. It would, as a practical matter, put to rest the corporate problems with which the fund directors were dealing. "I would be less than honest," wrote Bogle, "if I did not acknowledge that putting these problems to rest is one reason for raising the mutualization issue at this time. However, . . . the present controversy might be a 'blessing in disguise' in presenting an opportunity to engage in a total corporate restructuring."

Bogle concluded his memo with a capsule summary of six arguments in support of his proposal:

1.   "It is the *right* thing to do, given the environment we face outside, in our industry, and in our own company."

2.   "It provides substantial cost savings to the mutual fund shareholders."

3.   "It is not harmful, and could even be helpful, to the management company shareholders."

4.   "It could be beneficial—or at least be the best alternative—for the Wellington organization and its employees."

5.   "It is eminently doable today. We cannot be sure whether or not this opportune moment will again recur."

6.   "Last—and perhaps least—it would reverse the 1967 merger that was good for Wellington Management Company, uncertain in terms of its benefits to fund shareholders, and, apparently, personally difficult for the principals who put that merger together. Very importantly, mutualization would put to rest these management problems on a positive note rather than a negative one, with the considerable public relations value (with respect to clients, shareholders, employees, the investment community, etc.) that would be involved."

At 10:00 on the morning of January 23, the members of the Wellington Management Company board met at its office near Valley Forge. Fittingly enough, on the walls were engravings of the Duke of Wellington's military engagements. Present were Bogle and the four Boston partners, along with Walter M. Cabot, John B. Neff, Daniel S. Ahearn, William G. Gallagher, Philip H. Gwynn and David D. Ogden (both executives of TDP&L), and Richard E. Eisner (the only nonofficer director and a long-time friend of Doran's). Thorndike conducted the meeting.

In the morning the board dealt with routine business. Then, after lunch, Bogle—still hopeful that some of the directors would change their minds and vote against his dismissal—presented his proposal on mutualization. It seems puzzling that the Boston group would have allowed Bogle to propose taking over the management company when they were planning to ax him at that very meeting; however, it is likely that they believed it was better to let him air his views so that no one could later complain he had not been given a chance to speak.

Bogle suggested to the Wellington board that the proposal regarding mutualization and the personnel matter they were about to discuss—his firing—could not be separated. Firing him, he said, would make it more difficult to mutualize. Sounding skeptical, Doran wondered aloud what motivated Bogle to bring up the proposal at this time. He then suggested that more study of the idea was required—a polite way of trying to bury it. The board agreed and approved a resolution creating a four-member committee, consisting of Neff, Ogden, Ahearn, and James L. Walters (the inside counsel for Wellington Management Company), to study the matter.

The board finally got around to its most controversial piece of business, the proposed termination of Jack Bogle as head of Wellington

Management Company. The group was split into two distinct camps. The smaller one included only Neff and Bogle himself. The second camp, that is, the 10 other board members seated around the table, was loyal to the Boston Four. Doran announced that a decision had been made to dismiss Bogle, a decision that would have to be approved by the Wellington board.

Clearly, Root's threat to ask the fund boards to remove Wellington Management Company as their adviser had not been enough to dissuade Doran: "We knew that the dismissal carried significant risk," Doran said later, "but it was deemed the correct thing to do anyway. Certainly the fund boards had the authority to take extreme action against Wellington Management Company. They could have said: 'You've just fired Bogle, so we're going to fire you.' It could have happened, but we thought it was unlikely. The fact is, we just couldn't be sure what the independent directors of the funds would do."

With all eyes on him, Bogle began to speak. His strong voice masked the emotion he was feeling. He had three requests: that Thorndike yield the chair to someone else, that a full record be kept, and that any votes be secret. Perhaps, he thought, in a secret vote, board members would feel freer to support him. After a brief recess, Thorndike retained the chair but agreed to keep a full record and to hold secret ballots. Then, abruptly, he posed the crucial question:

"Well, Mr. Bogle, will you resign?"

It was the low point of Jack Bogle's career. The board was giving him a chance to leave the organization without being fired. He had to muster all his strength to face what was about to occur. He offered to consider the proposal, but he went on to assert that the board needed to know why he was being fired. Doran briefly outlined the reasons for the decision; there is no indication that he relayed Root's threat to the board. When he finished, Thorndike again asked Bogle whether he planned to resign. In response, Bogle took out a 28-page document—his plea, as he called it— which he read in its entirety.

"We are sitting here today," he concluded, "more as a 'kangaroo court' than as a board of directors, given the uneven, unfair, and *ad hoc* nature of the change of events . . . and the advance commitments that have been made." He then rejected the request for his resignation for four reasons:

1. No case had been made that his dismissal would be in the best interests of Wellington Management Company: "To the contrary, it could cause irreparable harm to the company."

2.   The method of his dismissal was "in violation of elementary standards of fairness and of accepted standards of corporate practice."

3.   The terms of the request were "both unethical and illegal."

4.   His acceptance of the request would involve a "serious misuse of the company's corporate assets and a breach of fiduciary duty" on the board's part.

"The process I have outlined might lend itself to a college fraternity or a social club," Bogle said, "but it hardly comports with how a board of directors of a company responsible for $4 billion of other people's money should act. If it were not such a serious matter, it would be a joke." He went on to argue, "This company's business strategy and its implementation . . . has been sound, solid, and successful." To have increased company earnings when few other competitors have done so in a period of market turmoil, he suggested, was a "considerable accomplishment." He asked the board, knowing that it was packed against him, to "proceed with a truly open mind, devoid of past ties, personal loyalties, school friendships, and regional prejudice."

Bogle's words fell largely on deaf ears. The board voted 10 to 1 to request Bogle to resign in return for the company's agreement to pay Bogle $60,000 a year until he found work elsewhere, then $20,000 a year until he received a total of $320,000. Bogle abstained from the vote because of his financial interest in the transaction. The one vote in Bogle's favor was John Neff's. "The measure of a man," Neff said years later, "is how he handles himself when things aren't going well. That was Jack's finest hour, the finest one I've witnessed. He was being fired. He couldn't have handled himself better."

Even after the vote was counted, Bogle refused to resign. When he rejected the proposal, a second vote was taken, this time firing him outright, with 10 votes in favor and 2 abstentions (Bogle and Neff). The board then voted to pay Bogle his current salary to remain as a consultant to advise the new four-member mutualization committee—a committee that was never heard from again. Doran was elected president and CEO of Wellington Management Company. The meeting ended at midnight, but no one alerted the media until a day later. No one was interested in revealing, any earlier than necessary, the company secret—that Jack Bogle was out of a job.

Even though he had had plenty of time to prepare for his dismissal, Bogle was heartbroken about the decision. He could not believe that the board had actually gone that far, leaving his career in shambles and turning over to others the company he considered his own. Nor could he appreciate that his dismissal was to be a crucial step in the creation of something new—The Vanguard Group of Investment Companies. Later, after the pain had subsided and the Vanguard experiment was under way, Bogle joked with people that he had left Wellington Management Company the same way he came to join his soon-to-be-created Vanguard—"fired with enthusiasm."

Bogle arrived home at 1:00 in the morning and told his wife, Eve, that he had just been fired. Eve was not surprised, for she knew of all the quarrels and friction and the Boston group's desire to get rid of her husband. She wondered how he would take the decision, but knowing Jack as she did, she knew that he would fight back.

CHAPTER 8

BOGLE PULLS
A COUP

T 6:00 AM ON JANUARY 24, 1974, the day after he had been fired by the Wellington Management Company board, Bogle and his assistant, Jim Riepe, were on the train to New York, where the board of the funds was meeting that day. During the train ride, Bogle confided to Riepe, "I have two choices. I can fight this thing, or go quietly." Riepe sensed that Bogle was emotionally distraught, but there was no doubt that his boss had made up his mind. "If they want me out," Bogle said, "there will have to be a public hanging, not a private one."

Riepe tried to offer encouragement, but at the same time he felt awkward, for despite his friendship with Bogle, Riepe had responsibilities to Wellington Management Company. He fretted that sometime soon he would have to choose between Bogle and the firm. But the fretting did not last long; he knew that he could not abandon his friend.

Riepe wondered what action Bogle had in mind. An obvious option was a proxy fight, which would have required shareholders to choose sides between Bogle and his rivals in a vote over whether Bogle should have been fired; but Bogle had always said that he did not want to put the company through the expense of such an undertaking. (Some of the independent directors of the fund boards later expressed disappointment that Bogle did not mount a proxy fight, feeling he could have won; others

65

felt that such a fight would only have caused more disruption for the funds.) Changing the minds of the Wellington Management Company directors seemed impossible. At this point, it was unclear what action Bogle was contemplating, but the most promising option seemed to be to enlist the support of the independent directors of the funds.

Under federal law, the fund boards had to include a majority of directors who were independent of the management company. While the Wellington Management Company board was packed with Boston-oriented directors, Bogle had more support among the members of the fund boards, although votes would have been pretty evenly divided: Of the 11 members, 3 were Wellington Management Company officers (Bogle, Thorndike, and Doran), and the remaining 8 were independent. Of these eight independent directors, there were five who had earlier served solely on the boards of funds managed out of the Philadelphia office (Richard F. Corroon, Barbara Hauptfuhrer, John Jackson, James Mitchell, and Charles Root), and three who had earlier served solely on the boards of the funds managed out of the Boston office (Daniel S. Gregory, John T. Jeppson, and James O. Welch, Jr.).

If decisions were made by the fund boards along geographic lines, Bogle would have a chance of winning, for at least some of the independent directors wanted him to remain in place. He thought a vote of 6–5 in his favor might lie in prospect. His chances improved when Root, noting the conflicts of interest facing Bogle, Doran, and Thorndike, recommended that none of the three vote on issues that affected either them personally or Wellington Management Company. The board agreed, and the potential favorable vote, in Bogle's opinion, moved to 5–3. His chance of winning had risen.

The question was whether he could count on the support of the independent directors whom he considered his allies. They had the power to oppose the Wellington Management Company board, but for any of them to take up Bogle's fight would have required considerable courage. One of Bogle's supporters was John Jackson, who later said, "I deplored the whole situation. I didn't want to see Jack leave because I figured that if Jack left, the Boston group would have eliminated everyone in Philadelphia." Bogle's strongest ally, though, was Charles Root, who had long taken a dim view of the Boston group's investment abilities and who had threatened to recommend to the fund boards that they remove Wellington Management Company as the investment manager of the funds if Bogle were fired. Indeed, of all the supporting actors in Bogle's story, Root displayed the greatest courage, taking on an industry taboo by standing up to a management company for the first time in the industry's history.

Before the official board meeting commenced, the fund directors met in an executive session and heard from Doran and Thorndike about Bogle's dismissal. Root was convinced that Doran expected the boards to approve the dismissal without discussion and to immediately relieve Bogle of his posts as chairman and president of the funds. Root, however, had no intention of being bullied by the Wellington Management Company board members. He had too much respect for Bogle's abilities, integrity, and management style, and he felt that Bogle was necessary to the organization's survival. Like Bogle, he sensed what the rest of the industry up to that point had not: that the fund boards had power over the management company that as yet had not been exploited. The ace up their sleeve was the legal right to select for the funds not only their own chairman and president but whatever management company they desired.

■ ■ ■

Once the official meeting began, the directors conducted a wide-ranging discussion. With Bogle's dismissal hanging in the air, the directors thought it legitimate to raise a whole set of issues, all revolving around the relationship between the fund boards and Wellington Management Company. Should the fund boards continue their relationship with Wellington Management? If so, who should be responsible for the investment advisory function? Should other investment managers be asked to handle some of the funds? Although there were no easy answers, what was significant was that the questions were being discussed at all. The most urgent question, however—whether Bogle should continue as president and chairman of the fund boards—had to be answered immediately.

Bogle weighed in with his own views. "You don't have to fire me," he insisted. "This is your corporation. You oversee these mutual funds on behalf of their shareholders. Wellington Management Company doesn't own the mutual funds. This is a great opportunity for us. The funds ought to have their own voice." Bogle must have sensed some support around the table, for he went on to argue for his mutualization proposal. Some at the meeting were amazed at his boldness. For one thing, Bogle was hardly in an objective position. If by some chance the boards adopted his proposal and swallowed Wellington Management Company, Bogle would more than likely win back the titles taken from him the night before. For another, it seemed unthinkable for the head of the funds to advocate so radical an idea, given the lock that management company boards had historically maintained over their fund boards.

The Boston partners were cynical. Under other circumstances, they might have actually welcomed a chance to disconnect themselves from the faltering mutual fund business. But they saw Bogle's mutualization proposal as nothing more than a clever, last-minute tactic designed to salvage a job for himself. Bogle anticipated the attack and defended himself by pointing out that he had raised the issue several years earlier. In fact, in a July 1972 profile, *Institutional Investor* had reported that "Bogle had explored the possibility of mutualizing all or part of Wellington Management Company . . . to have the management company largely owned by the funds," and that he had questioned whether "a business like ours should be publicly owned and try to make a lot of money."

After asking Doran, Thorndike, and Bogle to absent themselves, the independent directors returned to executive session to thrash out these issues. Root and Hauptfuhrer insisted that the Boston partners could not "do this to us"—the *this* referring to Bogle's dismissal, the *us* referring to Bogle's supporters on the fund boards. Eager to retain Bogle and prepared to ignore Wellington Management's wishes that he be fired, the independent directors arrived at a bold solution. They concluded that Bogle should direct a major study—which would be called the Future Structure Study—that would examine whether and how the Wellington complex should be restructured. Bogle would be paid his regular salary and, along with Root, Hauptfuhrer, and Jim Welch, would examine the means by which the funds "might best obtain advisory, management and underwriting services in the future." It turned out that this ad hoc committee would hold only one perfunctory meeting to plan the strategy for the study; all further evaluation was conducted by the full fund boards.

Among the options to be studied by the fund boards were:

1. Continuing the present relationship with Wellington Management Company.
2. Splitting up Wellington Management's investment counseling and mutual fund management businesses.
3. Seeking one or more new investor advisers, managers, or underwriters.
4. Internalizing the funds' services by acquiring Wellington Management Company's mutual fund management assets.

Doran and Thorndike agreed that Wellington Management Company would continue to pay Bogle's salary and provide him with an office while he conducted the study. It was an incredible turnabout: Yesterday they had fired Bogle; today they were agreeing to keep him around and let him supervise a study that could result in the partial or complete dismantling of Wellington Management Company.

The most likely explanation for this turn of events is that Doran and Thorndike now understood something they had failed to understand the night before: that the fund boards were serious about opposing Wellington Management Company's decision to fire Bogle. While the fund boards could not be expected to overrule that decision, they wanted to retain Bogle in some capacity. Unless the Boston group dropped its efforts to remove Bogle entirely, the fund boards were ready to move against Wellington Management. In short, Doran and Thorndike probably concluded that agreeing to the Future Structure Study would give them time to devise a new strategy aimed at getting rid of Bogle.

The fund boards' decision to have Bogle launch the Future Structure Study was a remarkable event in the history of the mutual fund industry. By threatening war against a management company, the fund boards asserted their independence and established themselves as a separate entity rather than as a servant of the management company. The Future Structure Study was Charles Root's threat to the Boston partners made good, the opening shot in a war to be fought over who would control the funds— their boards or the management company's board. Despite the enormous implications of the Future Structure Study, a news release drafted by Bogle announcing the boards' actions attracted little media attention. Unlike today, business intrigue, however dramatic, was then of scant interest to the media, so Wellington's infighting remained largely a company secret.

Even as the story began to leak out, there was considerable confusion as to what was actually going on at Wellington Management Company. The confusion was exemplified by a *New York Times* article published on March 10, 1974. The headline in the early edition stated: "Ousted Fund Man to Come Back." But the headline in later editions was modified to ask: "Ex-Fund Chief to Come Back?"

Doran and Thorndike were devastated by the fund boards' decision. They had never taken Root's threat seriously, remaining convinced that the fund boards would never take on the management company. All along they thought they had solved the "Jack Bogle problem" and that Bogle would not fight back. Misreading him had cost them dearly, for now he appeared to be in a strong position to eviscerate Wellington Management Company. Mutualization was no longer pie-in-the-sky; it had a chance to become a reality. The significance of Bogle's coup was that now he could get his hands on the management company's most precious assets—the funds themselves.

As Bogle boarded the train back to Philadelphia later that day, accompanied by Riepe, he was emotionally spent and physically exhausted. He burst into sobs, not quite comprehending that his coup, against all odds, now had a real chance of success. His entire life to this point, however, had been a kind of finishing school for the past 24 hours. The cards he had been dealt—his family's financial setback during his childhood, his heart problems, the failed merger—had tested his mettle. Yet not only did he emerge from these skirmishes motivated to succeed, he found them uplifting. He loved getting up from the floor, dusting himself off, and delivering a knockout blow to his adversaries. The Boston partners had no idea what hit them.

CHAPTER 9

THE FUTURE STRUCTURE STUDY

AFTER THE FUND BOARDS MEETING on January 24, 1974, Jack Bogle seriously questioned whether he really wanted to stay with the Wellington organization. He had fought hard to remain in charge of the funds, but he wasn't sure he had enough tolerance left for the conflict and controversy that no doubt lay ahead. The closest he came to leaving Wellington was in the spring of that year, when he considered a leveraged purchase of Delphi Management, Inc., headquartered in Wilmington, Delaware. Delphi, owned by the Du Pont family, managed the Sigma Funds. While assets of these four mutual funds were less than $100 million, Bogle loved the mutual fund industry, and he thought he would enjoy the challenge of building up the Sigma funds without the contention he had endured at Wellington.

Making the decision to leave more difficult, however, was the fan mail he received from leaders in the mutual fund industry. Wrote the president of one firm, "Am shocked—and speechless—Can I help in any possible way? Good luck!" Chapman Clark, vice president of Auerback Pollak & Richardson, Inc., of New York, wrote: "Just wanted to let you know that your friends on the Street find the situation a little unbelievable—Wellington is Jack Bogle to most of us."

Bogle began to realize that there would be a price to be paid if he left Wellington to head his own firm: Doing so would allow the Boston partners to snatch victory from the jaws of defeat; he would be giving up the battlefield to them. Moreover, he was about to undertake the Future Structure Study, and he was curious to learn whether he could turn a study into a reality. What finally convinced him to stay, though, were the smirks he must have imagined would be on the faces of Doran and Thorndike if he decided to depart.

The timing of the Future Structure Study was, as a practical matter, propitious. From a high of 1052 in January 1973, the Dow Jones Industrial Average had plummeted to 800 in February 1974, and was to bottom out at 580 in October 1974. Wellington Management Company's stock price dropped from a high of $40 per share in 1967 and was on its way to $5 per share. This decline in the price of the company's stock was particularly galling to the Boston partners, who had acquired 148,000 Class A shares in the merger—once worth $1.5 million to each of them but worth just $185,000 at the low.

As mentioned earlier, Wellington Fund, the company's flagship fund with $2 billion in assets under management in 1966, had shrunk to $900 million in assets by the end of 1973. Assets of the once-hot Ivest Fund, nearly $400 million at their high, were less than $200 million. Shareholders were leaving in droves; 1974 would be the second year in a row of net capital outflow. Total fund assets had fallen from $2.6 billion late in 1972 to $1.5 billion in 1974, and the end was not yet in sight. Times were desperate, and anything that had a chance of improving the prospects of the Wellington Management Company funds seemed worth trying.

Bogle had no way of knowing whether the Future Structure Study would produce the kind of restructuring he advocated, but he was convinced that restructuring the mutual funds' relationship with Wellington Management Company would benefit fund shareholders. He pointed out, for example, that the CEO of the management company was also the CEO of the funds, and that the management company directed the entire package of services—administration, investment advisory, and distribution. Together, these two critical factors created what he derisively called a "Gordian knot" that bound the funds to the management company. Only by cutting the knot and distancing the funds from Wellington Management could the funds negotiate lower investment-counseling fees, either with Wellington or with other investment advisory firms. Costs could also be kept low by shifting ownership from the publicly held management company to the funds themselves, eliminating the need to generate profits and dividends for shareholders of the management company.

Bogle began preparing the Future Structure Study a few weeks after the January 24 board meeting. The funds' independent directors held numerous meetings with the key personalities, including Bogle, Doran, and Richard Smith, special counsel to the independent directors. Smith played a significant role in shaping the outcome of the study by insisting that the final decision by the fund boards' independent directors be unanimous. Smith knew that Wellington Management Company would do its utmost to block Bogle's mutualization proposal, which, if successful, would dismantle Wellington Management—but only after years of court battles. When Bogle learned of Smith's position, his heart sank. He knew that mutual-ization was now a long shot for the near future, since he was unlikely to get unanimous backing for it by the independent directors.

Proposals on other options flew back and forth, and the paperwork piled up. Bogle was relentless: He would prepare 50-page memos, outlining arguments the very least of which he knew the Wellington Management Company group would find outlandish. A Wellington representative would then write rebuttal memos; Bogle, in turn, would rebut the rebuttals. Jan Twardowski, Bogle's assistant at that time, called the whole process a little scary: "These guys . . . were at each other's throats . . . At the time it seemed petty, now it seems ridiculous . . . The big guys would meet upstairs and we toads, the workers, were downstairs . . . having a few drinks while the fighting was going on."

As the weeks unfolded, the study began to take shape under Bogle's direction. If Bogle was the architect of the study, however, Philip Fina, legal counsel to the fund boards and a partner at the Philadelphia law firm Stradley, Ronon, Stevens & Young, was the master craftsman. Fina's was the hand that organized Bogle's concepts into the charter of The Vanguard Group, Inc., spelling out the formal arrangements between Vanguard and the individual funds and drafting the application for exemptive approval by the Securities and Exchange Commission.

At the next meeting of the fund boards, on February 20, 1974, Bogle discussed with the independent directors the objectives of the proposed restructuring. Most important, he stressed that all of the myriad issues boiled down to one critical factor: independence—the independence of the funds to make decisions solely on the basis of the interests of their shareholders. The question was whether the status quo was really the best structure to serve the fund shareholders. As Bogle noted in his remarks to the fund board, "as the Funds perform more activities on their own behalf—rather than having them performed by Wellington Management Company—they not only become increasingly independent, but they can save massive amounts of dollars." Bogle went on to outline seven options for structuring the relationship between the funds and Wellington Management Company:

1. Continuing the existing relationship.
2. Internalizing any administrative functions that the funds would need to perform if distribution of fund shares and investment management were temporarily suspended. Wellington Management Company would continue as underwriter and investment adviser.
3. Internalizing all administrative and distribution functions. Wellington Management would continue as investment adviser.
4. Internalizing all administrative, distribution, and investment management functions by having the funds themselves acquire the fund operations of Wellington Management. (This was the radical mutualization step that Bogle most desired.)
5. Internalizing administration and distribution, with investment management supplied by a new adviser(s).
6. Replacing Wellington Management with a new external management company.
7. Internalizing administration, distribution, and investment management by creating a completely new internal organization.

By the end of the meeting, it was clear to Bogle that the independent directors wanted to focus the analysis on options 2 and 3; in their view, the latter options were too sweeping to be considered seriously.

RISING TO THE CHALLENGE

If the independent directors of the fund boards had shown their mettle earlier in the year by making sure that Jack Bogle remained as head of the funds, these same directors showed themselves to be even more committed and zealous in dealing with the Future Structure Study. For the most part, mutual fund directors were "one-day-a-month" participants, but with the Future Structure Study the fund directors likely spent more time and engaged in more rigorous analysis of the issues than any fund board had ever done. The steps they were considering were virtually without precedent, and they wanted to be sure they were upholding their fiduciary responsibility to do what was best for the shareholders of the funds.

As the study progressed, regular monthly meetings of the fund boards, which might normally have lasted only seven hours—from 9 AM to 4 PM—often became day-and-a-half to two-day sessions, lasting long into the night. In addition, there were numerous special meetings and committee meetings. Thousands of pages of documents were presented to the fund boards for analysis. Board member John Jackson became a particularly vital player. At one stage in June, Jackson huddled in New York City with the major participants for two consecutive days, working on the final shape of an accord, deciding who would stay with Wellington Management Company and who would work for the funds directly. Jackson's role, in the words of one participant, was to broker the deal that was put together: "By his doing so, we all avoided a confrontation and an outcome that no one could have lived with."

Accordingly, Bogle met with the directors at the next fund boards meeting, on March 20, and presented a fresh study entitled "The Future Structure of the Wellington Group of Investment Companies." The study first reviewed the economics of the current relationship with Wellington Management Company. Implicitly, it took for granted that a continuation of the existing relationship was now out of the question, so it analyzed the merits of the three most likely outcomes:

Option 1: Wellington Management Company would continue to provide the funds with investment management and underwriting services, but the funds would provide for themselves all administrative services.

Option 2: Wellington Management Company would continue to provide the funds with investment management services, but the funds would provide for themselves all administrative and underwriting services.

Option 3: The funds would acquire all of the investment company activities of Wellington Management Company, thus internalizing all investment management, administrative, and underwriting functions.

The independent directors' agreement that any decision on their part should be unanimous would, in Bogle's judgment, likely preclude Option 3. By gaining control of the three tasks integral to running a mutual fund company—administration, distribution, and investment advice—the funds could stand on their own feet and garner substantial cost savings for the fund shareholders. Thus, even though he suspected that the radical step of mutualization was dead for the moment, he continued to press this proposal, hoping to negotiate down to what he regarded as the next best alternative—internalizing the administration and distribution functions. He was interested in controlling the investment management function— where the profits were earned—but at least control of the distribution function would give him the truly arm's-length advisory relationship with Wellington Management Company that he wanted.

This compromise would still represent a radical change, for Bogle knew that attorney Richard Smith was concerned that the SEC might not allow the funds to pay for distribution directly out of shareholder assets. Bogle countered that the management company was already indirectly using shareholder assets to cover the cost of distribution, and it was charging higher advisory fees to cover those costs.

At the March 20 meeting, Wellington Management Company representatives opposed Bogle's mutualization plan on a number of grounds. They argued that Bogle was exaggerating the savings to be gained by the various options. They also maintained that if each fund shared in the cost of a common internal management organization, conflicts would arise: "The allocation of such costs would raise serious new conflicts between the shareholders of the different funds. Each fund's share of the management and distribution costs would depend on the method of allocation. The intensity of this conflict may well require that each fund have separate boards of directors."

Wellington Management Company also maintained that, as a diversified and integrated management company, its fund activities could not be severed from its counseling activities as easily as Bogle's proposal suggested. Trying to do so, representatives said, could drastically affect the quality of services provided to the funds. Insisting that they had provided the funds with "outstanding administrative services and produced a highly credible [sic] record of investment performance," they added that "a newly created internal management organization is hardly in a position to maintain existing management services, much less to strengthen them and adopt innovations."

Finally, the Wellington representatives noted that internalization would neither give the funds more independence nor diminish conflicts of interest between the funds and their management company. "It would," they argued, "only make the funds more dependent on their internal management and substitute new and novel conflicts of interest for the well-recognized and regulated ones posed by external management."

STARING OUT THE WINDOW

At the annual meeting of Wellington Fund shareholders on April 30, a "rump" movement to reinstate Bogle as president and CEO of Wellington Management Company arose. Thomas P. Emmons, a one-time vice president of a Wellington subsidiary, offered the resolution. Bogle claimed that he knew nothing about the proposal in advance.

As chairman of Wellington Fund, Bogle presided over the meeting and the shareholder vote. No one had the temerity to ask him to excuse himself from the chair while the vote was being conducted. To avoid catching the eye of anyone who might think that he was trying to influence the voting, Bogle stared out the window. By a show of hands, the shareholders voted 30 to 2 in favor of the resolution to reinstate Bogle. Fund counsel Andrew B. Young disparaged the vote as a popularity contest and told the shareholders, "You can tell Wellington Management Company what to do, but you can't require it to do it." The vote, however, sent a signal to the management company: Bogle remained popular with the fund shareholders.

■ ■ ■

By June the fund directors had neared a decision. After five months of dissecting and evaluating the options, they were prepared to determine the fate of the Wellington organization. If the Boston partners had been hoping that the study would end with Bogle's departure from Wellington, they were wrong, for he emerged from the study in a strengthened position. Though he had failed to persuade the independent directors that the funds should take over Wellington Management Company, he had persuaded them to make changes in the relationship between the funds and the management company, stripping the latter of some of its powers. The consensus of the independent directors was to recommend that the funds take over administrative functions, but that the distribution and investment counseling functions remain in Wellington Management's hands (in essence, to adopt Option 1 from Bogle's study). This less controversial change would realize the primary goal of the study, which, in Bogle's words, was to grant the funds corporate and business independence in order to provide "consistently superior performance . . . optimum cost-effectiveness . . . and new share distribution arrangements, through an incentive-oriented organization . . . with a corporate structure consistent with an environment of consumerism, new standards of business ethics, and increasing regulatory surveillance."

The board's decision, by the unanimous vote Smith had sought, was reached on June 20, 1974. The press release that announced the proposed new accord read in part:

> The Boards of Directors of Wellington Management Company and the Wellington Group of Investment Companies [i.e., the funds] jointly announced today that they have reached an agreement in principle concerning the future structure of relationships between the Company and the Funds.
>
> The agreement contemplates, in substance, the assumption by the Funds of the internal corporate administrative functions heretofore performed by the Company. Wellington Management Company will continue to serve as the investment advisor and principal underwriter for the Funds. The Funds and the Company are continuing to negotiate . . . a reduction in the management fees paid by the Funds.
>
> When the proposed restructuring becomes effective, it will mark a significant departure from the prevailing practice in the mutual fund industry, in which the mutual fund's manager typically furnishes a mutual fund with most of its required services including portfolio management, sales and distribution, and internal corporate administration.
>
> John C. Bogle, President of the Funds, commented that "the restructuring will give the Funds substantial independence in the negotiation and implementation of their investment advisory relationships."

The directors had, in the end, decided on the most conservative and least contentious option: investment advice and distribution would be left to Wellington Management, administration to the funds themselves.

On July 22, Charles Root traveled with Phil Fina to the SEC offices in Washington to update the SEC staff on the proposed restructuring of the relationship between the funds and Wellington Management Company. They were greeted with skepticism. "Well, what's in it for the management company?" the SEC staff kept asking. Root and Fina had difficulty explaining that the restructuring was not meant to benefit the management company, that it was supposed to benefit the funds' shareholders. Two days after the meeting with the SEC, the fund boards gave their formal approval of the restructuring plan, the day after the board of Wellington Management Company had formally approved it.

Bogle was pleased that he had won something, even if it was a side of the business that was not very interesting to him. In retrospect, he realized that he had been thrown only a few crumbs, for the more glamorous distribution and investment advisory functions still eluded him. He would be, at least for the moment, little more than the "chief clerk" that Doran had earlier envisioned. Still, his partial victory was a remarkable achievement for someone who only six months earlier had been fired from one of his jobs and was about to be fired from the other, and he knew that he now had something to build on. "Everyone must have known I was going to try to make something more out of this," he said. He was already planning to expand his responsibilities, even if some of them had not been formally agreed on. For example, while his staff was not supposed to give investment advice, one of its chief tasks would be to examine whether the funds were getting the best bang for the buck from their investment advisers. And, while the fund directors had committed to retaining Wellington Management Company as distributor, he had some ideas about how the funds could assume this role over time. Bogle guessed that a future, more sweeping reorganization could result in a reduction of at least several million dollars in the advisory fees paid by the funds to Wellington Management Company.

An immediate problem was to define what constituted administrative functions. Wellington had been administering the funds for years, so the question had never arisen. Now, however, the fund boards and Wellington Management Company had to be specific about who was going to do what. What became known as the "belly-up theory" became the guiding principle: The funds would be responsible for any function that, if left unfulfilled, would force the company to go belly up—to cease operations. Accordingly, all tasks that had to do with legal compliance, financial accounting, shareholder records, assuring that the funds' prices reached the newspaper on a daily basis, and balancing and auditing the books were to be handled by the funds.

Bogle tried to argue that the funds had been given more independence than was actually the case, observing that they would have substantial corporate self-sufficiency from Wellington Management. In reality, they still depended on the management company for investment advice and distribution. This was the conclusion drawn by the *Boston Globe* when it examined what it called the Wellington Compromise: "Bogle wanted mutualization. In the compromise he gets a base of operations, a staff . . . that work for him in Philadelphia, while the Wellington advisers in Boston keep $7 million in fees. The terms are not a dramatic shifting of power to the funds at the moment. Most of the fund employees already are based in Philadelphia. The management company retains the sales function since it was believed that distribution and investment management go arm in arm and fund shareholders should not have to subsidize the losses accrued from investment counseling."

■ ■ ■

It was not an ideal time to be devising novel concepts in the mutual fund industry, for the climate was pretty dismal. As chairman of the fund boards, Bogle wrote to shareholders of Ivest Fund that the 28 percent decline in the value of the unmanaged Standard & Poor's 500 Stock Index for the fiscal year ended August 31, 1974, was the largest drop for any similar period in the index's history, which dated back to 1926. Ivest Fund had done even worse; its net asset value fell by 43 percent. With his typical candor, Bogle wrote, "We (the management) regard the Fund's performance as unsatisfactory." When Daniel S. Gregory, a member of the fund boards, read what Bogle had written, he told Bogle in no uncertain terms that he had gone too far. Telling the whole truth about poorly performing funds, he argued, was dangerous and foolish. Shareholders, he believed, might sue the fund.

Wellington Management Company's other funds were not helping the organization. Technivest had been a disappointment; its assets shrank steadily and it was merged into Ivest Fund in 1973. Explorer's performance was even worse than Ivest's, and Morgan's was almost as bad. In just two years, Explorer's assets fell from $28 million to $9 million, Morgan's from $128 million to $67 million. Wellington Fund continued to provide sluggish performance; even Windsor Fund was a disappointment in 1973–74, although it would recapture some of that performance gap in 1975–76. Among the company's major fund offerings, only Wellesley Income Fund had performed with even relative distinction in the difficult stock market environment.

In short, the Wellington Compromise was precarious. No mutual fund had ever tried to assume its own executive and administrative functions; if the new structure became too chaotic, investors might pull their money out of the funds. Uncertainty hung in the air, and people were forced to take sides.

One person who was caught in the middle of the conflict was Raymond J. Klapinsky, now Senior Vice President and General Counsel of the Vanguard Funds. A University of Delaware Law School graduate who had worked as an attorney on the staff of the Securities and Exchange Commission, he joined Wellington Management Company in 1969. Klapinsky is one of the longest-tenured members of the Vanguard crew, and was both a first-hand witness to, and an active participant in, the formation of The Vanguard Group. Klapinsky was one of the few senior members of the Wellington staff who signed on with Bogle, and he soon proved to be a critical member of the new Vanguard team.

Bogle, for his part, placed a high value on Klapinsky's talents. "We started off with a mandate to perform only legal, accounting, and shareholder service functions," he said, "and it was critical that we perform them flawlessly. Ray has a strong legal background, a good head on his shoulders, an appetite for detail, and a great sense of balance and equanimity. He lived up to our highest expectations—and beyond."

Recalling the early days of the Wellington Compromise, Klapinsky emphasized "The biggest risk was that this thing (the Compromise) was going to fall flat on its face, that it just wouldn't work, that employees wouldn't attach to it because it was not the traditional way of doing things." In an effort to entice Klapinsky and others to their side, the Boston group played on those fears, warning the group that the small "compromise staff" would always be titular, with little to do. They pointed out that since they still provided the investment advice—the most powerful function in any mutual fund operation—in reality they continued to run the funds. Klapinsky and his colleagues feared that the Boston executives might be right. "At the time, there really wasn't much to running the daily operations of a mutual fund," Klapinsky observed. "Ninety percent of the job was investment advice." The administrative function, he concluded, was a nothing kind of job.

At the end of the summer, George Lewis, one of the Boston group, asked Bogle, "Aren't you going to be bored in your new job?"

Bogle thought to himself, little does he know what's coming.

FROM THE
DECK OF HMS
VANGUARD

ON FRIDAY, AUGUST 1, 1974, Bogle was driving north on the New York Thruway with his 14-year-old son, John Jr., to their summer home in Lake Placid. At the same moment, back in Philadelphia, the fund directors were debating whether to retain the Wellington name. The informal title of the 11 funds, the Wellington Group of Investment Companies, had been used to identify them as the property of Wellington Management Company. At issue was whether Wellington Management Company would continue to use its corporate name or whether the funds could use it as their group identification.

The issue was not a trivial one to either Bogle, Wellington Management Company, or the fund board members. Certain members of the fund boards, still bitter over the struggles earlier in the year, wanted to deprive Bogle of the Wellington name's goodwill. Others, however, were concerned that if the group had to take a new name, the funds would in essence be starting from scratch as a mutual fund company; all of the name recognition that had been built up over the years would evaporate. For its part, Wellington Management Company saw the Wellington Compromise as the start of Bogle's attempt to take control of all the funds' activities. For him to demand use of the Wellington name seemed presumptuous.

Bogle stopped at a rest area on the thruway and put in a call to Charles Root and Richard Smith, who gave him the bad news: the directors had agreed that Wellington Management Company should not be required to change its name. The funds could not continue (even if they wished) their use of the Wellington Group name, though the name Wellington Fund would remain. Livid, Bogle told them: "This is the last straw. That is such a stupid decision. I'm out of here. I'm going to resign. Leave the whole business."

Nothing in his past suggested that Bogle was that impulsive. He had not resigned when the Boston partners maneuvered behind the scenes against him, nor when they asked him to resign, nor when the board yielded fewer powers to the funds than he had hoped. Still, Bogle left Root with the impression that the "name thing" was the last straw. Root and Smith tried to calm him in a telephone call to Lake Placid early the next morning. "We've come all this way," Root said. "Forget the name. The name isn't important. You can call the new firm any name you want. Then go out and make it the best name in the mutual fund industry."

Bogle quickly reconsidered the matter and relented. He chose, however grudgingly, to take the sensible course and search for another name. Most of the names he thought of reflected the historical tradition of the Duke of Wellington. And the ones he liked best began with the letters W or V. At one point he considered the name Victory in honor of Admiral Horatio Nelson's flagship HMS *Victory,* on which Nelson had died at the Battle of Trafalgar in 1805. Bogle concluded, though, that under the circumstances the name seemed a little too much.

He finally came upon a name by accident. The fund directors had pressured the management company to allow him to keep his old office, but the prints on his walls, which were the property of Wellington Management Company, had been removed. He needed to replace them. An art dealer happened to call on Bogle in September to show him some Napoleonic War prints. Bogle bought a dozen, including six that depicted the Duke of Wellington's land campaigns and six, taken from a book published in 1825, that depicted Lord Nelson's naval battles. In appreciation the dealer gave him the book, which had several pages that explained each battle. Browsing through it, Bogle came upon some stirring words Nelson had penned nearly 200 years earlier: "Nothing could withstand the squadron under my command. The judgment of the captains, together with the valor and high state of discipline of the officers and men of every description, was absolutely irresistible." Nelson wrote these words from the deck of his flagship, fresh from an overwhelming victory over the French fleet at the historic Battle of the Nile in 1798; the flagship was HMS *Vanguard.*

Feeling that he, too, had been through a battle and had let nothing stand in his way, Bogle wanted to command a modern-day Vanguard, a name that to him resonated with themes of leadership and progress—of being "in the Vanguard." He was proud of his selection of The Vanguard Group as the new collective identifier for the funds. His decision was ultimately, if reluctantly, endorsed by the directors, who were apprehensive about the name. Thinking back, Bogle said, "The name Vanguard was almost too good to be true. It's as if it jumped off the page."

Bogle thought it was imperative to create a new core corporate entity, which made more sense than having each fund handle its own administrative chores independently. Accordingly, he created a new corporation, formally named The Vanguard Group, Inc., which would be owned jointly by the 11 funds and, in keeping with the Wellington Compromise, would provide administrative services to them. The company's expenses, including the salaries of its employees, were to be charged to the funds at cost, and the company would make no profit. No SEC approval was needed to create the new company, though the company did have to apply to the SEC for the right of the funds to share administrative costs. Pending SEC approval, The Vanguard Group of Investment Companies was incorporated on September 24, 1974. The 380,000 shareholders of the funds— Wellington, Windsor, Ivest, Explorer, Gemini, Trustees' Equity, Exeter, Wellesley Income, Morgan Growth, Westminster Bond, and Fund for Federal Securities—would be served by the new company.

With a staff of 59—of which 19 were in the executive and administrative groups and 40 in the fund accounting group—Bogle continued as president of each of the funds, earning the same salary that Wellington Management Company had been paying him, that is, $100,000 annually. The portfolios of the funds continued to be supervised by Wellington Management Company, which also continued to distribute the shares to the public through stockbrokers. Vanguard was responsible for keeping the funds' books and records, filing tax returns and official reports to government agencies, and handling other administrative functions that Wellington Management Company had previously performed. "Maybe a little on the dull side," Bogle confessed, but it had to be done to perfection for the company to continue to function. Typical of the administrative functions the company took on were shareholder record keeping and share transfers, which an outside vendor had handled for Wellington but which Vanguard decided, soon after its charter was approved by the boards, to internalize.

Bogle knew that founding a new company was not going to be easy. Although he had held leadership positions at Wellington, he had worked in the shadow of Walter Morgan and subsequently was hamstrung by the Boston partners. In a sense, when he started Vanguard he was starting from scratch, and he wanted others to judge him as a business leader based on his efforts at Vanguard. Many others had started businesses by identifying a consumer need, finding capital, and setting up shop. Bogle, however, had no interest in starting just another business. He portrayed the creation of Vanguard as the outcome of a titanic struggle, as the final act of a morality play, and he wanted the new company to be a beacon of light in an industry that, in his view, had lost its way.

He talked of the Vanguard funds as the only "mutual" mutual funds, a noble experiment, a test of whether a mutual fund complex could flourish under a new method of corporate governance, a new set of rules, and a new philosophy. Because The Vanguard Group was owned by its constituent funds, any profits it earned would be returned to the funds. While most mutual fund companies existed to make profits, Vanguard was unique in that it operated at cost, with only the interests of fund shareholders in mind. Bogle was determined to do what he believed many others in the industry had not done—give the shareholder a fair shake.

Bogle was careful, though, not to accuse others in the industry of totally overlooking the interests of their shareholders. He knew that other mutual fund firms maintained—indeed, had a fiduciary duty to maintain— that the interests of their fund shareholders were of primal importance to them. When a senior executive from a Vanguard competitor said to him, doubtless in jest, "By giving the client a fair shake, you're going to destroy this industry," Bogle knew that he was on the right track—that too many mutual fund executives were putting the desire to earn profits for their management companies above the desire to earn profits for their fund shareholders. On another occasion, the same executive exclaimed, "Bogle, if you had to get into charity, why did you have to pick this [expletive] industry?" Bogle decided that in addition to launching a new firm, he was going to launch a crusade to transform the mutual fund industry.

■   ■   ■

Bogle would have preferred to start his new enterprise when the economy was flourishing, but unfortunately it was in the throes of a serious recession. Although the stock market was just starting to shake off the effects of the severe 1973–74 bear market, the net cash flow of the Wellington—now Vanguard—funds had been negative for 40 consecutive months, a trend that would continue for 40 more long months, until January 1978. "The ghastly period of attrition," Bogle called those 80 months, when vastly reduced fund purchases by new investors were overpowered by huge redemptions from existing shareholders. In total, the net cash outflow was $930 million, equal to 36 percent of the funds' assets when the avalanche began. From its very creation, then, there were serious questions about whether Vanguard would survive and whether the fledgling company would have enough capital to keep the operation growing—in short, whether the Vanguard experiment would work. Though it was not an auspicious time to found a company, Bogle said he looked forward to getting "the fund shareholders out of the back seat and into the driver's seat."

The Vanguard Group immediately sought to establish a new, more independent relationship with Wellington Management Company. By diminishing Wellington Management's administrative responsibilities, the new arrangement quickly allowed Vanguard to reduce by $1 million—from $7.4 million to $6.4 million—the annual fees it had been paying Wellington. Beyond that, Bogle's goal was for Vanguard to be able to terminate part or all of Wellington's investment advisory services if required because of poor performance, high costs, or service quality. In fact, the funds already had that power, because their contracts with Wellington Management Company, like similar contracts in the industry, could be canceled with 60-days' notice. In reality, though, the management company held the funds hostage by retaining the distribution function it performed for the funds collectively. As long as Wellington Management Company distributed the funds' shares and absorbed the costs of doing so, the fund directors felt they could not simply pull the plug on any individual fund's investment advisory contract.

Although Bogle wanted, as he said, "independence from our investment adviser and corporate and administrative self-sufficiency for the funds," he denied that the funds intended to abandon Wellington Management altogether. At the time he said, "Don't interpret [the Wellington Compromise] as a halfway step in replacing Wellington Management Company. That's not been contemplated. We're trying to put our funds in the same posture as any pension fund, university, or foundation with money to invest, giving the funds the ability to deal with Wellington Management Company at arm's length. Under the new setup, our adviser will have greater incentive to perform because the contract is at stake." He added that Vanguard's eye would be solely on "the shareholders' interests in terms of the funds' expenses, the investment advisory fees they pay, and the funds' performance."

On February 19, 1975, the company announced that the SEC had approved its proposal to reorganize itself as The Vanguard Group of Investment Companies. Proxies were soon distributed to shareholders, whose approval came at meetings held on April 22. Vanguard began operating on May 1, 1975, the newest player in an industry comprising 390 U.S. mutual funds, whose combined assets totaled $45.9 billion. The board of directors of the funds remained in place, becoming the new Vanguard board—an arrangement that troubled Bogle, for it meant that two of his adversaries, Doran and Thorndike, would still face him across the board table. With no intention of ceding to them any of his powers as president of the funds, Bogle developed a good rationale for removing them from the board: "If we're going to be independent," he told the board, asking for Thorndike's removal, "let's really be independent. Let's not have any Vanguard director associated with any fund's investment adviser." The board concurred: Thorndike left the board in 1976, Doran in 1977.

■ ■ ■

Early in its existence, Vanguard struggled with name recognition. Although many people recognized the name Wellington, few had any idea who or what Vanguard was. Because of the company's lack of identity, many of the staffers at Vanguard were afraid that the new arrangement would not work—and year after year of declining assets seemed to confirm those fears. At the same time, a sense of exhilaration somehow penetrated the gloom. The very fact that there was no real path or model to follow in their building of Vanguard created in the staffers a sense of camaraderie that helped them overcome the difficult days at the company's founding.

There was a lot of grunt work at the beginning, little of it terribly creative, but no one seemed to mind. One example: In the aftermath of the internalized administration, Ray Klapinsky had to prepare proxies for the shareholder meetings of the 11 funds, and revise and update all of the funds' prospectuses. But even such nitty-gritty work was performed with enthusiasm. Said Karen West, who became vice president and controller at Vanguard, "We all thought it was very exciting, all this Wall Street activity. You'd listen to the news . . . and think that this could affect what I'm doing tomorrow. You felt a part of things. You were not just making widgets."

The Vanguard Group needed this sense of excitement, for as a private company, owned by the funds, it was not a candidate to go public. Given Bogle's aversion to company executives cashing in at the shareholders' expense, no one there was going to get rich quickly. Some were surprised. Ian MacKinnon, who would arrive at Vanguard in 1981, admitted, "I didn't realize until a year later that there wasn't a piece of the action to get, that I had signed up with a mutual fund company where there was no equity. I discovered, not to my dismay but to my surprise, that this was not a small investment company, but a small mutual company owned by the funds themselves, owned by the shareholders of the funds." Word got around the mutual fund industry that one paid a financial penalty by going to work for Vanguard. Vanguard did little to dispel that reputation, but within a few years would develop a unique plan that made every employee a partner, sharing in the firm's profits. Nonetheless, Bogle continued to believe that the members of his crew shared his idealism and worked toward a higher purpose: the welfare of fund shareholders. Bogle had gotten his way.

11

CUTTING THE GORDIAN KNOT

DURING THE LATE 1970s, the only bright spot at Vanguard was its money market mutual fund. Introduced by Vanguard in 1975, it invested in very short-term (typically 30 to 90 days to maturity) high-quality debt securities such as certificates of deposit, high-grade commercial paper, and U.S. Treasury bills. With yields rising to as high as 16 percent and a net asset value of $1.00 per share that was expected to hold stable, money market funds had become an attractive alternative to low-interest bank accounts and even equity funds. They changed the face of a troubled mutual fund industry. By the end of 1981, the assets of Vanguard's money market funds had grown to $1.6 billion, representing 40 percent of the total assets of the company.

The rest of the mutual fund industry had also come to rely primarily on money market funds. Traditional long-term stock funds were in the doldrums, and Vanguard's stock funds were no exception. As the stock market recovered from the 1973–74 crash, Vanguard fund assets grew nicely—from $1.45 billion in 1974, to $1.78 billion in 1975, to $2.05 billion in 1976. While cash outflow slowed—from minus $127 million in 1976 to minus $89 million in 1977—Vanguard's investors continued to redeem more shares than they purchased, and fund assets fell back to $1.85 billion by the end of 1977. With investors still focused primarily on stock funds, Vanguard's competitors were attracting far more assets than the new company, which was stronger in bond and money market funds than in equity funds.

Early in 1976, only eight months after Vanguard had officially begun operations, Jack Bogle began to formulate a plan to reverse Vanguard's disappointing performance. Under the current arrangement, Vanguard was responsible only for the administration of the funds; distribution and investment advice were still in the hands of Wellington Management Company. Bogle's goal, no matter what he may have said publicly, was to make Vanguard fully independent of the management company by ultimately assuming control over these two functions. He decided to continue slashing at the Gordian knot that he had described earlier as binding the funds to the management company. He would do so by taking over the distribution function.

Vanguard—and the Wellington funds before its creation—had been content to allow Wellington Management to handle the distribution of its shares. While vital to the company, distribution was essentially a profitless task, and the management company had been willing to do it at cost, or even at a loss, because it helped to increase the company's assets under management, generating higher advisory fees. Further, the management company knew that distribution was a valuable card. Bogle, however, knew that by taking the distribution function out of the hands of the management company, Vanguard would be free to negotiate advisory fees, terminate existing contracts, and hire any adviser it wanted to. And, because the largest profits in the mutual fund business arise from the fees paid to the investment adviser, Vanguard's freedom to choose its invest- ment adviser would have a direct, adverse impact on Wellington Management's pocketbook.

"To confront that issue directly," said Bogle, "to say we're going to pay a distribution fee and a management fee separately so that we can deal with the manager at arm's length, was our goal. We were trapped because you can't really fire the investment manager. If you did, who would distribute the fund's shares? By taking over the distribution, we would basically shift the control over the operation to . . . Vanguard. It would then be only a matter of time before we started to do our own investment management, because our fund advisers in a couple of cases weren't doing a very good job and because the management fees were too high in areas such as money market funds, where high fees subtract directly and mean- ingfully from return, without any possibility that they will lead to better performance."

The key to taking over distribution, Bogle believed, was converting the funds to a no-load distribution system. So Bogle began campaigning to eliminate the funds' sales loads and market their shares directly to investors without a stockbroker acting as an intermediary. Wellington Management Company strongly opposed conversion to a no-load distribution system. Bogle, however, believed that the door had been opened for Vanguard to assume responsibility for this critical marketing area— just as had been proposed in the 1974 Future Structure Study.

As is the case today, mutual funds then could be purchased either directly from the management company, which sold its funds through advertising, mail solicitation, and word-of-mouth, or from an intermediary such as a stockbroker, a financial planner, or a bank. Funds that were sold through these intermediaries charged a sales commission, or load. (A sales load is paid by the investor to an outside party such as a broker, as distinct from the annual fees the funds paid to Vanguard directly for administrative services.) Generally, about 80 to 90 percent of the load went to the selling broker; the rest went to the management company to compensate it for distributing the funds. The companies that managed funds garnered large revenues from these sales loads, which, like Wellington's, started as high as 8.5 percent for purchases up to $10,000 and declined as the size of the purchase increased. Despite the revenues, sales loads placed an added burden on the management company: Because the sales load reduced the size of the investor's return by the amount of the load, the load funds had to perform significantly better than the no-load funds just to stay competitive. As Bogle often noted, the sales load meant that an investor running a 100-yard race was starting on the 108-yard line.

Bogle believed that for Vanguard to survive, the investment performance of its funds had to become more competitive. The best way to do that, in his view, was to make Vanguard the lowest-cost provider in the industry. That required not only maintaining minimal operating expenses and negotiating rock-bottom investment advisory fees, but offering the funds on a no-load basis as well. In the 1960s and early 1970s, though, when most mutual funds were equity funds, costs seemed to matter little to investors. Only when the money market segment of the industry began to burgeon in the 1970s did the issue of costs begin to command attention, since competition came to preclude most such funds from charging sales commissions. The timing seemed right for Bogle to bring his idea to fruition.

Bogle's decision to go no-load had almost the same revolutionary feel as his decision to establish Vanguard. By going no-load, Vanguard would no longer require the services of wholesalers, who for decades had been the link between the Wellington organization and the broker/dealer network. Employees at Wellington Management Company were used to the system, which had paid enormous dividends to them over the years. The firm had relied on the broker/dealer network to distribute shares of the funds, and load funds had been the traditional distribution method since the industry's inception in 1924. Eliminating the wholesalers and having investors bypass the broker/dealers to deal directly with Vanguard would be a radical change from past practice, one that would likely cause immense anger among the broker/dealers, who had been entirely responsible for bringing in the assets of the funds.

Bogle had long considered that no-load funds could have a profound effect on the industry. In a speech in 1971, he allowed that "the big competition in the mutual fund field will continue to be within the conventional system of dealer distribution . . . The dealer, after all, can help average investors cope with the complex issue of evaluation of which funds are most suitable for them." He went on to say, though, that "major inroads will be made by no-load funds at the expense of captive distribution (fund organizations which distributed through their own sales forces). The astonishing trend in this direction is little noticed thus far, but is one of the most significant in the mutual fund industry—the no-load funds are now outselling the captive distribution funds." In an *Institutional Investor* article in 1972, he went even further, saying, "If we [Wellington Management Company] cannot sell through broker-dealers, the alternative that is most in keeping with our philosophy is to go no-load." Now, just four years later, the issue was squarely on the table.

Bogle believed one of the powerful incentives for Vanguard to convert to no-load was the consumerism he had predicted in 1974: Cost-conscious consumers were becoming less willing to pay the 8.5 percent sales load, so eliminating it could be a way to attract them back to the mutual funds they had been leaving. A second reason was that in the long run it would become more and more difficult for fund organizations to get the broker/dealers to sell Vanguard funds, because the brokerage firms had a large and growing number of their own mutual funds to choose from and would soon begin to offer them through their broker/dealer networks. Third, and perhaps most important, Bogle thought that a major part of the future for mutual funds lay with institutional investors, which at the time represented only 20 percent of Vanguard's business—a figure he wanted to raise to 50 percent. Going no-load would encourage institutional investors to link up with Vanguard in larger numbers. Institutions were traditionally averse to paying a load; if Vanguard went no-load, its funds would automatically look more attractive to them.

The twin decisions—to go no-load and to assume distribution responsibilities—began to come together at Vanguard in June 1976, when a meeting was held at the New York office of Richard Smith, who had been special counsel to the independent directors of the funds during the tempestuous period of 1974. Attending the meeting were Bogle, Jim Riepe, Philip Fina, and two Wellington Management Company attorneys, James Walters and Richard M. Phillips. High on the agenda at the meeting was the issue of whether the funds should engage in the "separate pricing" of advisory and distribution services, paying Wellington two separate fees under two separate contracts, and whether the SEC would permit Vanguard to use fund assets to pay for distribution in that fashion. Fina thought that the SEC would, but he urged caution. Smith persuaded Bogle to proceed more slowly than he would have liked. Nonetheless, for the next six months the issues of internalizing distribution and going no-load were consuming subjects at board meetings.

Once again, Bogle had to face some old adversaries. Bob Doran and Nick Thorndike were still on the fund boards (though they would soon leave), and the two forcefully opposed Bogle's plan to take on distribution responsibilities. They understood its devastating implications for Wellington Management: a further erosion of its hold over the funds and, more significant, the decrease in advisory fees that would be in store for them, since advisory fees had been used to subsidize distribution expenses. They contended that the dealer distribution network was vital because dealers could do a better job of distributing and marketing shares than Vanguard's staff could. And by going no-load, they argued, Vanguard would automatically give up crucial sales volume. According to Bogle, Doran had described the likely result of a conversion to no-load as "the holocaust." (Doran would only say, "I might have used that term. I just don't remember.") Doran stated that he had been positioned as being against no-load, when in fact he had not been opposed to using the no-load approach as part of a broader "variable pricing strategy," which might have included a low load or even no load on fixed-income products and the highest loads on the most aggressive equity products.

Whatever Wellington Management's stance on the proposal to convert to a no-load distribution system, Vanguard did not need Wellington's approval to implement either the separate pricing proposal or the internalized distribution proposal. Bogle, however, needed time to persuade the fund directors that the long-term rewards of this essentially irreversible strategy far outweighed the obviously substantial short-term risk of eliminating all sales through Wellington Management's network of broker/dealers before Vanguard could gain adequate distribution volume on its own. This problem was not trivial, because the funds would need an SEC exemption permitting them to bear the costs of distribution directly. Given the length of time involved to secure such an exemption, unless the funds were permitted to put the plan into operation on an interim basis, they would be dependent on Wellington Management's willingness to continue to finance a distribution effort out of its advisory fees.

Emotions ran high at the Vanguard board meetings over the next several months. The Vanguard board was split into three groups: one that had wanted to go no-load when the company was first formed; a second that objected to all forms of internalization, even administration; and a third that favored absorbing the distribution function but was worried that the SEC might throw a roadblock in Vanguard's way. Ray Klapinsky, secretary of the funds, recalled: "You'd come into a meeting, Jack would present something, and Wellington Management would have an opposite presentation. Wellington Management opposed us the whole way." Bogle argued that the wave of the future was no-load distribution, which would benefit shareholders and new investors. He further argued that the current distribution system was breaking down—that in fact it had been unprofitable to Wellington Management for a number of years and that distribution had been subsidized by Wellington out of the advisory fees paid by the funds.

Despite his compelling arguments, Bogle was not without concerns about taking such dramatic steps. His long experience with Walter Morgan had conditioned him to believe that the broker/dealer system was inviolate. Over lunch one day with Vanguard board member John Jackson, he confessed his fears. Recalled Jackson: "He was properly concerned, maybe frightened, by the notion that if we go no-load, get rid of the sales force, what happens if everyone redeems? Anybody whom Jack talked to in the brokerage business told him to forget about going no-load. They told him: 'You have to have a broker to sell the funds.'"

Bogle eventually set aside his fears, saying, "I don't see how we can do much worse than we're doing right now."

■ ■ ■

It was finally time for the Vanguard board to reach a decision on these issues. One critic of Bogle's proposals was Walter Morgan: "I was opposed to it," he said, "because I had so many friends who were in the investment business and they were somewhat annoyed that they might lose their commissions for selling Wellington Fund." Morgan, who did not have a vote in the matter, nonetheless did not try to dissuade Bogle; one of the most important lessons Morgan had taught Bogle was that if you believe you're right, press ahead, no matter what others say.

In late January 1977, the Vanguard board met and apparently came near a decision on the no-load distribution plan. Bogle was angered and frustrated when the board deferred the decision until a further review could be undertaken. In his view, internalized distribution had been studied to death—not only during the six-month 1974 Future Structure Study but also during the six-month period after the July 1976 decision to investigate converting to a no-load fund organization. Earlier in the month, Vanguard director Dan Gregory (who opposed internalized no-load distribution) had submitted a new list of questions to which Bogle and his staff had responded. To Phil Fina, it seemed that there just wasn't anything more to say or study about internalized distribution. Fina, in a letter to Jack Bogle many years later, recalled that day as if they were engaged in some great military battle and focused on Bogle's ability to rise above the bitter disappointment of the board's postponement of the issue.

Bogle, Fina, and the rest of the group pressed ahead, and when the board next met on February 8, 1977, again in New York, the discussion ran into the early morning hours. The issue was finally joined at 1:30 AM, when a vote was taken. The distribution plan proposed by Vanguard—and championed by Bogle—was adopted by a vote of 7–4. In the end, the chief reason for the board's favorable vote was the majority's agreement with Bogle's conviction that no-load distribution was the wave of the future in terms of consumer preferences and successful marketing.

Going no-load—and choosing Vanguard as distributor—also seemed a good way for the directors to address their concerns that Vanguard was too dependent on Wellington Management Company, and too weak to force the management company to mend its ways. By adopting Bogle's plan—replacing the old direct-distribution system with a no-load system, and replacing Wellington Management as distributor—Vanguard could take responsibility for its own actions. Although he was obviously pleased, Bogle, ever the competitor who hated to have things come too easily, was perversely disappointed that the vote was not closer. (In fact, he expected director Corroon, who finally voted in favor, to vote against. That would have made the vote 6–5, an outcome Bogle seemed to enjoy contemplating.)

In the wake of the decision, one Boston director, Daniel S. Gregory, resigned. He was not angry about the decision, but he disagreed with it and felt uncomfortable sitting on the board any longer. Jim Welch, too, had voted against the plan, but he remained on the board, eventually becoming a strong believer in Bogle's plan. But whatever each individual board member's personal beliefs, the issue had been decided. In effect, Option 2 in the Future Structure Study had been approved just three years after it had been rejected. The second step along what would be a three-step path toward full mutualization had been taken.

■ ■ ■

Cynics in the industry scoffed at Bogle's steps. Dreyfus ran full-page ads with its lion roaring "No Load? No Way!" Brokers were incensed, and Bogle and his staff took numerous calls from brokers who loudly announced their dismay and anger with the new arrangement, and threatened to recommend that their clients redeem their Vanguard fund shares. The day after Vanguard announced that it was going no-load, Jan Twardowski took such a call from the head of a brokerage firm who was placing a $1 million order for the Windsor Fund, an enormous order at that time. Recalled Twardowski: "He went ballistic. He had convinced his client that Windsor was the best fund ever, and he wasn't going to get paid for his work. Who could blame him?"

Indeed, the risks to Vanguard were large. As Twardowski said, "We didn't know if it would work or not. We didn't know how to advertise or do direct mail. We created the whole marketing operation from scratch. We hired people; but some didn't work out. None of us knew how to sell directly to investors." Vanguard's challenge was to find a whole new set of self-directed investors who could be lured into buying funds through direct mail and advertising, and eventually word of mouth. Bogle remained confident that, despite the interim peril, no-load was indeed the wave of the future and that he was going to ride that wave. Moreover, he was convinced that going no-load was simply the right thing to do for investors.

Through it all in those early days of no-load, the concern remained that broker/dealers who had sold Vanguard fund shares would direct their clients to redeem their Vanguard shares. Bogle insisted, though, that massive redemptions were unlikely. Brokers who redeemed shares without good cause could face trouble with securities regulations calling for fair practice on their part, and a fund's going no-load, he believed, did not constitute good cause. Besides, he argued, Vanguard was a small company with a thin budget and fewer than 60 employees, so it could survive even if its fund assets were cut in half. As it turned out, no significant increase in redemptions came to pass. Redemptions in the two years following the conversion to no-load averaged 1 percent per month—only barely above the 0.9 percent rate of the preceding two years—despite the poor returns of Wellington Fund and Ivest Fund, which continued to disappoint Vanguard, even in the market recovery from the lows reached in late 1974.

Aiding Vanguard significantly during the years following the conversion to no-load were the growing assets of the John Neff–managed Windsor Fund, which rose from $300 million at the end of 1974 to $600 million at the end of 1978. Bogle reasoned that Windsor's recent record, which had returned to top form in 1975 and 1976, along with Neff's growing reputation, would make brokers think twice about recommending redemption by their clients. Despite the elimination of the broker/dealer sales force, investor purchases of Windsor shares rose from a total of $48 million in 1975–76 to $117 million in 1977–78. Windsor supplanted Wellington Fund as the firm's largest fund—flagship of the Vanguard fleet—early in 1979, its assets growing to $625 million even as Wellington's assets declined. Growth continued apace, and Windsor crossed the $1 billion milestone early in 1982. There was nothing like a top-performing fund to ease the pain of transition, and Neff's contribution to Vanguard's early survival was little short of immense.

■ ■ ■

Accelerating Bogle's decision to go no-load was the company's impending plan to introduce Warwick Municipal Bond Fund, the first-ever multiseries municipal bond fund. The fund would offer investors different bond maturities and various kinds of strategies. An investor could thus select a long-term municipal bond portfolio, or an intermediate-term portfolio, or the equivalent of a tax-exempt short-term money market portfolio—the industry's first. Most directors agreed with Bogle that attaching even a 6 percent sales load to a portfolio of municipal bonds would make it more difficult—even disabling—for the investment adviser to produce good net returns for fund shareholders. A load also seemed deceptive, since investors would be paying for investment advice that was no doubt deemed essential at the time for equity funds but that mattered far less for high-grade bond funds with carefully structured maturity schedules.

Warwick Municipal Bond Fund began operations on September 13, 1977. The initial concern about who would provide the investment advisory function for the fund had been put to rest earlier in the summer. Vanguard had been able to take over the administration and distribution functions with relative ease, but providing investment advice was a skill that no one in the company could hope to master overnight. (Eventually, Vanguard would hire in-house investment managers, at least for the fixed-income side, where the firm's low-cost structure would provide the greatest advantage.) Until Warwick Municipal Bond Fund came along, Wellington Management had always performed the investment advisory function for the Vanguard funds, but Vanguard was trying to liberate itself from Wellington Management. So it broke with tradition and hired Citibank as Warwick's investment adviser. "That decision was significant," recalled attorney Phil Fina, "because it set in motion the possibility that Vanguard would be restructuring itself and making its own decisions."

Adding momentum to the recovery of the assets of the Vanguard funds was the success of its new money market fund. For the investor who was accustomed to dealing directly with a bank, Vanguard's no-load money market fund—originally named Whitehall Money Market Trust—had large appeal. At the time Vanguard's money market fund was introduced, the interest rate banks could pay on deposits was limited by federal regulation to 5.5 percent. As annual inflation rates soared into double digits, individual savers in bank accounts saw the purchasing power of their savings being quickly eroded. Money market funds gave individual investors a way to do what big corporations were doing—earning double-digit rates of interest on cash reserves invested in money market instruments such as commercial paper.

The growth of the money market segment at Vanguard was crucial to the company's overall growth, for once investors were introduced to the money market funds, they were more inclined to try out Vanguard's other funds. The strategy appeared to be working: In 1977, some $80 million had flowed out of the company's coffers; by the next year, $52 million had come in, and $280 million the year after that. By the close of 1979, Vanguard's assets had reached $2.4 billion and were on their way to surpassing the previous high of $2.6 billion reached late in 1972. By the close of 1980, assets had crossed the $3 billion mark.

In the meantime, Vanguard was introducing other new funds. The company expanded its bond fund offerings by introducing a high-yield municipal bond fund and a high-yield corporate bond fund late in 1978. One year later, a GNMA ("Ginnie Mae") income fund was added, the first such fund available on a no-load basis. In 1981, an international growth portfolio was introduced as a distinct component of Ivest Fund—with a new manager, London-based Schroder Capital Management International. It was among the first mutual fund portfolios investing in foreign securities.

(It would become a separate fund in 1985.) Vanguard's marketing plan—to build a comprehensive family of mutual funds—was beginning to take shape.

■ ■ ■

Now that Vanguard had assumed the job of selling and distributing its own funds, it had to figure out how to pay for it. To Bogle, the answer was obvious: the money should come directly from shareholder assets. Indeed, there was now no other possible source. For many years, the funds had been paying an overly large investment management fee to Wellington Management Company that was sufficient to subsidize Wellington's distribution costs. Now that Wellington would no longer be paying the distribution costs, Bogle saw nothing wrong with overtly using shareholder assets to pay reasonable sums for distribution. After all, distribution was required if fund assets were to grow and economies of scale were to be achieved for fund shareholders.

Bogle's stance was directly opposed to the prevailing industry practice, in which distribution costs were covertly subsidized by large management fees, and the profits that were realized from economies of scale were salted away by management companies rather than benefiting fund investors. Bogle reasoned that the interests of full disclosure would be served by laying distribution expenses out in the open rather than burying them in the management fees paid by the funds.

The problem was that the SEC had concerns about Bogle's plan, and Vanguard had to receive SEC approval to use shareholder assets to pay for distribution. In the early 1970s, the SEC had made a number of public pronouncements to the effect that the Investment Company Act of 1940 made it improper for mutual funds to bear distribution costs. The SEC believed that the management company, rather than the funds, should bear the costs. Ironically, the SEC's own studies at the time were demonstrating that industrywide distribution revenues (i.e., sales charges) were not covering the distribution costs. Therefore, fund investors were already paying the costs of distribution out of their assets through higher management fees. Vanguard's studies concurred with those conducted by the SEC. Bogle was determined that these distribution expenses should be brought out into the open.

On February 24, 1977, before it had introduced Warwick Municipal Bond Fund, Vanguard filed an application with the SEC, seeking an exemption from the portion of the Investment Company Act related to fund distribution. Bogle and his colleagues shuddered at the prospect of going before the commission. They knew that getting SEC approval on this issue could take a long time; in the meantime, a legal uncertainty would hang over the company. In fact, only once before had a mutual fund been granted an exemption from the Investment Company Act of 1940 by the SEC to allow its funds to jointly expend assets to pay for their costs of distribution. In 1972, and again in November 1976, the SEC had approved the Broad Street Group—one of the two historically significant "internally managed" groups of investment companies—to bear distribution expenses. Indeed, the SEC approved the very "asset-related" allocation that an administrative law judge would later disapprove in Vanguard's case. Vanguard's chances of winning approval were uncertain, but the fund boards amended the application a number of times to boost the chances of success.

On July 15 the SEC issued a Notice of Filing of the Application and stated that anyone requesting a hearing had to do so by August 9. Otherwise, it would grant the exemption 30 days later. The fund boards were eager to resolve the issue, so they scheduled a shareholders meeting for August 18, at which time they expected the fund shareholders to approve the new arrangement in which the funds would pay distribution costs. On July 19, a proxy statement for each fund was sent to its shareholders, seeking their approval for the internal distribution arrangement and noting that the arrangement was subject to SEC approval. Shareholders overwhelmingly approved the proposal.

In retrospect, some at Vanguard believed that Bogle's decision to accelerate the timing of the proxy statement mailings was a mistake. Vanguard was under no legal obligation to provide advance notification to its shareholders of the request for an exemption from the SEC. Although the SEC publishes such requests, it does so in obscure documents such as the *Federal Register,* where shareholders are unlikely to see them. Had the company waited until the SEC approved the request, the proxy statement could have said so, and it would have been too late for anyone to ask the SEC to hold a public hearing on the matter. But Bogle was too impatient for that.

Because Vanguard issued the proxy statement, though, a Philadelphia shareholder named Joseph Silberman filed a request for a hearing. Silberman, a pensioner and shareholder, presented himself as a representative for Wellington Fund shareholders—a designation the SEC expressly rejected. Silberman argued that as The Vanguard Group's largest fund, Wellington Fund would unfairly bear half of the group's distribution expenses—unfair, he argued, since the fund's poor performance record during the previous decade gave it little immediate opportunity to garner new sales.

On September 13, the SEC issued a temporary exemption in response to Vanguard's application but called for a hearing on the issue. The commission, however, placed one condition on the order: that Vanguard *not* describe its funds as no-load. The SEC believed that one issue that had to be determined in its hearing was whether a fund that bore distribution expenses should be permitted to describe itself as no-load. The order allowed Vanguard to proceed with its distribution plan and to use shareholder assets to finance it, but the company would have to wait for the SEC's final ruling before the arrangement would be permanent.

Sidney Mendelson, director of the SEC's Division of Investment Management, was the administrator in charge of the hearings. Silberman retained attorney Fred Lowenchuss, who also filed a civil suit in Federal District Court, urging the court to block Bogle's plan. When he heard about the suit, Bogle thought, "My God, the game is over." He was wrong. But the suit would be held in suspended animation for nearly four years as Vanguard awaited the SEC's final ruling.

The SEC hearings, under the aegis of SEC administrative law judge Max O. Regensteiner, were held in two stages. The first lasted from January 5 to February 3, 1978, five days a week, 8 to 10 hours a day—said to be the longest hearing ever on an application for an exemption under the Investment Company Act of 1940. On December 1, Judge Regensteiner weighed in with what the SEC calls an Initial Decision. He rejected the Vanguard proposal. Nonetheless, he indicated that he would grant the substance of the exemption if the terms were revised. Vanguard had proposed that each fund pay its share of distribution costs based on its relative net assets (each fund, then, would pay the same percentage fee), without regard to whether the distribution costs were incurred in its behalf. The SEC judge, however, termed the arrangement inequitable because it placed an excessive burden on the funds not directly benefiting from the expenditures. He also decided not to allow Vanguard to refer to its funds as no-load. He seemed to ignore the argument that, given Vanguard's at-cost operating structure, all the funds would enjoy any economies of scale, whether any individual fund's own assets were growing or shrinking.

When Bogle received the Initial Decision, he was furious; he even threw the document against the wall. The decision, however, was not a death blow to Vanguard. The temporary exemption remained in force, giving the company a chance to amend its application by proposing a more equitable allocation of costs that would meet Judge Regensteiner's test. Bogle and his staff moved quickly to meet the judge's demands. They tossed around new cost allocation arrangements, and on January 31, 1979, they submitted an amended application to the SEC, modifying the previous proposal. The new proposal, while it based the lion's share of the allocation of distribution costs on relative net assets, included a modest allocation based on distribution of shares. Thus, a slightly lower fee would be paid by funds that had lower sales volume, and vice versa. Four days of new hearings began on April 16, and on October 4 the judge issued a Supplemental Initial Decision, this time approving the application. He continued the ban on the use of the term *no-load,* but three and a half weeks later the SEC adopted Rule 12b-1, which for the first time expressly permitted an individual mutual fund to bear its own distribution expenses. (The rule did not deal with the critical issue of a complex-wide distribution fee, which was at issue in the Vanguard case.)

Whereas the SEC ruling allowed Vanguard to pass on the economies of scale that resulted from its future growth to shareholders in the form of lower operating costs, Rule 12b-1 had the opposite effect on the industry as a whole. In fact, the rule was later employed by other mutual fund companies to add a new layer of expenses to be borne by shareholders. While Vanguard's average expense ratio declined from 0.71 percent in 1974 to 0.31 percent in 1995, the industry's average expense ratio actually increased from 1.08 percent in 1974 to 1.10 percent in 1995. In a twist of irony, Bogle would later be tabbed as "the father of the 12b-1 fee," a moniker that infuriated him. As Bogle explained it, "It's sort of like Frankenstein's monster. I may have been Dr. Frankenstein, but the rest of the industry created the monster."

For some time following the judge's decision, Silberman remained a thorn in Vanguard's side. He appealed the decision, asking the SEC to review the case. It agreed, but finally, on February 25, 1981, the SEC ratified Regensteiner's verdict—it even allowed Vanguard to call its funds no-load. In light of the SEC's unanimous decision, the judge in Silberman's long-pending civil suit dismissed the case. In an action that some attorneys saw as unprecedented, the judge ordered Vanguard to pay Silberman's attorney a mere $85,000 in fees and $3,469 in expenses, far less than the $1.1 million he had been asking. The suspense that Vanguard had endured for four long years was over, with the battle to take over distribution finally won.

The SEC's opinion not only approved the decision of the administrative law judge but also provided a sweeping endorsement of the Vanguard distribution plan. To this day, Bogle revels as he recounts the words:

(The Vanguard plan) is consistent with the provisions, policies and purposes of the (1940) Act. The proposed plan actually furthers the Act's objectives by ensuring that the Funds' directors, with more specific information at their disposal concerning the cost and performance of each service rendered to the Funds, are better able to evaluate the quality of those services. Moreover, [the] applicants' proposal will foster improved disclosure to shareholders, enabling them to make a more informed judgement as to the Funds' operations. In addition, the plan clearly enhances the Funds' independence, permitting them to change investment advisers more readily as conditions may dictate.

The plan promotes a healthy and viable mutual fund complex within which each fund can better prosper; enables the Funds to realize substantial savings from advisory fee reductions; promotes savings from economies of scale; and provides the Funds with direct and conflict-free control over distribution functions.

In short, the SEC ruling had kept the Vanguard experiment alive. Bogle was ecstatic. It meant that Vanguard could now conduct genuinely arm's-length negotiations with its investment advisers. Following the ruling, Bogle's first objective was to reduce the fees paid to those advisers. When Vanguard began to distribute its own funds, Wellington Management no longer had a gun to the funds' head. The work was plodding, time-consuming, and contentious, but in the end advisory fees were reduced: first in 1977, from $7.4 million to $5.2 million, to take into account the funds' assumption of their distribution costs, and again in 1978 by an additional $700,000, reflecting the funds' new ability to negotiate advisory fees at arm's length. Together the fee reductions totaled $2.9 million, a 39 percent cut in the advisory fees paid to Wellington Management.

"HOW RIGHT YOU WERE"

When Charles Root retired from the Vanguard board, the other board members presented him with a retirement gift: a framed montage of a photograph of each of the fund directors. Under each director's photo was a personal statement. Jim Welch, the only member of the Boston group who remained on the board beyond 1977, and one of the more vocal opponents of the plan to switch to internal no-load distribution, wrote under his photo, "Chuck, how right you were." Those words, Root said later, meant a great deal to him.

Bogle's next objective was to internalize the critical investment advisory function. He had never envisioned Vanguard as a traditional equity money manager, but he could see great merit in running carefully defined, high-quality bond and money market funds. One motivation for this move was Citibank's poor performance as the investment manager for the Warwick Municipal Bond Fund. Another was Vanguard's ability to run both the municipal bond and money market funds at low cost. This time, in mid-1981, Bogle encountered less opposition from the Vanguard board, convincing them to approve his proposal that Vanguard serve as investment adviser to the two funds. The vote for the no-load decision in February 1977 had been 7–4. On August 15, 1981, the vote on internalizing advisory services for the money market and municipal bond funds was taken: eight in favor, two opposed. "It is simply impossible to overstate the importance of this decision in the growth that followed," Bogle said years later.

In effect, the board had now accepted Option 3 from Bogle's proposal of March 1974, and the process of full mutualization was, in substance, complete. It had taken seven years—from 1974 to 1981—to bring Bogle's cherished goal to fruition. Jeremy Duffield, senior vice president of planning and development, underscored the importance of the move: "Jack Bogle's decision to internalize the fixed-income management made our low-cost advantage stand out. As investors shopped for the best money fund or bond fund yields, costs began to matter. It wasn't long before new assets were rushing at us like waves breaking over the deck."

Of all the advantages gained by Vanguard's three-step conversion to full mutualization, none was more important to Bogle than the independence of the funds and the cost savings that resulted. At first, the savings were small, but in time they would climb to more than $1 billion annually, all passed on to Vanguard's shareholders. By the time the 1980s had gotten under way, the Vanguard experiment was proved. In Bogle's words, "It was just a matter of how successful it would be."

THE
18th-CENTURY
MAN

SOMETIMES IT SEEMS as if Jack Bogle has fallen asleep, drifted back in time, and awakened a few minutes after Lord Horatio Nelson trounced the French at the Battle of the Nile in 1798. "Jack likes the 18th century," noted T. Chandler Hardwick III, head-master of Blair Academy. "And what's true of the 18th century is that anything that is important has a moral authority [that] extends beyond a church or school . . . into every aspect of life, whether it's literature, music, or finance."

Bogle exudes this moral authority. It seems to grow out of his love of things past. He believes that Vanguard's unique corporate structure makes sense not only for Vanguard but for the entire mutual fund industry. There is no doubt in his mind that going no-load was not only good for his company but would be good for virtually all mutual fund investors. The first thing he said to the author in his interviews for this book was, "Vanguard by the year 2020 will have changed this industry and . . . unless they change their ways, too, Charles Schwab, Fidelity, will be footnotes." This was not just small talk. Bogle genuinely believes that he has a mission.

It is often said of Bogle that he has the mind of an economist but the personality of a preacher. His former aide Jim Riepe once gave him a clerical collar as a joke, but Bogle did not take offense. Bogle not only believes that he has seen the light, but he has a clergyman's zeal in making sure others know it. "It's fair to say I'm a missionary," he commented. "Give me a cause and I will run with it as far as it will go. That comes with idealism." He cannot help sounding as if his function in life is to preach to the masses. Asked by SEC chairman Arthur Levitt what he would do if he were SEC chairman, Bogle replied, "[I would] get on my bully pulpit, like Teddy Roosevelt, and say to the directors of mutual funds: 'Do your job. Save some real money for the shareholders that you were selected to represent. Put the shareholders first, not the management company.' " In a 1990 speech to the Vanguard crew, he sounded like a preacher when he said, "Vanguard stands alone (we like it that way!), not much concerned about growth in the short run, confident that we shall do well in the long run. It is, for us, a luxury to act on the principle that the best growth is organic and not forced, coming naturally from within. I am in fact elated to have Vanguard as the 'test case' on whether 'the different drummer' of trusteeship can succeed in a world of industry and commerce."

Because of pronouncements like these, Bogle and the Vanguard name have become synonymous with something approaching moral rectitude. Zealously, Bogle adopts the role of preacher when making the most important point in his mission statement: that Vanguard does the best job of any mutual fund company of guarding the interests of shareholders. He knows that he is not the first mutual fund executive to make this claim, but he is adept at making it seem as if he is the only one who actually does it.

One interesting aspect about Bogle is that he has been right so often that he is understandably convinced that the only way to do things is his way. Actually, says his most recent assistant, James M. Norris, "there are two ways to do things, Jack's way and the other way. And the other way will inevitably be the wrong way." Bogle admits that he has a domineering personality. Although he constantly holds meetings, tossing ideas back and forth and seeking the opinions of others, in the end his view is generally the one that prevails. For example, the direct responsibility for proposing new funds lies with Jeremy G. Duffield, Vanguard's senior vice president of planning and development. Yet Bogle acknowledges that Duffield has probably been "miffed" at his rejection of some of Duffield's proposals for new funds, including a high-yield short-term bond fund and international funds concentrated in areas such as Mexico and South America, where Bogle thinks the risks are too high and the payoffs to investors too uncertain. At the same time, Bogle swept aside opposition when he ordered the formation of other new funds—often index-related and generally conservative—most recently including a series of bond index portfolios holding long-term, intermediate-term, and short-term bonds. Clearly, Bogle has had the last word on new fund formation, no matter how the operating structure looks on paper. Said George Putnam, one of Bogle's close friends in the industry and the chairman of Boston's Putnam Funds, "Jack is in many ways a one-man gang."

Bogle seems to enjoy being right, especially when he can show that the rest of the world is wrong. "There is no question he has a holier-than-thou attitude," said Norris. None of this escapes Bogle, who admits to being a bit self-righteous. He also thrives on being a contrarian. "The worst argument you can make to Jack," says F. William McNabb, senior vice president of Vanguard's institutional group, "is to say, 'Everybody else is doing it. Don't you think we should do it?' He'll say, 'We should look at it, but it doesn't mean we should do it.' I've never seen anyone with such courage in going against the trend."

"WHENEVER JACK SAYS . . ."

Jim Norris, who helped Bogle craft his 1993 book, *Bogle on Mutual Funds,* wrote a small primer of items categorized into two groups: "Whenever Jack says . . ." and "What Jack means is . . ." Norris presented it to Bogle at a dinner attended by Bogle assistants, past and present. In the weeks after the dinner, many of the former assistants phoned Norris to add to the list he had drafted. The following are some of the items from the final listing:

Whenever Jack says:	What Jack means is:
"I know it's not your fault."	"It's your fault."
"I need this whenever you get a chance."	"I meant to ask you to do this yesterday, so now I need it in five minutes."
"Have you double-checked these numbers?"	"There's an error."
"You decide."	"Do what I would do."
"Could you take a whack at writing this?"	"I'll rewrite your version later."
"I haven't had a chance to read it."	"I've memorized it."

Bogle can be subtle. While he does not raise his voice often, few of his associates mistake his subtlety or calm demeanor for going soft or letting his guard down. Strangely enough, one way he gets the attention of his associates is to avoid saying what he means, leaving it for the other person to figure out. In meetings, he often asks questions about details others think are petty. In conversations, he is often a model of brevity, assuming that his associates are coming at the issues from his own perspective. In all, his communications are multi-leveled and complex.

All of this makes Bogle seem like an overpowering figure. Kenneth G. Martin, managing director of Hay Management Consultants in Philadelphia and someone who has done extensive personnel consulting for Vanguard, says that "most of the people who have direct contact with Bogle are very intimidated by him. They respect him, but he scares them. They dread going to his meetings, because they're going to be called to task for something . . . [or] challenged to defend something . . . Jack Bogle is not a modern-day participative manager. There's a little trembling in the boots in dealing with him."

Martin adds, though, that Bogle is "seen very much as a man of the people, really caring about people. He's viewed as accessible. For years and years he knew the names of most employees and their families, and he tried to make them feel good . . . He has come to be seen as this really benevolent, all-powerful guy."

Jim Norris's feelings about his boss reflect the complexity of Bogle's relationship with many of his Vanguard associates. On the one hand, Norris proudly makes clear that there is no one else in the world he would rather work for. But then he adds that Bogle can on occasion be "impetuous," "callous," "uncaring," and "mercurial," and that he "can make you feel absolutely stupid." Norris attributed most of these ups and downs to Bogle's health: "When he's not having a good day, you're not either."

Norris recalled one time when he was working on some revisions for an article Bogle was writing for the *Journal of Portfolio Management*. Bogle agreed earlier that he did not need the revisions until the next day, but at four o'clock in the afternoon on the same day he popped into Norris's office and asked: "Do you have the revisions to the article? I want to look at them tonight." When Norris stated that he did not have the revisions and reminded him of their earlier conversation, Bogle was nonplussed: "There's no possible reason why I would have said that. What reason could I have? We have a whole night now that's absolutely wasted. Well, I guess we'll just have to persevere."

Commented Norris, "When things like this would happen, you'd find yourself wondering if your mettle was somehow being tested, since Jack forgets nothing. On the other hand, he loses everything you give to him, so you learn quickly to make copies of everything or suffer the consequences. It can be maddening to work for him. By the same token, I wouldn't trade jobs with anybody; I've learned the ins and outs of this industry from the very best." Norris has also found no one more loyal or appreciative of the work that is done for him. To the charge that Bogle was demanding, Norris replied that he had a right to be demanding and that it is hardly absurd to expect something to be done correctly.

None of the comments about his managerial style ever seemed to disturb Bogle. "I don't think any institution ever achieved real success by being run by a committee. Apparently I'm known as intimidating," he said. Then, with a twinkle in his eye, he added, "I can't imagine my being that way." Jeremy Duffield, also a former assistant to Bogle, acknowledged Bogle's demanding style: "The man is a fierce competitor; his combative nature comes out in debate, in negotiations, in one-on-one battles, as spokesperson for his beliefs, and in other fields of endeavor, from crossword puzzles to the squash court."

■　■　■

Bogle boasts that his large ego has been a source of competitive advantage for Vanguard, pointing out that because of his self-confidence in stating his position, he was often quoted in the press, giving his new company free publicity. "Ego is not a weakness but a necessity when you have to build something from scratch," he remarked.

To his credit, Bogle is able to poke fun at himself for having such a big ego. In a 1994 speech, he quoted an employee who, he said, had written him a note that read: "If I had but 20 minutes left on earth, I should like to spend it listening to one of your marvelous partnership speeches— honest, enlightening, philosophical, sonorous, and powerful." As Bogle was reveling in the note, he observed the writer's instruction to turn the page over. There Bogle read, "It would seem like an eternity!" Bogle then confessed that he had made up the story.

Bogle has done more than flaunt a giant ego. The truly great preachers know how to communicate, and ever since Walter Morgan placed him in charge of investor and public relations for the Wellington organization in the 1950s, Bogle has managed to communicate with great effectiveness a set of messages to employees, shareholders, and the public. "Everyone here," says Jeremy Duffield, "feels they owe Jack Bogle a debt for creating a vision that they feel part of. They've gotten enriched in believing they work for something that's larger than just a company."

Ken Martin, the management consultant, emphasizes the numerous dividends Bogle's sense of focus has paid Vanguard: "When I think of Jack's role in the organization, I think of the importance of being focused and staying the course. There are all kinds of examples where he had easy opportunity to stray from the course but he didn't, especially the go-go 80s, when all financial services firms were getting into a million different things. He has been badly criticized for being too conservative, for being too focused, for not getting into high-growth sorts of things, for not trading on the Vanguard name to get into new businesses. But he never veered."

■　■　■

For a man with serious heart problems, being a workaholic would not seem to be the wisest course. Yet Bogle sank himself into each day as if it were a gift, often putting in 13-hour days, six and sometimes even seven days a week. Because he was fiercely competitive, Bogle was determined to reach his goals. Hating to admit defeat, he had framed on his office wall a quotation presented to him by former assistant Jan Twardowski. It carries the words of Georges-Jacques Danton, the French revolutionary: *"De l'audace, encore de l'audace, toujours de l'audace"* ("Audacity, more audacity, always audacity"). Bogle once said, "I wouldn't want on my tombstone that I ran the most efficient mutual fund company in America," as if efficiency were a sin. "Efficiency could be taken as meaning sterility. I would want on my tombstone that I ran the *best* company."

Bogle's son, John Jr., grew up knowing that his father always had business on his mind. One image that John Jr. retained into adulthood was of his father spending a part of each weekend seated in his study, an enormous stack of reading material piled on the floor next to his desk. "I'd walk by thousands of times," said John Jr., "and watch him just constantly reading books on the desk, on the floor, on his lap, constantly reading, constantly trying to learn more things." John Jr. also remembers his father's passion for doing things right. He recalled that when he and his father put up a tree fort in their backyard, it was not thrown together but rather "done with a high degree of precision, using the proper tools, making sure everything was exactly level, perfectly aligned."

On occasion, Bogle took up outside interests. He noted in the 25-year reunion yearbook of the Princeton Class of 1951 that his interests included sailing and that he was an avid squash player. But it was the details of his business that fascinated him more than anything else. He wanted to be involved in anything that he felt could have an impact on how the company was run or how it was perceived from the outside. Take, for example, the letters that came to him personally, an average of 150 a month. Most CEOs delegate to a staffer the task of answering letters. Bogle, on the other hand, read each letter carefully; any that he could answer on his own he answered almost immediately, perhaps one-fifth of the total. The others he sent to department heads with requests that they respond, making sure that the shareholder was told that Bogle had reviewed the letter. He called these letters his Bogle Barometer, an intelligence file that gave him a high-level measure of Vanguard's service and performance. Even one complaint was significant to him, for it might touch on a simmering problem that others had not yet voiced.

Bogle was so involved with the details of the business that he even proofread his messages in the annual shareholder reports, checking for typographical errors before the reports were sent to the printer. He boasted that he was the best proofreader at Vanguard. "Catch those mistakes," he admonished his staff repeatedly. In later years, Bogle was aware that his hands-on attitude might have created some ill will in the company. He could almost hear some Vanguard employee saying, "For God's sake, do we really have to clear *that* with him?" The answer, of course, was yes.

■   ■   ■

Bogle's conservative streak, forged during his depression childhood, extended to his personal life. He had an aversion to material things and discussions about money, refusing, for example, to answer journalists' questions about his salary. Some media reports in the 1990s estimated his salary at several million dollars, but he scoffed at such reports, calling them highly exaggerated. "I've accumulated a decent amount of wealth," he said tersely. "Nothing like the industry billionaires. But I'm not poor."

Bogle has always eschewed the "good things" in life. When he traveled, he flew coach. His home in Bryn Mawr, Pennsylvania, is not ostentatious. He has stuck with his 1987 Honda Acura for nearly 10 years. "I wouldn't dream of buying a Jaguar or a Mercedes," he said. "It would seem like I was trying to show off."

While styles changed, Bogle remained happily locked in the past. The crew cut he wore beginning at age 13 made him in the 1980s look like a boy playing hard-driving executive. (His hair grew long during an extended hospital stay in late 1993, and he decided to keep it at a more conventional—if short—length thereafter.) Blue or white button-down shirts were part of his dress code long after men's shirts turned sporty. "For him," says Jim Riepe, "it was a big departure sometime in the 1970s when he wore a yellow shirt. You'd think he was wearing a zoot suit." Ever frugal, he wore dark wool ties, not light-colored silk (wool lasted longer, and dark colors could be cleaned promptly and put right back in use), and off-the-rack (although Brooks Brothers) suits. He is said to have worn the same belt for something like 20 years.

One often retold incident perfectly illustrates Bogle's conservatism and frugality. He was checking in to New York City's plush Plaza Hotel in 1984 and asked for the cheapest room in the house. The clerk informed him that the cheapest room was $230 a night (before a 20 percent corporate discount). "There is absolutely no way I'm going to pay that price for a room," Bogle said. "Whenever I've come to the Plaza, and I've been coming here for 15 years now, I've always had the cheapest room in the house, and it used to be less than $100. I'd like that now." The clerk offered a small room next to a noisy elevator shaft.

"How much?" Bogle asked.

One hundred dollars.

"Do I get the corporate discount?"

No, said the embarrassed clerk.

"I'll take the room anyway."

Meanwhile, a long line was forming behind Bogle. An impatient man behind him asked, "Aren't you John Bogle?"

"How on earth would you know that?"

"I'm a stockholder in Vanguard funds. I've seen your picture."

When Bogle apologized for creating a delay, the man replied, "Oh no. Don't feel that way. At first I didn't understand what you were doing. Now that I see who you are, I understand completely. Vanguard—low costs, no loads, isn't that right?"

■ ■ ■

If Bogle has seemed like a man out of the 18th century, it was in part because he has a deep sense of history. He is a man of ideas, and he wants to be counted among the intellectual classes. Speeches to the crew gave Bogle a chance to bathe himself in history. In one speech at the 10th annual Vanguard Partnership Plan celebration, delivered under a large canopy at the Philadelphia Zoo, he worked in references to Victor Hugo ("An invasion of armies can be resisted, but not an idea whose time has come"); T. S. Eliot ("April is the cruelest month . . . stirring dull roots with spring rain"); and Ralph Waldo Emerson ("Speak what you think today in hard words"). His other speeches, too, were sprinkled with historical quotations and lines from inspirational songs. Some examples included:

- President Calvin Coolidge: "Nothing in the world can take the place of persistence—press on."

- Sportswriter Grantland Rice: "The one Great Scorer . . .marks— not that you won or lost—but how you played the game."

- Economist Joseph Schumpeter: "There are three entrepreneurial motives more powerful than money. (1) The will to found a dynasty; (2) the will to conquer, to succeed, not for the fruits of success, but for success itself; and (3) the joy of creativity, of exercising one's energy and ingenuity."

- Ecclesiastes: "The race is not to the swift nor the battle to the strong . . . but time and chance happeneth to them all."

- "The Impossible Dream": "This is my quest, to follow that star, no matter how hopeless, no matter how far."

- "My Way": "The record shows we took the blows and did it our way."

Bogle's intellectual yearnings manifested themselves in his love of the written word. At times it seemed as though he was as much a writer as he was the head of a mutual fund company. In 1970, to create distance between the funds and the external management company, he began writing nearly all of the annual reports for the mutual funds, and in the mid-1990s he was still writing some 30 annual reports each year. He insisted on writing them not only to give shareholders an honest view of the funds' performance but also because he loved putting words on paper. He would rarely allow any staffer to prepare drafts for him. And when he did, he typically edited it to such a degree that it was as if he had written it anyway. "You would think," said Bogle's brother-in-law Jay Sherrerd, a founder of the investment management firm Miller, Anderson, and Sherrerd, "that he wouldn't have time . . . but those reports are very important to the organization, and Jack knows that while others can do them, they won't do them as well as he does. He's not an unduly modest guy. If he thinks he can do it better than anyone else, he'll do it."

Ever the wordsmith, Bogle has long loved crossword puzzles. Every Sunday for years he timed himself to see how long it took him to complete the *New York Times* puzzle, the toughest of them all. His best time: 36 minutes. He rarely needed more than 60 minutes.

WRITING POETRY

Between annual reports, Bogle even wrote poetry, as he did in 1994 for John Neff on his 30th anniversary as portfolio manager of the Windsor Fund. A few of the nine stanzas:

> From America's heartland he joined us
> And soon took o'er Windsor Fund's reins.
> What a job he has done for us since then
> With rare common sense and with brains.

> He's one of a much-honored triad—
> There's Neff and there's Buffett and Lynch.
> Paradigms of investment performance,
> To copy their records' no cinch.

> So here's to a treasure we savor
> With investment acumen so deft.
> The Lord surely did Vanguard a favor
> When He matched Windsor Fund with John Neff.

Given his preoccupation with precision in the use of language, Bogle became something of an English teacher around Vanguard. A 20-volume set of the second edition of the *Oxford English Dictionary* sat just outside his office, and it was not unusual to see Bogle's tall frame leaning over it, trying to squeeze out of the dictionary the precise meaning of a word. Jim Riepe, Bogle's former assistant and now managing director of T. Rowe Price, Inc., a major manager of no-load funds and perhaps the competitor most respected at Vanguard, had a habit of using the word *irregardless*. Sounding like a high school English teacher, Bogle finally could stand it no longer and said, "Jim, you've got to stop using that word." When Riepe asked why, Bogle, in a gesture he has become known for, tossed his wallet on the table, and he and Riepe made a small wager on whether the word existed. Riepe looked the word up in a style manual Bogle had on his bookshelf and never lived down his discovery that usage of the word *irregardless* was labeled "illiterate."

Jan Twardowski recalled what it was like to turn a draft document into Bogle, the editor: "I learned to expect that he would shred my writing . . . even to appreciate it. I would give him an analysis he had requested, only to have it edited to within an inch of its life. From Jack, I learned precision, how to make complex things understandable, and how to create a document that the reader could follow." To Bogle, words mattered, precision mattered.

In fact, Bogle believed deeply that the choice of words could shape the character of an organization. He banned the use of words such as *products* (too much like a retail business; he preferred *mutual funds* or *investment portfolios*), *employees* (too demeaning; use *crew*), and *customers* (implies a short-term relationship; use *clients*). He would often observe with irony, "For an enterprise without products, or employees, or customers, we've come a long way."

"HAIL TO THE CEO"

After noticing contradictory uses of the term *CEO* in the media, Bogle wanted to know how it had come to signify the number one person in the company. He wrote a letter to *New York Times* columnist William Safire, asking him where the phrase *chief executive officer* had come from—never expecting that the columnist would answer his question in a column. On September 28, 1986, Safire did just that. In his letter to Safire, Bogle wrote, "The boss used to be either president or chairman of the corporation and no modifier was considered necessary . . . It might be interesting to research the origin of CEO."

In an amusing column entitled "Hail to the CEO," Safire noted that the idea for the column had come from Bogle, both "Chairman and Chief-You-Know-What of The Vanguard Group." Safire went on to provide all sorts of detail about how the term *CEO* had developed, even how it had become corrupted in one major U.S. company to refer to the second-in-command, not the first.

And the mind mattered, too. Bogle loved to massage both his mind and the minds of others. He was always challenging others to come up with information, testing them to find out if they were up to his level. It was not easy to keep up with him as he suddenly switched thought in midsentence and posed tricky questions to associates. Duncan McFarland, another former Bogle assistant and now president and CEO of Wellington Management Company, recalled one such test that has become part of Bogle folklore. Bogle put a series of numbers up on a board and asked the group gathered around him what number was missing. Most were stymied, but someone finally blurted out the correct answer, recognizing that the numbers on the board were the subway stops on the Lexington Avenue line in New York City. "This is obviously a guy who focuses on the question," Bogle said admiringly.

Burton Malkiel, a professor of economics at Princeton University and a Vanguard board member, expressed great respect for Bogle's ability to take apart issues: "Jack really has a researcher's instincts. A lot of his speeches are extremely well-researched. There's a lot of good research in his book. We'll sometimes have arguments, really good discussions on academic issues . . . That's one of the things that makes him unique."

Evidence of Bogle's research abilities appeared in the articles he wrote in the 1990s, serious articles laden with charts and statistics, theories and analysis, that were published in financial journals of weight. Four of Bogle's articles appeared in the *Journal of Portfolio Management,* including "Investing in the 1990s," "Occam's Razor Revisited," "Selecting Equity Mutual Funds," and "The 1990s at the Halfway Mark—Occam's Razor Is Tested." In 1960, he was so eager to get his article "The Case for Mutual Fund Management" published in the *Financial Analysts Journal* that, when a colleague pointed out that using his own name might violate industry self-advertising standards, he submitted it under a fictitious name.

The best example of Bogle's love of writing was the publication of *Bogle on Mutual Funds* in 1993. Bogle labored tirelessly to get the book just right. His goal was to produce a book on mutual funds that could hold its own with Benjamin Graham's 1949 classic on investment strategy and security analysis, *The Intelligent Investor*—in Bogle's view the best book ever written on common stock investing. To remind potential readers that he was trying to equal, if not outdo, the Graham classic, Bogle subtitled his book *New Perspectives for the Intelligent Investor.* "I wanted to write a book that would not only help investors make sound decisions but would change the mutual fund industry," he said. "This industry can have lower costs for customers, create much better disclosure, have honest advertising, and be overseen by more responsible directors. There is so much room for improvement."

Bogle's 18th century perspective on moral authority was again in evidence.

C H A P T E R

THE VANGUARD MANUAL

FROM THE TIME HE WAS A STUDENT at Princeton University, Jack Bogle had a clear picture of the problems that confronted the mutual fund industry and the best ways to overcome them. His senior thesis provided a theoretical framework for solving the industry's problems: the primacy of the interests of fund shareholders, candor and fair dealing with clients, innovation in the development of new funds, and a focus on low costs.

This Bogle philosophy began to come into sharper focus during the 1980s. For Bogle, the shareholder always came first. When he founded Vanguard, he might easily have taken the position that a mutual fund's sole job was to maximize the value of the investor's portfolio and then focus on ways to gain a competitive advantage over other fund companies. But in each investor who called Vanguard, Bogle may have seen something of his father and mother, caught in the turmoil of the depression and hoping that someone would look after their savings. Or perhaps he understood that doing what's best for the shareholder was simply good business. Whatever his motivation, the invisible, faceless shareholder was at the center of Bogle's philosophy. He wanted to make shareholders come alive, often referring to them as "down-to-earth, honest-to-God human beings, with their own hopes, fears, and aspirations."

Others in the industry also claimed that they focused on the share-holder, but their words rang hollow to Bogle, for they pocketed consid-erable sums of money for themselves that in his view rightfully belonged to the fund shareholders. Bogle wanted the Vanguard experiment to make the words *focus solely on the interests of the shareholder* a reality. Yet, because he had no way of knowing whether his radical experiment would succeed, he held back from preaching too loudly about ways to transform the industry until the experiment had passed a series of tests—the hard-ships of the 1970s, the battle to make the funds no-load and the assumption of fund distribution responsibilities, and the campaign to assume invest-ment management responsibilities. In all, Vanguard had made its mark.

As he and his company passed each test, Bogle felt a growing con-fidence that the success of the Vanguard experiment was no longer in doubt. One way this confidence manifested itself was his decision to incorporate the Vanguard name into the company's new funds. In mid-1980, Westminster Bond Fund, Warwick Municipal Bond Fund, and Whitehall Money Market Trust dropped their "British W" first names and, along with First Index Investment Trust, became the first Vanguard Funds. (By 1993, all the funds had incorporated Vanguard into their names, as Wellington Fund became Vanguard/Wellington Fund, and so on.)

Bogle was convinced, too, that the company's organizing principles made better sense than ever. One of those principles was "Easy does it." As a child of the depression and a student of Walter Morgan, Bogle was nothing if not conservative in his investment approach. He saw no virtue in wild-eyed, reckless investment strategies whose goals were to make a killing overnight. As he learned the hard way from the go-go funds Wellington Management acquired in its merger with TDP&L, too many investment managers had adopted strategies that served shareholders well in the short run but ran the risk of something akin to ruin—or at least inferior returns—over the long haul. If Bogle seemed out of step with those who viewed the mutual fund industry as an opportunity to get rich quickly, it was because he marched to a different drummer.

In particular, Bogle avoided many of the trends that dominated the industry in the 1980s. One was a kind of price war in reverse, which Bogle described as "a paradoxical battle to increase, beyond any reasonable level, the prices investors pay to own mutual funds, so that fund managers can undertake massive marketing expenditures to generate sales commissions, and so on." A second focused on new investment "products," as companies scrambled to introduce more and more new funds, many of them specu-lative, all of them untested. In Bogle's view, the worst of these trends, however, was the performance war, "a contest to see which funds can add the most 'hype' to their records—by reaching to the very extremities of prudence and beyond for the largest equity returns and highest bond yields."

For the most part, Vanguard stood alone in its approach to the mutual fund industry. Rather than raise prices, Vanguard lowered them; rather than introduce speculative funds, it introduced conservative, relatively predictable funds; rather than trumpet yesterday's performance miracles, it committed itself to a modest advertising program that spoke common sense. As the Vanguard philosophy emerged, Bogle wrote its tenets down in what he titled "Vanguard's Manual for Officers and Crew." These tenets included:

1. Above all, provide value, keeping operating costs paid by investors at the lowest levels in this industry and offering fund shares to investors without loads or hidden sales charges.
2. Hold to our course, concentrating our primary focus on the industry we know best: mutual funds.
3. Innovate soundly and sensibly, making intelligent bets on the future while never ignoring the lessons of history.
4. Generate rewards for our clients, consistent with the risks they expect, and generally surpass competitive norms.
5. Maintain a crew of dedicated people who have "signed on" to Vanguard's mission.

For each of these tenets, he gave a one-word summary description: value, concentration, innovation, performance, dedication.

"A FAIR SHAKE"

A traditional investment adviser used an array of benchmarks to plot its own success, from the profits it earned for its manager-owners, to the value it created for its private owners, to the price of its stock if it traded in the marketplace. In contrast, because it provided its services on an at-cost or non-profit-making basis, Vanguard had goals that were more difficult to specify and quantify. Bogle recognized this in a memorandum he wrote in December 1987: "What the financial objective of our firm is, is very hard to say. Certainly we don't have financial objectives in the customary sense, where someone would say we've got to get a 12 percent— or 100 percent—return on capital. But I guess I'd say it is to be

> an enterprise that gives the customers—clients, as we call them—
> a fair shake. And that means high-quality funds—with objectives
> that at least have the hope of being achieved—low costs, and a
> high service component. It sounds a bit like motherhood."

■ ■ ■

At the forefront of Vanguard's philosophy was keeping costs low, a
tradition that traced its roots to the early 1950s, when Bogle joined
Wellington Management Company. At that time, Wellington Fund was
one of the first mutual funds to provide a "sliding scale" of fees that
declined as assets rose, enabling the fund to share economies of scale with
its clients. In a memo to Walter Morgan in 1959, Bogle proudly noted:
"Wellington Fund's rank in the mutual fund industry in keeping expenses
low has improved from 12th to 7th among 151 funds."

It appears that Bogle never forgot his early lessons in cutting costs.
In its first years, Vanguard had been at a distinct disadvantage compared
to other mutual fund companies. While most fund companies had large
sums of money to spend on advertising, Vanguard did not. Vanguard,
though, turned this weakness into an advantage, suggesting that keeping
costs low was not only good in and of itself but part of a sound investment
policy. Bogle conceded that actively managed equity funds may have
needed higher-priced management talent, but the funds could absorb these
higher costs only as long as huge profits were produced for fund shareholders. He argued, however, that costs were a critical issue in money
market and bond funds, where investment managers had less ability to
demonstrate their skills in selecting securities. Any mutual fund company
that could run these funds at lower cost would enjoy a distinct yield
advantage, and it was no coincidence that the funds in which Vanguard
most excelled were the ones in which cost savings mattered the most.

With money market funds, for example, differences in yields among
various funds were almost entirely the result of differences in expense
ratios, which take into account the total cost of a fund's operations,
including management fees and administrative expenses for a given year,
expressed as a percentage of average fund assets. Expenses, Bogle argued,
accounted for 95 percent of the differences in the performance of money
market funds and 80 percent of the differences in the performance of fixed-
income funds; for stock funds, he estimated the figure at about 65 percent
of the differences in performance, at least over the long term. "Given this
cost–return relationship," Bogle explained in a speech, "one can easily
contrast the returns of two investors, each of whom places $10,000 in a

fund providing a total return before expenses of 10 percent a year over 20 years. If the first investor's fund has an expense ratio of 0.30 percent, or 30 basis points, the investor in this fund will earn 9.7 percent annually, and will accumulate $63,700 after 20 years. If the second investor's fund has an expense ratio of 1.20 percent, or 120 basis points, this investor will earn 8.8 percent, and will accumulate just $54,000, or $9,700 less, a difference equal to almost the entire $10,000 initial investment. This substantial extra return comes simply as a result of a lower expense ratio."

Bogle boasted that the secret to Vanguard's low costs was shareholder ownership. Because shareholders of the funds owned Vanguard, no profits had to be extracted from fund returns and paid to a parent company or management company. Bogle explained: "We started with the structure and our strategy evolved very naturally. You want to be low cost. You certainly don't want these sales charges. You want to put the shareholder first in terms of service . . . You don't want to spend a lot of your shareholders' money on expensive and misleading ads. Advertising doesn't benefit anybody but the adviser. The outside adviser gets the big profits if he brings additional money into the funds, and we aren't that kind of a company. We don't get the profits. We operate at cost. So a lot of our discipline in marketing flows from this structure."

Vanguard also benefited from its ability to negotiate fees with invest-ment advisers at arm's length, avoiding the conflicts of interests that are inevitable for traditionally structured fund companies. Bogle noted that, as Vanguard's funds began to grow in asset size, Vanguard was able to negotiate favorable fee rates and still pay the dollar level of advisory fees that was necessary to attract the most talented investment managers. At the same time, by having its money market and bond funds managed internally on an at-cost basis, the company was able to further reduce its expenses. These funds received enormous benefits from economies of scale. All told, by mid-1995 it was costing Vanguard just $8 million a year to manage its $75 billion in money market and bond portfolios, a ratio of less than one basis point, or 0.01 of a percentage point.

In addition to low costs, the other anchor of Vanguard's philosophy was candor, which meant, above all else, being straightforward about how a mutual fund was performing. Bogle sometimes referred, only partially in jest, to candor as an important Vanguard marketing strategy that dif-ferentiated the company from others in the industry. Candor became a critical part of Bogle's approach to the business. He disliked the marketing focus and guile that others used to get ahead in the industry, and he railed at those who profited from misleading advertising. At the same time, he suggested that it was far better to do business with a firm like Vanguard, which presented a full and accurate picture of each fund's performance results.

If a Vanguard fund had not done well during a particular period, perhaps because an entire market segment had underperformed, Bogle specifically mentioned this fact in the next report to shareholders and cautioned them that such performance might continue for a period of time. Recall that in 1974, when Bogle noted in his chairman's letter in the fund's annual report that Ivest Fund's performance had been unsatisfactory, fund director Daniel Gregory had been infuriated by Bogle's candor and feared that it would encourage a shareholder lawsuit. At a typical mutual fund company, where the chief executive officer of the funds and the management company were the same individual, such a comment would have been virtually without precedent. Bogle felt no such inhibitions.

This pattern of candor would continue at Vanguard. In the annual reports in 1989, Bogle cautioned clients not to expect in the coming decade a repeat of the golden decade of the 1980s, when the returns on financial assets were the highest in history. As soon as 1990 got under way, the stock and bond markets declined, and the declines grew worse that summer as the war in the Persian Gulf loomed. Bogle wrote: "Shareholders who followed our advice—always own some stocks, some bonds, and some cash reserves—easily weathered the storm, perhaps bloodied, but nonetheless unbowed."

In 1991, when health care stocks were performing exceptionally well, Bogle wrote a letter to shareholders of Vanguard's Health Care Portfolio, cautioning them about the risks of sector funds and noting that "it is highly unlikely that such absolute returns—or even the Portfolio's relative performance advantage—will be matched in the future. The Portfolio's performance resulted from the particularly favorable returns of health care companies as a group. Experience has shown that such periods of superior performance by an industry group do not continue indefinitely. Indeed, periods of outperformance are often followed by periods of underperformance."

The history of Vanguard is peppered with many similar examples. In 1990, a booklet entitled "Plain Talk about High Yield Bonds" was sent to all investors in Vanguard's High Yield Bond Fund. Among other things, the booklet warned that "clearly, given their risks, high yield bonds are not for (a) the faint hearted, (b) short-term investors, nor (c) income-oriented investors depending heavily on bonds as the source of their income." Most recently, in the 1995 annual report for Vanguard Index

Trust—following a year in which index fund returns surpassed the returns of actively managed funds by a wide margin—Bogle stated emphatically, "I again caution you . . . stay *off* the indexing bandwagon if you seek short-term performance results. There *will* be years in which more funds outperform the Index than underperform it."

Some competitors doubtless saw Bogle's honesty as lunacy, but the financial press loved it, and, judging by their letters to Vanguard, shareholders seemed to appreciate his forthrightness. Vanguard board members, who supported Bogle's directness, even kidded him that the tougher and more candid his message, the more money poured into the funds.

Bogle's candor had a trickle-down effect throughout the company, as the rank and file took their cue from him. Bill McNabb noted that Bogle's sense of ethics "makes a big difference in how this place is run. You find yourself in situations where you ask, 'How would Jack Bogle look at this?' The other day we had money come in from one of our institutional accounts and we invested it . . . We didn't do it exactly right. The client's directions were a little vague, and we could have made the case that the vagueness had forced us to make the error . . . We said, 'Forget the vagueness. We screwed up.' So we said we'll make it whole . . . At another institution, I might have had my head handed to me for owning up because I would have negatively impacted the bottom line. I couldn't imagine Jack playing those games. When we know something is wrong, we say so. It gives people here a great deal of comfort, and it makes it easy to make the right decision because you know . . . you won't be second-guessed for doing what is right for the client."

CREATING LOYALTY AND RESPECT

IT WAS NOT ONLY BUILDING client loyalty and respect simply by doing what was right that concerned Bogle. One of his sternest tests, given his domineering, I-know-what's-best-for-us personality, was whether he engendered the loyalty and respect of his employees. He knew that if they failed to sign on to his and Vanguard's values, he would have no chance of widening his base of support beyond the company. To instill a sense of pride in the company, Bogle took the unique tack of making the headquarters look and feel like a 200-year-old British warship, embarked on a crucial mission led by Commander Jack Bogle. Bogle admitted that the nautical theme may have seemed a little corny, but he believed that it was essential for "the captain" to give "the crew" the sense that they were not working for just another mutual fund company.

There is a certain irony to the British naval imagery, given that Vanguard's headquarters is only a few miles from the spot where George Washington's army spent the icy winter of 1777–78. Bogle, however, seemed oblivious to the heroic exploits of the Founding Father. Moreover, he had never skippered more than a sailboat, never longed for a naval career. His romance with things naval had more to do with a love of battle than with the functioning of ships. Because he was enthralled with the symbols of Admiral Nelson's Battle of the Nile and other naval battles, a visitor to Vanguard headquarters driving down Vanguard Boulevard soon crosses Admiral Nelson Drive, where a sign for the parking area indicates SHORT-TERM CREW PARKING. Across the way, in an area where a new building is going up, the sign reads No CREW MEMBERS BEYOND THIS POINT. Walking into Vanguard's headquarters, the visitor might mistake it for a naval museum. Immediately to the left inside the main entrance is a scale model of HMS *Vanguard* in a glass case. To the right are six circular medallions with anchors, ships, and flags. The main building is named Victory, after Nelson's last flagship. Other buildings bear the names of other Nelson ships that took part in the Battle of the Nile: Zealous, Majestic, Audacious, Swiftsure, and Goliath.

Virtually every aspect of the company's headquarters is part of a modern-day HMS *Vanguard*—from the cafeteria (the Galley) to the fitness center (Ship Shape), from the company store (the Chandlery) to the telephone numbers Vanguard clients dial (1-800-662-CREW for client services, 1-800-662-SHIP for investor information). Antique prints of British naval battles adorn the walls throughout the sprawling complex.

The commander's office, too, seems like a museum. Behind Bogle's desk are engravings showing the Battle of the Nile, the Battle of Waterloo, and the Duke of Wellington (a gift from Walter Morgan). Also on the wall is a map of the Battle of the Nile. Three biographies of Nelson, a telescope, a sextant, and an antique print depicting the only meeting between Nelson and Wellington made visitors feel as though the room were rocking gently at sea. "Sometimes we thought he overdid that a little bit," said director Charles Root, but on the whole the crew found Bogle's love affair with naval imagery a plus. It galvanized them, making them think they were part of something larger and nobler. Most important, it reminded the crew that Bogle and his company were not just on a mission but were at war. "I *love* crisis," he once said, "not only because crisis brings out the best in us, but also because a crisis environment has been one in which Vanguard has thrived."

Bogle used the naval imagery to craft a family atmosphere at Vanguard. He seemed to think of each crew member as part of his extended family. In some cases, his assistants became almost as close to him as his six children—none of whom, incidentally, ever worked full-time at Vanguard. He almost always hired young people in their 20s without extensive business experience but with solid academic credentials from the nation's top schools. As a result, Vanguard has a young feel to it: Of the company's

3,700 employees in the spring of 1995, only 8 had been with the company since its inception in 1974.

Bogle liked to hire those who could be molded, learn on the job, and develop strong loyalty to him and to Vanguard—without being yes-men. While he believed that he was usually right, he wanted young people around him who could think independently and speak up when they opposed his viewpoint. He wanted to hear what they had to say, to know all sides of an argument before making a decision. He threw a great deal of responsibility his assistants' way, then watched them sink or swim. They learned quickly. Three of his assistants—Jim Riepe, Duncan McFarland, and Jack Brennan—went on to head mutual fund companies themselves. Others also built accomplished careers, including Jeremy Duffield, senior vice president of Vanguard; Daniel R. Butler, president of CSC Networks; and Jan Twardowski, president of Frank Russell Securities.

Until 1989, all of Bogle's assistants had been hired from outside the company. The only internal hire was Jim Norris, Bogle's current assistant. Norris, who had joined Vanguard in 1987 following his graduation from Saint Joseph's University in Philadelphia, was working as an accountant in 1989 but had plans to leave Vanguard. Jack Brennan, Vanguard's president, had gotten wind of Norris's impending departure and convinced Bogle to talk to Norris about the recently vacated assistant's position. Norris urged Bogle to give him a shot, and Bogle, impressed with his past performance and potential promise, did just that. Norris was just 25 at the time, and he became the longest-tenured of Bogle's assistants. He currently is a 1997 MBA candidate at the Wharton School.

Of the externally hired assistants, two had Harvard MBAs (Brennan and David A. Hamra); one had an MBA from Dartmouth's Amos Tuck School of Business (Thomas E. Chapin); two had graduated from Penn's Wharton School of Business (Jan Twardowski and Jim Riepe); and one came straight from Ohio Wesleyan College (Daniel R. Butler). Jeremy Duffield had graduated from the University of Virginia and briefly worked at the Federal Reserve Bank of Richmond before joining Bogle; Duncan McFarland arrived straight out of Yale.

"THE SVENGALI EFFECT"

Jeremy Duffield first caught Bogle's attention at a conference in New York at which he (Duffield) was the speaker. Duffield's speech was based on a paper he had co-authored while at the Richmond Fed, one of the first papers to recognize the potential economic significance of money market mutual funds. Bogle recalls being "overwhelmed" by the event. "Here this 24-year-old—and even younger looking—man gives a powerful, carefully reasoned, highly articulate speech to his elders, with all of the composure and poise of a veteran. At the lunch break, I asked him to eat with me, and was even more impressed." It wasn't long after that meeting that Bogle persuaded Duffield to sign on with Vanguard.

Following a two-year stint as Bogle's assistant, Duffield was elevated to vice president of planning and development in 1982, and in 1985 was appointed senior vice president. During his tenure, Duffield would oversee the introduction of 72 new Vanguard Fund portfolios, whose assets in June 1995 exceeded $70 billion. Bogle was impressed not only with Duffield's intellect and integrity ("both quite out of the ordinary"), but with his drive and determination as well. "He has been with me almost since the beginning of Vanguard," Bogle said, "and was one of 'we happy few, we band of brothers' who struggled through those early days of dire adversity that finally ended in mid-1982. He is a battler, and has been great fun to have at my side."

Duffield reciprocated Bogle's esteem. In a letter to the author, Duffield expressed his heartfelt praise for Bogle's leadership, including his ability to command loyalty.

"Over the years, I have seen Jack Bogle work his magic on countless people. I call it 'the Svengali effect' (without the evil overtones). A few (usually clever and amusing) words, a winning smile, and a deep laugh and they're hooked. They know there's something special in this package and they feel some of the magic rub off on them. They'll listen to him, they'll laugh with him, and they'll follow him wherever he wants them to go.

"One of the keys to our survival and prosperity has been the support of the Crew throughout. They shared the exhilaration of growth and shared the sense of mission, even of crusade, that Jack Bogle fostered. I think he was a marvel at building this support and it's one of his greatest attributes as a leader.

"It's a classic story, but one rarely played out as well as in this case. A leader develops a vision that he believes in fervently and that his troops can buy into. It contains a social purpose they identify with and contains the seeds of their own success. Jack used every opportunity to communicate the message. A speech at every billion-dollar mark in the early days. Twice a year, at least,

William Y. Bogle, Jr., Lieutenant,
Royal Flying Corps of Great Britain,
1917.

Josephine Lorraine Hipkins, 1921.

Marriage of William Yates Bogle, Jr., and Josephine Hipkins Bogle, September 20, 1924.

Josephine Bogle and her children (from left: William, John, David), 1932.

John, David, William Bogle, 1936.

John Bogle graduated *Magna Cum Laude* from Princeton University. "Nassau Herald," 1951.

John Bogle, 1959.

Walter L. Morgan, founder and first president of Wellington Fund, formed in 1928.

Joseph E. Welch, Walter L. Morgan, and John C. Bogle, 1960.

"The Whiz Kids Take Over at Wellington," *Institutional Investor*, January 1968. Represented here: John C. Bogle, W. Nicholas Thorndike, Robert W. Doran, George Lewis, Stephen Paine.

John Bogle, 1970.

Robert W. Doran (left) and W. Nicholas
Thorndike, Wellington Management
Company Annual Report, 1974.

John Bogle and James S. Riepe, 1981.

David, John, and William Bogle at dedication of Bogle Hall, 1989.

Bogle Hall, Blair Academy, 1989.

Publication of *Bogle on Mutual Funds: New Perspectives for the Intelligent Investor.* John Bogle, James Norris (right), 1993.

"The Assistants" convene. (From left) Standing: Jeremy Duffield, James Riepe, Daniel Butler, Jan Twardowski, Duncan McFarland. Seated: John Brennan, Mortimer (Tim) Buckley, John Bogle, James Norris, 1993. Not Pictured: Thomas Chapin, David Hamra, and Walter Lenhard.

Vanguard Board of Directors, 1995 (From left) Standing: Robert W. Cawthorn, Burton S. Malkiel, Bruce M. MacLaury, John J. Brennan, Alfred E. Rankin, J. Lawrence Wilson, John D. Sawhill. Seated: Barbara B. Hauptfuhrer, John C. Bogle, James O. Welch, Jr.

John Bogle, 1995.

John Bogle and Louis Rukeyser, *Wall Street Week*, 1991.

"The Succession:" John J. Brennan, John C. Bogle, Walter L. Morgan, 1996.

"The Battle of the Nile." Engraving by Thomas Sutherland after painting by Whitcombe. From "The Naval Achievements of Great Britain," by John Jenkins, 1818.

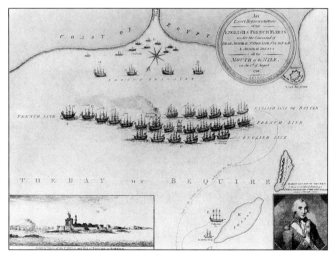

The Battle of the Nile. "An Exact Representation of the English and French Fleets." Published by Laurie and White, October 1798.

"The Army and the Navy." Only meeting of the
Duke of Wellington and Lord Nelson. Engraving of
1818 by S.W. Reynolds after painting by
J. P. Knight, ARA.

Scale model, HMS Vanguard, by Alfred Oxspring,
1983.

The Vanguard Corporate Campus, Malvern, PA, 1994.

John J. Brennan (left) and John C. Bogle at groundbreaking for Vanguard campus, 1992.

Charles D. Root, Jr., 1980.

John B. Neff presenting the "Good Scout Award" to John Bogle, 1992.

John J. Brennan (left) and John C. Bogle at Vanguard's $5 billion milestone celebration, August 28, 1982.

John C. Bogle, *Money Magazine*, 1986 (© 1987 Nina Barnett).

> he hosts a Vanguard celebration, a partnership picnic and a holiday event to gather everyone together and to get the point across in a 15-minute speech. The message and the success are eerily consistent. The chairman's values become the Crew's values and they support the whole enterprise, binding a company with an unusually strong corporate culture. It's a virtuous cycle: motivated crew leads to strong service ethic and happy clients, which in turn leads to success with a share to the crew, which helps create a motivated workforce, and so on. It helps that Jack Bogle is a magnetic personality, with a sense of humor and a well-known concern for the Crew that endears him to the group."

The veteran assistants have formed themselves into a more or less permanent club, having met with Bogle once a year since the early 1980s for squash, dinner at a Philadelphia restaurant, business talk, and mutual needling. The latter is said to approach the outrageous level, but is expected to be taken by the victim (often Bogle) in good grace. The yearly get-togethers, without wives, may run from three o'clock in the afternoon until near midnight. Bogle's traditional toast, sounded every year, begins, "You, sirs, are a tribute to my good judgment about the human character."

■ ■ ■

It was no secret that Vanguard's growth through the early 1980s had no substantial effect on the personal wealth of its employees. Had Vanguard been a publicly held company, employees would have had access to stock options and similar compensation programs. To head off discontent and to put Vanguard on more of an equal footing with other mutual fund companies, Bogle and his colleagues in 1983 instituted a yearly bonus program for senior executives, designed to provide an equitylike participation in Vanguard's success.

In every speech Bogle gave to the crew when a major milestone was reached, he emphasized how critical it was for Vanguard to drive its expense ratio even lower relative to the expenses of other complexes. The goal, he reminded each crew member, was to maintain and enhance the firm's standing as the lowest-cost provider of services in the entire mutual fund industry. Even as Bogle talked about the need to press for efficiency, he sensed that crew members were beginning to equate low cost for Vanguard clients with miserly compensation for them. As he became more concerned, he discussed the issue at length with Brennan. Out of his experience with Johnson Wax, Brennan suggested that perhaps all crew members should have a chance to participate in the plan. Bogle immediately agreed and promptly developed a program in which crew members would be rewarded, in large part commensurate with Vanguard's asset growth and its ability to keep costs at the minimum level consistent with first-class service. So, in the very next year (1984), the earnings participation provided in the executive plan was extended to include every member of the crew. It was called the Vanguard Partnership Plan.

Vanguard took a novel approach to calculating distributions under the plan. In publicly held companies, bonuses were paid out of profits. Because it operates at cost, however, Vanguard disclaims having profits. Instead it counts as profits the money it saves shareholders by keeping its costs well below those of its competitors. Put differently, Vanguard's savings are equivalent to the profits that a management company would have earned by reason of operating at a higher cost than Vanguard.

Because it is not a public company, Vanguard does not publish an earnings statement. It does, however, publish its "profits" based on the extent to which its traditionally low expense ratios provide shareholder value relative to the expenses of its major competitors. This difference is then applied to Vanguard's average assets for the year—creating larger earnings as its cost position improves and as its asset base grows. This figure showed that in 1994, Vanguard served its shareholders at an overall cost ratio of 0.30 percent of assets, compared to 1.05 percent for the industry. As a result, the profits earned by Vanguard for fund shareholders totaled some $969 million—its expense advantage of 0.75 percent multiplied by average assets of $129 billion. A specified portion of this savings goes into the Partnership Plan pool and is adjusted for any value created by the Vanguard Funds' returns relative to the returns of other mutual funds with comparable investment policies.

Given Vanguard's increasing cost advantage and rapidly growing asset base, "profits" have burgeoned, as have the Partnership Plan distributions. The company distributed $500,000 to the crew in 1985, $1.8 million in 1987, $3.9 million in 1989, $8 million in 1991, and $16 million in 1993—all through the Partnership Plan. Bogle estimated that "profits" would grow to over $1 billion in 1995, and that more than $25 million would be distributed to the crew. The remaining 98 percent of profits, of course, would go to the direct benefit of fund shareholders.

The Partnership Plan was, not surprisingly, an immediate success with the crew. As Bogle would later note, however, "money isn't everything." The plan helped get people working together as a team and signing on to Vanguard's mission. But it was supplemented by an enhanced program of better communications within the organization; better facilities (in 1993, the new campus); and an enlightened program to respond to the crew's needs (including an open-door policy and an open-channel policy, providing for ready access to senior executives to discuss company policies).

Bogle felt strongly that too many companies demanded loyalty without giving loyalty in return. "Loyalty," he stressed, "must run both from the individual to the institution and from the institution to the individual." In message after message to the crew, he returned to the themes of mutual caring and respect between each individual member of the crew and Vanguard as an institution. "Caring," he noted in one speech, "is a mutual affair," calling attention to Vanguard's responsibility, as an institution, to provide each crew member with "respect as an individual; opportunity for career growth, participation, and innovation; an attractive environment in which to work, corporate information through a meaningful communications program, and fair compensation." In return, he said, quoting Dean Howard W. Johnson, chairman of Massachusetts Institute of Technology, "we need people who have a deep sense of caring about the institution . . . Caring is an exacting and demanding business . . . and the burden must be borne by all who work for it, all who own it, all who are served by it, all who govern it."

An important part of caring, Bogle believed, called for Vanguard to recognize outstanding individual achievement by members of the crew, especially those who were performing lower-level but essential administrative tasks. In 1984, the Vanguard Award for Excellence was created to honor service above and beyond the call of duty. Candidates for the award are nominated each quarter by crew members, and nominees are considered on the primary basis of "making a difference" at Vanguard, taking into account such traits as exceptional courtesy and professionalism, outstanding job performance, creativity, enthusiasm, and self motivation. A group of senior officers evaluates the quarterly nominees and makes final recommendations.

The awards are presented either at an all-company meeting or in the winner's department, with Bogle personally bestowing the prizes on the winner: credit for dinner and two tickets to a theater or sports event; a contribution to the winner's favorite charity; and a handshake for the men, a kiss for the ladies. The award itself, a plaque engraved with the winner's name, depicts HMS *Vanguard* and carries a quotation from Bogle: "I believe that even one person *can* make a difference." Bogle describes the days he presents the awards as among the most rewarding of his career.

In a 1988 speech he titled "Tradition," Bogle reaffirmed that the traditions established by Walter Morgan for Wellington—conservative investing in a balanced portfolio, focus on the long-term investor, fair dealings with clients—remained an integral part of Vanguard's operations. He made it clear that loyalty to the people of Vanguard should be added to the list of traditions. "It is really incredible," he said, "that it has taken so many American corporations so long to realize that it is simply *not right* to ask those who do the daily work to be loyal to the corporation without making the same commitment, with the same fervor, that the corporation will be loyal to them in return. That concept of 'two-way' loyalty—of mutual caring—must itself become another Vanguard tradition."

■ ■ ■

Bogle also was faced with the challenge of gaining respect outside the company. Because his ideas were revolutionary and because he adopted the stance of a preacher, he took it for granted that he would alienate many of his listeners in the industry. He knew that he faced a hard task in winning the respect of the members of the financial community, who would collectively define the company's image and reputation.

Wisely, Bogle focused first on winning over the media. While he knew that any attempt to create loyalty would be not only out of the question but also inappropriate, he believed that Vanguard's unique structure and mission, if handled with complete candor, could generate favorable media attention. Few business executives were as skillful as Bogle in handling the press. Essentially his own spokesman, he enjoyed talking to the press and, perhaps because of his own experience as a newspaper stringer in the summer of 1949, seemed to understand the needs of reporters better than most. He was brimming with controversial ideas, yet he spoke in simple, easy-to-understand sentences, providing numerous quotes that would add color to a story. He was always happy to take a call from a reporter, whether Vanguard was involved in the story or not. Even if the topic of the story was benign, Bogle, always the contrarian, found a way to make it controversial, not by design, but because of Vanguard's unique perspective. At the very least, he provided background that enabled the reporter to grasp the story's true relevance.

Bogle's candor was of great appeal to journalists, whose tolerance for windbags and prevaricators was low. Journalists had long found the mutual fund industry arcane and confusing, and hence of little interest. Bogle prodded them to begin asking probing questions of industry leaders and to write stories on subjects that had long been taboo, such as the need for accurate disclosure of fund performance or for highly paid board directors to exert their influence on behalf of the mutual fund shareholders, whose sole interests they were supposed to serve. To the members of the media who had long taken the industry's secretive behavior patterns for granted, Bogle was a breath of fresh air. It was no coincidence that the same reporters who found Bogle such a good source of quotes began writing favorably about the news topic closest to Bogle's heart—The Vanguard Group.

Bogle's accessibility to the press was a pleasant contrast to the doors that frequently slammed in the faces of journalists trying to talk to other industry leaders. The media found it so easy to reach Bogle that Brian S. Mattes, a Vanguard principal responsible for public relations, had little reason to call press conferences. Bogle preferred going one-on-one with a reporter; he enjoyed the give-and-take, and saw the occasion as a chance to educate the writer, particularly about Bogle's own likes and dislikes.

High on his list of dislikes was advertising, a practice that the preacher found practically sinful. Bogle genuinely believed that if someone built a better mousetrap, customers would beat a path to his door. (One of his speeches was titled "If You Build It, They Will Come," drawing on the theme of the movie *Field of Dreams.*) Bogle felt that mutual fund companies should have a trustee relationship with their clients, and he wanted to distinguish mutual fund distribution from the way products like beer or toothpaste were typically sold. "Bringing out new funds because the public wants new things is fine for Bloomingdale's," he said. "But supposing the public wants a fund that's a lousy investment? Does that mean we have to go out and sell it to them? I don't think so."

Given Bogle's strong views on advertising, it's not surprising that Vanguard spent relatively small sums—and those grudgingly—on getting word of its funds out to investors, while its rivals, principally Fidelity, were outspending the company many times over. In 1991, Vanguard spent $6 million on advertising; Fidelity was said to have spent some $50 million. By 1995, Fidelity had upped its advertising budget to an estimated $100 million; Vanguard, in contrast, was still spending its same old $6 million. For Bogle, advertising was not just expensive, but often tainted as well. "Most advertising," he said, "takes the thrust that a particular fund is 'first in performance' and is therefore a good investment. The fund sponsors know . . . that today's 'first' may be tomorrow's 'last,' and that the odds strongly favor a future return that is more or less average."

If Bogle was going to stake out the high moral ground on advertising, however, he knew that he still had to find some way to attract the attention of potential investors—if only to let them know a better mousetrap had been built. One way to do so was to ensure that the message Vanguard communicated to investors was clear, sharply focused, and attractive. Beyond that, however, giving good quotes, supplying reporters with useful background information, and in general being contentious all became part of a conscious business strategy to win Vanguard continuing media attention. Jack Brennan, Bogle's recently appointed successor as CEO of Vanguard, confessed: "Bogle's relationship with the press, being the first to be called on a lot of subjects, is a tremendous asset. It's worth millions of marketing dollars every year to us."

Bogle always tried to draw a line between Vanguard's corporate affairs and his own personal affairs. For the most part he was successful, but Bogle was thin-skinned when it came to what he considered an invasion of his privacy. The problem came to a head in 1992. Daniel F. Wiener, a former reporter for *U.S. News & World Report,* ran a two-year-old newsletter called *The Vanguard Adviser.* With a circulation Wiener said was 15,000, the newsletter was devoted largely to recommendations about selecting from among the various Vanguard Funds. In the fall of 1992, Wiener told *Forbes* magazine his estimate of Bogle's salary: $2.6 million in salary plus substantial incentives. "When the story came out," Wiener recalled, "Bogle apparently hit the ceiling. Here was a guy who had made his reputation on being cheap, pushing low expenses, and saying we don't waste shareholders' money. How does it look that he makes $2.6 million a year?" Bogle reports that his salary was but a fraction of Wiener's estimate; in fact, only about 20 percent of the reported figure. The lion's share of his compensation was represented by incentives based on Vanguard's profits returned to fund shareholders and the relative performance of the Vanguard Funds. In any event, the *Forbes* story emphasized that Bogle's pay was in fact subpar, headlining the article "In the Vanguard, Except in Pay." In reference to Wiener's estimate, the article stated that "in today's boom in this industry, that's pretty small stuff."

Shortly thereafter, Vanguard sued Wiener's publishing company, insisting that it stop using *The Vanguard Adviser* as the title of its newsletter. Bogle claimed that angry letters and phone calls had come in from shareholders who had received solicitations from Wiener and assumed that Vanguard had sold their names and addresses to the newsletter. Wiener, in response, accused Vanguard of trying to put him out of business. He argued that Bogle was upset not by his use of the Vanguard name but by the *Forbes* report. "If the name was a problem, where were they for two years—were they asleep at the switch?" He issued a news release giving his version of events, and the press latched on to the story. In time, the matter was settled when Wiener agreed to change the name of the newsletter to *The Independent Advisor for Vanguard Investors*. Despite this concession by Wiener, Bogle remained furious, dismissing him as a "publicity seeker." He said that publishers who profited by purporting to provide advice on switching funds within fund families were "parasites" but, he added, "in the final analysis, irrelevant."

When it came to negative press reports about Vanguard, Bogle was so wedded to his company's values that if the reports were not solidly grounded in fact, they could infuriate him. For example, in its May 1, 1975, issue, *Forbes* magazine ran an article entitled "A Plague on Both Houses" about the events leading to the birth of Vanguard. Enraged, Bogle grabbed a yellow pad and scribbled a six-page letter to editor James W. Michaels. "I hardly know where to begin in evaluating an article which is so breathtaking in the scope of its unfairness and its inaccuracy." He assailed the magazine for becoming a "self-appointed antagonist to the mutual fund industry." One of his chief complaints was that *Forbes* had used faulty research and thus unfairly criticized the performance of Vanguard's funds. Beyond that, he wrote, "the real tragedy of your article is not that you distorted and slanted some facts and figures. It is that you failed to take advantage of an opportunity to say something positive about a forward step for mutual fund investors. There is no doubt in my mind that our new structure is the beginning of a substantial change in our industry."

Bogle prides himself, though, on not holding grudges. *Forbes* was in his line of sight again after a May 8, 1995, article entitled "Vanguard's Achilles' Heel," criticizing the company's equity fund performance. Bogle called the article "grotesquely unfair and incorrect," but rather than writing a letter to the editor, he wrote a blistering rebuttal addressed to the Vanguard directors and sent copies to the writers of the *Forbes* article. A week later, *Forbes* was writing an article on the fees paid to mutual fund directors. A reporter called, and Bogle agreed to talk to her about the issue.

"I'm surprised you're willing to talk to me," the reporter said to Bogle. "I saw the rebuttal letter you sent to your directors."

Bogle replied, "I would be willing to talk about anything . . . We're not going to boycott the press no matter how awful the coverage is." Sounding Trumanesque, he concluded, "If you can't stand the heat, you ought to get out of the kitchen."

15

THE CREST
OF THE WAVE

URING THE 1980s and the first half of the 1990s, the mutual fund industry enjoyed an era of explosive growth, a 15-year stretch in which industry assets soared, from $95 billion to $2.5 trillion—a compound growth rate of 24 percent annually. Vanguard rode the crest of the wave, with assets rising from $2.4 billion as 1980 began to $155 billion in June 1995—an even faster growth rate of 31 percent annually.

Certainly the principal reason for the industry's growth was the great bull market in financial assets that began in the summer of 1981. What followed was a period in which stocks, bonds, and cash reserves provided the highest returns for any comparable period in U.S. history. Stocks provided a total annual return of 16 percent; long-term bonds, 15 percent; and U.S. Treasury bills, 7 percent. A portfolio composed of one-third in each asset class at the outset of this period would have provided an average annual rate of return of 13 percent, compared with a long-term annual return averaging 7 percent since 1926 for a comparably weighted portfolio. This was truly the halcyon era for financial assets.

From a level of just under 800 in mid-1982, the Dow Jones Industrial Average rose almost unremittingly and broke the 5,000 barrier in late 1995. It was the longest and strongest bull market in this century, and it continues to run today. Traditionally market-sensitive, the mutual fund industry was probably the major beneficiary of the bull market. Merely being a part of the industry virtually assured double-digit asset growth, no matter how well-run (or ill-run) the fund complex. Underscoring this distinction, Jack Bogle was fond of saying, "Never confuse genius with luck and a bull market."

A second reason for the mutual fund industry's phenomenal growth was that a new generation of investors was entering the financial markets and witnessing firsthand the extraordinary returns. Before the 1980s, individual investors were inclined to stay away from the securities markets, believing they lacked the knowledge to cope with its fluctuations and uncertainties. But 77 million baby boomers came of age in the 1980s. Better educated than previous generations, they placed increasing faith in stocks and bonds, in portfolio diversification, and in the skills of professional investment managers. Once the province of the rich, the securities markets were becoming democratized, and the middle class, with more spare cash to invest, was joining the more affluent in those markets.

A third impetus behind the industry's growth was the gargantuan leap ahead in information technology. The creation of the 800 telephone number and the spread of computers made it possible for a single fund complex to process thousands of calls in a single day. As communication costs dropped and the availability of information rose, the pool of investors grew and large mutual fund complexes were able to handle millions of accounts, generally with considerable ease.

A fourth factor was the growing innovation of mutual fund managers, in contrast to their more conservative counterparts in other segments of the financial services industry. The one-fund mutual fund complex became a relic of the past, replaced by multifund firms that often managed scores of funds. The money market fund, which came into existence in 1974, had by 1979 become the single largest component of the mutual fund industry. This remarkable innovation introduced mutual funds to millions of first-time investors, who were seeking to ease the pain of double-digit inflation with a dose of double-digit investment returns. Vanguard's experience was typical. In 1977, only 1 percent of the firm's $1.8 billion in assets was invested in money market funds; in 1982, just five years later, $2.2 billion, or 39 percent, of Vanguard's $5.6 billion in assets was held in money market funds. Between 1977 and 1982, nearly $2 billion flowed into the company's money market funds, compared to only $900 million into all of its other funds combined.

Similarly, as short-term interest rates began to drop in 1983 and money market yields tumbled, investors sought the higher yields available in bond funds. Bond funds had not held a substantial portion of the industry's assets since the 1930s, and had been but 10 percent of the industry's asset base in 1975. But in an environment of higher interest rates, and because of a federal tax law that enabled the creation of fund investments in tax-free municipal bonds, by the mid-1980s bonds had become a major component of the industry, accounting for 20 percent of its asset base.

Stock-oriented funds composed 90 percent of industry assets at the outset of the devastating 1973–74 bear market, and it was 1982 before stock funds were to convert cash outflow to cash inflow, giving a further impetus to industry growth. What's more, new, usually more speculative, equity funds were created as the bull market whetted the public's appetite for higher returns. By mid-1995, industry assets of $2.8 trillion comprised 45 percent equity-oriented funds, 30 percent bond funds, and 25 percent money market funds, a diversity that minimized the industry's traditional full exposure to equity market risk.

Finally, the growth of retirement accounts provided an extraordinary stimulant to the popularity of mutual funds. In 1974, federal tax law created the individual retirement account (IRA) to encourage people to save money on a tax-deferred basis for their retirement. Mutual funds were perfect for IRA investors, who could get professional management and diversification with a maximum tax-deductible investment of $2,000 a year, as well as tax-deferred earnings on the account. In 1978, the emergence of the 401(k) thrift plan, named after the section of the tax code that enabled its creation, opened a massive market of investors who could deduct a portion of their salary before taxes and invest it, with the earnings tax-deferred for retirement. By 1995, 30 percent of all mutual fund investments were in long-term retirement plans, a total of $636 billion, which included some $342 billion of IRA assets and $186 billion of 401(k) assets, along with $108 billion in other types of retirement plans.

In sum, the bull markets in stocks and bonds of the 1980–95 era provided a remarkable environment for mutual fund companies in every market sector, whether money market funds (in the early years), fixed-income funds (in the middle years), or equity funds (in the later years). The real spark for the explosion came, as Jack Bogle put it, on a hot Thursday afternoon in August 1982 when Wall Street economist Henry Kaufman predicted, among other things, that interest rates were about to drop. And so they did. The drop in interest rates, accompanied by a slowing of inflation, sent the stock and bond markets soaring. Remarkably, the rise since then was virtually uninterrupted. Even the disasters of 1987—the bond market fiasco of April and May and the October stock market crash—and the disappointments of 1994—a bad year for bonds and a year in which equity returns were neutral to negative—did not stem the tide. Far more confident about the economy, less worried about inflation, and more interested in long-term investments than they were in the 1970s, investors placed their money not in hard assets such as real estate, diamonds, and gold, but in mutual funds.

The explosion in equity mutual funds led to a common misconception that they dominated the U.S. stock market. The reality was that, despite their growth, mutual funds held less than 20 percent of the nation's nearly $6 trillion in corporate equities in 1995. The holdings of households, private pension plans, and state and government pension plans accounted for a far larger share of the market. Still, the past 15 years was a glorious period for mutual funds. If they lacked the liquidity or the stability of other financial instruments, few worried, for mutual funds enjoyed a reputation for integrity, and their patrons at the Securities and Exchange Commission were viewed as protecting investors and assuring full disclosure of past returns, potential risks and current costs. For all the anxiety investors had felt about them in an earlier era, mutual funds increasingly became the investment vehicle of choice.

The mutual fund industry responded to—and even accelerated—this boom. New firms entered the field and existing firms created new funds at an ever-rising pace to meet the perceived demands of the marketplace. "Product proliferation" was the buzzword of the era. The number of individual funds rose from 600 in 1980 to 3,100 in 1990 to 5,800 in 1995. In particular, funds with narrower, more speculative investment goals were rapidly supplanting more traditional funds, and funds with new investment strategies were copied just as fast as they attracted investor assets. In many cases, market demand replaced common sense. Bogle spoke derisively about "government-plus" funds (creating phantom income by selling call options on their portfolio bonds), "global short-term" bond funds (capitalizing on a temporary boom in international interest rates), and adjustable-rate mortgage funds (purportedly offering higher yields than money market funds, but without added risk). All of the fad funds had their heyday before their investment promises proved illusory and assets plummeted.

■   ■   ■

Vanguard, too, aggressively expanded its product line, but it eschewed the untried speculative funds and simply ignored the transitory fads. Still, the firm added some 60 new fund portfolios from 1980 through 1995, bringing the total number of funds it offered to 80 by mid-1995. It focused on funds with conservative strategies, forming 8 new money market funds, 18 market index funds, 14 new equity funds, and 20 clearly defined "asset class" bond funds. In June 1980, for example, Vanguard introduced the first no-load Ginnie Mae (GNMA) fund—although the fund hit an early bump in the road. Jeremy Duffield recalls that the fund was one of the first developed after he joined Vanguard, and it was introduced just after a decline in interest rates. When interest rates suddenly rose sharply, the price of the Ginnie Mae fund plummeted. "It was a helluva shock for a new guy," he said. "This was something that was supposed to be relatively safe, since the U.S. government guaranteed the payment of interest and the principal value at maturity. I still remember seeing letters from people who wrote: 'Where do I write the U.S. government to get my principal back?' " As interest rates declined over the next few years, though, the fund grew to $7 billion, one of the largest in the industry.

While Vanguard's early foray into the institutional business had a major impact on its success relative to other fund complexes, perhaps the most pervasive trend in favor of Vanguard was the growth of the direct marketing (usually no-load) segment of the industry. During the 15 years from 1980 to 1995, while the industry as a whole grew at a 24 percent annual rate, funds controlled by, or distributed by, brokerage firms grew at a 20 percent rate, and the direct marketing segment grew at a 26 percent rate. As mentioned earlier, Vanguard's assets grew at an ever higher rate— 31 percent annually—and its share of the industry-leading direct marketing segment increased from 9 percent to 21 percent.

Clearly, Vanguard's risky 1977 decision to eliminate all sales charges was vindicated. If Vanguard had grown at the load segment rate during this period, its assets in mid-1995 would have been $40 billion; at the industrywide growth rate, its assets would have been $63 billion; at the direct marketing growth rate, $84 billion. Instead, as mentioned earlier, Vanguard assets totaled $155 billion at mid-1995.

Although Vanguard prospered from the mutual fund boom and from the direct marketing boom, it was Vanguard's other attributes that earned it the highest growth rate of any major mutual fund firm: the appeal of its low-cost funds in an era of consumerism, the performance of its funds relative to comparable competitors, its reputation as a provider of high-quality investor services, its unique role in market index funds, and the public awareness of the Vanguard name and the values it stood for— abetted by remarkably favorable press coverage. No matter how you looked at it, it was an era of incredible growth.

Above all else, it seemed to be Vanguard's low costs that caught the public's eye. Until Vanguard came along, no fund complex had staked a claim as the industry's lowest-cost provider. In fact, judging by the steadily rising expense ratios of the industry's major fund complexes during this period, it seemed that most companies were in a race to raise their fees.

Ironically, when Vanguard started out on its own in 1974, its costs were slightly higher than competitive norms, with an expense ratio of 0.71 percent versus 0.70 percent for the average large fund complex. By 1995, Vanguard was by far the lowest-cost provider, having sliced its expense ratio to 0.30 percent while that of the average large fund complex rose to 0.92 percent.

Vanguard's huge cost advantage was due to the combination of its unique "at-cost" corporate structure, its general operating efficiency, its economies of scale, its disciplined marketing and advertising expenditures, and its ability to bargain at arm's length in setting the fees paid to its external investment advisers. Whatever its cause, low cost had struck a chord with investors, and they beat a path to Vanguard's door.

■ ■ ■

When the company opened its doors, it was largely an individual or retail business, with only modest institutional trade. What little institutional business there was (pension fund management) remained the responsibility of TDP&L, the Wellington Management Company subsidiary. Vanguard's push to aggressively expand into the institutional business in the late 1970s would prove a major factor in its growth.

"A PAIR OF ACES"

As Vanguard struggled during the late 1980s to expand its institutional business, Bogle and Brennan looked outside the company for an experienced manager to spearhead the institutional effort. The search ended in 1989 with the hiring of James H. Gately as senior vice president of the institutional division.

Gately, a 1962 graduate of Wesleyan University, with a Harvard Business School MBA, had been running the asset management subsidiary of Prudential Insurance Company. When he took over the reins of the institutional division, its assets totaled $10 billion—roughly 30 percent of Vanguard's total assets. Under Gately's direction, Vanguard became one of the dominant firms in the institutional business, as its assets grew to nearly $70 billion by mid-1995.

When asked about Gately's contribution to Vanguard's growth, Bogle responded, "Jim Gately did a remarkable job in developing our business with institutional investors—especially in the 401(k) thrift plan arena. He integrated our highly complex record-keeping

activities with our marketing efforts, and developed a first-class
team around him. He's a very smart guy, a man loaded with
business sense, investment sense, and common sense."

In a reorganization of Vanguard's business lines in 1995,
Gately left the institutional division to assume leadership of the
individual division. His replacement in the institutional division
was F. William McNabb, Jr., who had worked closely with Gately
since 1990 in developing the unit's strategic initiatives, and had
direct responsibility for all marketing, education, and sales activities. Leaving behind an assistant treasurer post at Chase Manhattan Bank, McNabb was hired at Vanguard in 1986 by Jeremy
Duffield as a manager of insurance contracts.

Like Gately, McNabb had excellent academic credentials:
Dartmouth College (1972) and a Wharton MBA. Bogle described
McNabb as, "A real comer from his first day on the job. He's
bright, great with people, and a visionary thinker. Along with Jim
Gately, we have 'a pair of aces' running our two lines of busi-
ness—institutional and individual—truly a class act."

In the 1970s, the traditional corporate retirement plan was a defined
benefit plan. This meant that the employer was responsible for investing
retirement dollars in any way it saw fit—mutual funds, banks, under the
mattress—and then paying its retired employees a fixed pension. Bogle
believed that defined benefit programs were a source of opportunity for
Vanguard. As it turned out, however, the real growth would come in
defined *contribution* plans, including profit sharing and 401(k) plans, in
which the employer turned the responsibility for managing retirement
assets over to employees, allowing them to direct their own contributions
to whatever investments—including mutual funds—met their needs.
Corporations eventually latched on to the 401(k) because it was cheaper
to fund than a defined benefit plan and shifted the risks of investing from
the company to the employee.

The trend toward defined contribution plans was critical to the success
of the major mutual fund companies, for most defined benefit plans had
been privately managed and rarely invested in mutual funds. By 1995, one-
half of all corporate retirement plans were defined contribution plans, and
in ever-increasing numbers, companies were trying to eliminate their
defined benefit plans in favor of 401(k)s. For mutual fund firms like
Vanguard, these plans were highly profitable, giving the company immediate access to millions of new investors.

Bill McNabb explained how the company won over a sizable chunk of the 401(k) business in the early 1980s: "It started out as a very entrepreneurial enterprise, and Vanguard was again a pioneer in the field. We took our retail computer system and modified it to do the administrative functions that were required in the 401(k) environment. The big thing we did differently . . . was to treat the participants in the 401(k) plan the same way as the other investors in our funds. This meant valuing their accounts every night, giving them an 800 phone number, and allowing them to switch from one fund to another." At that time, only a few mutual fund companies had matched Vanguard in pushing for 401(k) money, including T. Rowe Price and Fidelity. Vanguard's success was substantial, and its institutional business accounted for $70 billion in assets as of June 1995, almost 40 percent of the total assets under the company's management.

Vanguard's institutional business posed a few problems that did not exist on the individual side. Vanguard had to continuously sell itself to institutional plan sponsors amid stiff competition. In the company's formal business proposal to prospective clients, senior officials at the institution had the chance to confront Vanguard executives and ask tough questions about the funds. They closely examined Vanguard's record-keeping service, its commitment to technology, and its ability to quickly and efficiently transmit information about a variety of investment plans to the institution's vast number of participants. Individual investors, in contrast, increasingly took it for granted that Vanguard offered high-quality service; their sole concern was the funds' investment attributes and performance accomplishments.

As Vanguard gained strength and presence in both the individual and institutional markets, its asset growth began to compound. The first major milestone came on September 17, 1980, when the company reached $3 billion in assets under management, more than doubling the $1.4 billion initial asset base in 1974. Bogle threw a champagne party, and all 300 Vanguard employees squeezed into one room to hear him give a congratulatory speech while standing on a table. It had taken 31 years—from 1928 to 1959—for Wellington Fund, the Vanguard funds' original flagship, to reach $1 billion. Total assets of all of the Vanguard (then Wellington Management) funds had first crossed $2 billion in 1965, a milestone that was long forgotten when the dark days of the early-1970s arrived and that Vanguard would not reach again until 1979. After that, the milestones were passed rapidly: $4 billion in 1981, $7 billion in 1983, $10 billion in 1985, $25 billion in 1987, $100 billion in 1993, $150 billion in May 1995.

While Bogle did not chase after growth, he accepted it as one of the best measurements of success. He appreciated the value of all those company milestones as employee morale boosters, and he made sure that there were celebrations and speeches to mark each occasion. He feared the consequences of growth, however, especially the development of a stultifying bureaucracy that would erode the flexibility and warmth to clients that smaller funds could retain.

But he knew that growth was essential, citing in one speech the words of John Cardinal Newman: "Growth is the only evidence of life." He saw in 1975 that Vanguard ranked 10th in asset size among the giants of the day—including Fidelity, the Capital Group, Dreyfus, Merrill Lynch, T. Rowe Price, and Putnam—and he knew he had to compete against those firms and others that would emerge. Above all, he wanted Vanguard's success to be determined by the strength of the investment performance it delivered, the quality of its service to clients, and the fair shake it gave them on costs. He refused to compromise his values by adopting investment strategies that might have increased assets but were, in his view, too risky. The fundamental strategy followed by Vanguard during the 15 years of industry growth would be best described as "no thrills or chills." If people want thrills and chills, Bogle said, "This is not a good place for them to be."

In short, it was the combination of a conservative investment strategy, fund performance that exceeded competitive norms, by far the lowest operating expenses in the industry, the 1977 no-load decision, and high-quality service that took Vanguard to the crest of the wave of the industry's extraordinary asset growth. In fact, Vanguard was doing more than merely riding the wave; it was among its principal creators. Bogle, however, ever the pragmatist, was candid about the role of luck in Vanguard's growth during this period. He acknowledged that even as the firm delivered on the mission it had sought for its clients, its success was partly the result of events over which the company had no control—especially the emergence of money market funds and tax-favored retirement plans. Reminiscent of his comments about luck and a bull market, in a speech he delivered in June 1989, Bogle stressed: "Never underestimate the role of good fortune in our success."

16

NO THRILLS
OR CHILLS

TO FULLY IMPLEMENT his no-thrills-or-chills investment strategy, Bogle believed that Vanguard ultimately had to control the portfolio management of its fixed-income and money market fund portfolios. As a result, with each passing year, Bogle sought to further disconnect Vanguard from Wellington Management Company. The April 1981 SEC decision allowing Vanguard to use shareholder assets to pay for distribution costs solidified Vanguard's conversion to a no-load system and the assumption of all distribution-related responsibilities. Later that same year, the company took another step toward the fulfillment of Bogle's vision of complete independence for the Vanguard funds.

In early 1980, Wellington remained the principal adviser to the funds, managing about 90 percent of their total assets. Bogle envisioned greater control over investment policies and larger cost savings to Vanguard if it could assume some of Wellington's investment management functions. Accordingly, in September 1981, Vanguard took the major step of internalizing the investment advisory function for its money market funds. At the same time, it took over the reins of the municipal bond fund portfolios that Citibank had managed since the fund's inception in 1977. Together, these fund portfolios had assets of $1.5 billion, roughly one-third of the company's total assets under management. From then on, Vanguard provided the investment advisory function for these funds at cost, gradually cutting annual portfolio advisory costs for each portfolio from about 0.20 percent of assets prior to the 1981 internalization to about 0.01 percent by 1995, when these assets had risen to $45 billion. The cost differential would amount to the staggering total of $85 million of annual savings to investors in the fund portfolios.

After taking over the distribution function (and even before receiving the SEC's final blessing of the Vanguard distribution plan), Vanguard also enjoyed new opportunities to hire external investment advisers other than Wellington Management Company for its equity funds. Pursuing this arm's-length strategy, Bogle focused on Dean LeBaron, one of the better known and most creative figures in the money management field and founder and chief executive of Batterymarch Financial Management. Bogle had read Batterymarch's annual report and thought that LeBaron would be an intriguing figure with whom to do business. The creation of Trustees' Commingled Equity Fund in 1980—with Batterymarch serving as the investment adviser—provided Vanguard with its first opportunity to use an external adviser other than Wellington. Shortly thereafter, Vanguard appointed Schroder Capital Management International of London to manage a newly created international component of Ivest Fund, Vanguard's first foray into international markets. By 1995, Vanguard had come to retain 14 different independent investment advisers to manage its equity funds.

■ ■ ■

In 1981, Bogle knew it was unrealistic to try to internalize the entire investment advisory function. Talented equity fund managers like John Neff were in short supply—and even Neff, though based in Philadelphia, was part of Wellington Management and served on its board. So, with the exception of the passively managed Vanguard Index Trust, all of Vanguard's funds were run by outside advisers.

Bogle's objective was to internalize the management of the bond and money market funds but to continue to retain external advisers for equity funds. Such a move would lower shareholder costs in the fixed-income fund arena, where low costs and a no-load distribution system would be critical to providing the high net returns that would attract new investors. The major problem was that there was no one working at Vanguard at the time with the expertise to manage the bond and money market funds. So Bogle conducted a search for some new talent and soon hired Ian A. MacKinnon to be Vanguard's first internal investment manager.

Born in Niagara Falls, New York, MacKinnon graduated from Lafayette College in 1970 with a B.A. in economics. Later he earned a master's degree from Penn State. He worked for a year as an economist with Mathematica, Inc., in Princeton, New Jersey; then, beginning in 1975, MacKinnon spent six years with the Girard Bank of Philadelphia, where he was a portfolio manager and head of the bank's $3 billion fixed-income group. He was largely satisfied with his job at Girard and was less than enthusiastic when a headhunter approached him about the job at Vanguard. He finally took the job when Bogle and Jim Riepe agreed to hire him as the head of the new division and to let him hire his own staff.

Embryonic is the best way to describe the "division" that MacKinnon was about to head up. On his first day at work, he discovered that his "office" consisted of a table pushed against a wall. Behind him were rows of auditors going through reams of computer paper. On the wall was a rotary phone with a take-out pizza menu tacked up next to it. On November 16, 1981, $1.7 billion of fixed-income assets came into his "possession." Having handled twice that amount at Girard, MacKinnon was not overly impressed. Nonetheless, it was a hefty sum. "You kind of mentally lop off the zeros so you can sleep at night," he said. Vanguard was, as MacKinnon recalled, "dirt poor" in terms of revenues and therefore had a high expense ratio—by Vanguard standards, if well below industry norms—of some 60 basis points (or $6 annually for each $1,000 in assets). But with each dollar that came in, the expense ratio dropped. "We were pinching pennies with pliers," said MacKinnon, who was turned down the first time he asked Riepe whether he could hire a municipal bond analyst.

Spartan, primitive, exciting, risky—it was all an experiment, and whether MacKinnon was trying to fix the air-conditioning or manage the money, he wondered whether the company was ever going to become a major force in the industry. Yet he found it an exhilarating ride, and by 1995 he had built the division into one of Vanguard's major engines of growth, with $62 billion in assets, 39 portfolios, and a staff of 42.

Bogle's vision for Vanguard's foray into active portfolio management was to offer fixed-income and money market funds that maintained clearly defined investment policies, quality standards, and maturity standards. Their names would characterize their policies, as in Vanguard Long-Term Municipal Bond Portfolio, Vanguard Intermediate-Term U.S. Treasury Bond Portfolio, and Vanguard Short-Term Corporate Bond Portfolio. As Bogle noted, "The trick is to tell investors what the fund will do and describe the risks, and then just do it. And tell the truth to them in your annual reports." Later, he would designate the Vanguard money market and bond funds as "defined asset class funds."

VANGUARD'S DEFINED ASSET CLASS PORTFOLIOS

The following table provides an overview of the portfolios included in Vanguard's defined asset class strategy, including the number of portfolios and the aggregate assets held in each in mid-1995.

DEFINED ASSET CLASS PORTFOLIOS
Assets at June 1995
(Millions of Dollars)

Portfolio (Number)	
Money market	
Taxable (4)	$24,706
Tax-exempt (6)	7,600
U.S. Government bond (7)	5,244
Corporate bond (5)	9,470
GNMA (1)	6,359
Tax-exempt bond	
National short-term (2)	3,190
National longer-term (5)	10,026
State-specific (7)	4,584
Total (37)	$71,179
Percentage of Vanguard Total Assets	46%

As 1981 ended, Vanguard offered 10 portfolios in its defined asset class group, including 7 that it managed internally. It added 19 more by 1990, and another 8 since then. By 1995, Vanguard offered 37 bond and money market fund portfolios—each designed to provide steady, relatively predictable returns compared to appropriate benchmarks—with total assets of more than $71 billion. Vanguard's fixed-income group managed $59 billion of this total. The remaining $12 billion—in the GNMA, long-term corporate bond, preferred stock, and high-yield bond portfolios—was managed by Wellington Management Company.

The funds would be managed by a staff of professionals under MacKinnon's direction but would neither hold high-risk securities nor make major bets on interest rate movements. By maintaining tight quality and maturity standards, Bogle reasoned, the Vanguard fixed-income and money market funds would gain their yield and return advantage over competitive funds by virtue of their at-cost structure. They would also add a note of clarity for investors and provide them with returns that were consistent relative to those of the markets in which they invested.

Fueling the engine of growth for Vanguard was the creativity that Bogle and his development team, led by Jeremy Duffield, showed in devising new funds, including the Ginnie Mae fund, a short-term bond fund, a high-yield bond-fund, a municipal money market fund, and state-specific municipal bond funds. This novel strategy had begun in 1981, and Vanguard became the first mutual fund company to offer its shareholders the opportunity to choose from among three tax-exempt portfolios invested in short-term, intermediate-term, or long-term bonds rather than a single, vaguely described "managed municipal bond fund."

Bogle was enthusiastic in his praise of the job MacKinnon had done for Vanguard: "He is a man of considerable intelligence and unimpeachable integrity," Bogle said. "Not only his investment skills, but his management competence, were quite out of the ordinary." MacKinnon had quickly signed on to Bogle's notions of disciplined, high-quality investing, and, Bogle said, "made the most of any opportunities to consistently enhance the performance margins that Vanguard's low-cost operations provided against the competition." MacKinnon had built, in the words of *Morningstar Mutual Funds,* "one of the best investment research staffs in the United States." Under MacKinnon's leadership, Vanguard's defined asset class funds had earned the firm a major role in the money market fund field, along with almost uncontested dominance in the direct-marketing bond fund arena.

Although Vanguard did little advertising over the years, the better mousetrap theory was working; people began to learn that Vanguard was offering investment opportunities that other mutual fund firms were not. Ironically, the advertising that other fund firms were doing helped Vanguard. If these firms enjoyed some competitive advantage by getting the word out about themselves while Vanguard remained silent, they also encouraged those who saw their ads to engage in comparison shopping. In mid-1995 Vanguard was number two (behind Fidelity) in terms of total assets under management. It offered 80 investment portfolios, 52 of which were managed internally. According to Bogle's defined asset class model, the breakdown of the company's assets included 46 percent in defined asset class funds (bond funds and money market funds); 17 percent in index funds; and 37 percent in actively managed, usually conservative, stock and balanced funds. The firm's no-thrills-and-chills strategy was firmly in place.

■ ■ ■

Bogle experienced some moments of personal loss in the 1980s. One concerned James Riepe, his handpicked successor. Of all the men and women who had worked at Vanguard, Bogle felt closest to Riepe. And although in 1982 Riepe had tremendous respect for Bogle and wanted nothing more than to succeed him, at age 38 Riepe was running out of patience. Bogle was only 53 and, despite Bogle's heart problems, Riepe could not count on stepping into his shoes anytime soon. Yet Riepe hungered for the chance to run his own show: "I was only a half-generation removed from Jack. He was still young and active and in my view was going to be in place for a long time. I felt a little bit of a need to prove to myself what I could do on my own."

Riepe got his chance when an offer came from T. Rowe Price to run its mutual fund business—with assets of $8 billion at the time—and to serve on the company's four-member management committee. Riepe could not refuse the offer. What he liked was the chance to be surrounded by internal investment managers: "What I enjoyed in coming here to T. Rowe Price," Riepe said in July 1995, "was to have a much larger professional group than we had back then at Vanguard. Jack gave me plenty of intellectual stimulation; but it's not like having a whole group of investment people around."

Bogle put a great deal of pressure on Riepe to stay, but he understood the rationale behind Riepe's decision to leave. Bogle always regretted losing Riepe; the two remained close friends and saw one another at least twice each year for dinner and a round of squash, as well as at the annual dinner for former Bogle assistants. On Riepe's departure, Bogle presented him with a bronze sculpture of a squash player with a plaque inscribed: "Partner. Competitor. Friend." In return, Riepe gave Bogle a nautical clock inscribed with a phrase from *The Prophet:* "It is when you give of yourself that you truly give." Their mutual respect and affection never diminished.

When Riepe left, Bogle's assistant Jeremy Duffield moved up to become head of new fund development, and Bogle sought a new assistant. The mantle fell to John J. Brennan, also known as Jack, who had joined Vanguard in July 1982 from Johnson Wax in Racine, Wisconsin. Before he joined the firm, Brennan had never even heard of Vanguard; he had grown up in Boston, where the mutual fund industry was synonymous with the name Fidelity. Brennan barely had time to settle into his new position when Vanguard was confronted with a crisis.

In May 1982, Vanguard had bought from Lombard Wall (a bond dealer) U.S. government guaranteed ship-financing bonds for its federal money market fund. In August, Lombard Wall declared bankruptcy. When the bonds matured later that month and it came time for Vanguard to be paid for them, Vanguard learned that the subcustodian bank, Chase Manhattan, had neglected to reregister the bonds in Vanguard's name; the securities were still registered in the name of Lombard Wall.

For a brief period, Vanguard did not know whether it would be paid for the ship-financing bonds. It had paid Lombard Wall back in April, but the transfer agent had not acknowledged the payment because it was still showing the bonds as belonging to Lombard Wall. A lot of money—about $15 million—was at stake. Although the sum represented just 3 percent of the assets of Vanguard's Federal Money Market Portfolio, without it the portfolio might not have been able to maintain its net asset value of $1.00 per share, a potentially devastating outcome.

MacKinnon and Bogle were constantly on the phone to Vanguard's law firm and custodian bank, Philadelphia National Bank. In the end, Vanguard received its money back from PNB, which had received the money from Chase, which in turn had received the money from the transfer agent. Still, it was a frightening start for Brennan: "I didn't understand the mechanics, but I saw the look on Jack Bogle's face and on Ian MacKinnon's face, and I knew it was a significant, potential problem for us." But what Brennan remembered most vividly was Bogle's coolness under fire and the way he kept his focus on the interests of Vanguard's shareholders, not resting until the crisis was resolved satisfactorily. Those early years with Vanguard were, he recalled, "arguably the most exciting time for Vanguard . . . The company was growing, and we had the feeling of explosive growth. But we were doing it with largely homegrown talent. There were battlefield promotions all over the place. New funds were coming out continually. It was a tremendous time to be here."

It was hard to imagine that Vanguard had started in 1974 as an obscure firm providing corporate, legal, and accounting services to a handful of mutual funds. Fifteen years later, that same obscure firm was handling all shareholder account administration, all marketing responsibilities, and a major chunk of the investment management services. In Vanguard's 1990 annual report, Bogle wrote, "The Vanguard Experiment set out to prove that mutual funds could operate independently, and in a manner that would directly benefit their shareholders. The Vanguard Experiment . . . has been successful beyond our wildest dreams."

CHAPTER 17

"THE DEVIL'S INVENTION"

VANGUARD'S DEFINED ASSET CLASS STRATEGY FLOURISHED after it was put in place in 1981, becoming the largest single component of Vanguard's asset base. It provided the no-thrills-or-chills approach to investing that Bogle favored; at the same time, it delivered consistently superior returns relative to competitive funds for investors in the Vanguard money market and municipal bond funds. Eventually, the industry took notice. Virtually unnoticed, however, was an even earlier Vanguard pioneering innovation that was to drive the firm's growth during the 1990s—the formation in August 1976 of the industry's first "market index" mutual fund, initially called First Index Investment Trust. Indexing is the ultimate no-thrills-or-chills investment strategy, providing, as it does, fully assured participation in the ups and downs of the financial markets.

The traditional approach to equity portfolio management, and the one that remains the industry's modus operandi today, is to identify specific stocks that the fund manager believes will best achieve a fund's investment objectives and, most important, will perform better than "the market" itself. In this model, the adviser actively manages the portfolio by buying and selling stocks as perceived relative values change.

Vanguard's introduction of First Index Investment Trust represented a complete reversal of this active management approach—that is, a passive management approach, under which the manager, in effect, buys stocks in percentages representing the particular market to be emulated, essentially holding the securities on a permanent basis and hoping to replicate the performance of either the overall market or a predetermined, discrete sector of the market. Under the passive approach to investing, an index fund should perform about as well as the market it tracks. Active investors as a group—fund managers, individuals, pension managers, and so on— should also match the performance of the market; indeed, as a group, they *are* the market. But active fund managers as a group end up underperforming the market for their shareholders, largely by reason of their funds' advisory fees, operating expenses, and transaction costs, not to mention any sales loads paid by their investors who purchase the funds' shares.

Proponents of the passive school, in which Jack Bogle often seems to be the lone member from the mutual fund industry, argue that for the overwhelming majority of funds, active management works only in the short term, and then only for the gifted or the lucky. Ultimately, the returns on a mutual fund regress to the mean and then end up below the mean when expenses are taken into account. Even as a Princeton student, Bogle had written in his senior thesis: "The funds can claim no superiority over the market averages." Later, he was amused by the classic assertion that Burton Malkiel—later to become a director of the Vanguard funds—made in his 1973 book, *A Random Walk Down Wall Street:* "A blindfolded chimpanzee throwing darts at *The Wall Street Journal* can select a portfolio that can do just as well as the experts."

In contrast with many of his colleagues in the mutual fund industry, Bogle was attuned to the efforts of academicians like Malkiel, whose quantitative studies seemed to confirm what is known as the efficient market theory. According to this theory, the price of a company's share of stock immediately reflects all available information, as well as investor expectations, related to the company. Efficient-market theorists contend that because financial markets are perfectly efficient, it's extraordinarily difficult to beat the stock market over the long haul. As Bogle liked to say, "There is only so much return that the market gives, and it's simply not possible for every manager to beat that return." Bogle might have been remembering Stephen Paine's boast in 1967 that he could provide a 25 percent annual return on Explorer Fund. Over the 27 years from its inception in 1967 through mid-1995, the fund was to provide an average annual return of just 9 percent, not only far below Paine's projection, but well short of the 11 percent annual return on the unmanaged Standard & Poor's 500 Stock Index.

Bogle examined the past performance records achieved by both the active and passive schools. He also examined the costs of each type of management. He concluded that a fund was far more likely to produce above-average returns under passive management than active management. He based his conclusion on two factors:

1. All investors collectively own all of the stock market. Because passive investors—those who hold all stocks in the stock market—will match the gross return (before expenses) of the stock market, it follows that all active investors as a group can perform no better: They must also match the gross return of the stock market.

2. The management fees and operating costs incurred by passive investors are substantially lower than the fees incurred by active investors. Additionally, actively managed funds have higher transaction costs, because their managers' tactics drive them to buy and sell frequently, increasing portfolio turnover rates and therefore total costs. Since both active and passive investors achieve equal gross returns, it follows that passive investors, whose costs are lower, must earn higher net returns.

Putting numbers to this theory, the cost difference is dramatic. Vanguard was saving its index fund investors about 1.8 percent per year—the expense ratio of the 500 portfolio was 0.2 percent versus 2.0 percent for the average equity fund (expenses plus transaction costs). To put that amount into perspective, in a market with a 10 percent annual return, an index fund might provide an annual return of 9.8 percent, while a managed fund might earn an annual return of 8.0 percent. If so, over 20 years a $10,000 initial investment in an index fund would grow to $64,900, while an identical investment in a managed fund would grow to $46,600, a difference of more than $18,000 in the accumulated account value.

In sum, Bogle believed that while some investors might profit from active management in the short run, those above-average profits would evaporate in the long run, as performance inevitably regressed to the mean. History shows that precious few managers will beat the market, and they are virtually impossible to identify in advance. Passive management, in contrast, is certain to provide an investor with at least the same return as the overall market. On the presumption that the stock market will exhibit a positive trend line in the long run, passive management was, for Bogle, a sound, strategy. He further believed that many investors shared his views on indexing and would be willing to shift their assets from actively managed mutual funds to passively managed mutual funds if the returns provided by passively managed funds were more consistent in the short run.

Indexing itself was not Bogle's invention. The new Vanguard fund was modeled on index-oriented accounts that banks had operated since the early 1970s for giant pension funds. Vanguard's innovation was to make indexing work in a mutual fund format. At the time Vanguard was formulating its index fund, the Dow Jones Industrial Average was the most familiar stock market benchmark to investors. However, because of the growing acceptance and sound construction of the Standard & Poor's 500 Composite Stock Price Index—a weighted index that reflects the total market capitalization of 500 of the largest companies in the United States—Bogle adopted it as the tracking standard that First Index Investment Trust would emulate.

Indexing and Bogle were ideally suited for one another, for indexing and low costs are, in a sense, two sides of the same coin. Vanguard boasted that in 1995 it was saving its index fund shareholders nearly $300 million annually, largely because index funds make light demands on a mutual fund firm's management skills, keeping costs down. It takes no time or thought, for instance, to decide which 500 stocks to buy—or how much of each stock to buy—for an S&P 500 stock index fund. The composition of the index itself dictates those decisions automatically.

Despite the compelling merits of indexing, Bogle engendered little enthusiasm for the idea when First Index Investment Trust (now the 500 Portfolio of Vanguard Index Trust) was formed in June 1976. The Vanguard board, lukewarm to the idea, supported it only because Bogle was such a firm believer. The reaction within the industry, though, was decidedly more negative: "the pursuit of mediocrity," one commentator called it; "un-American," said another; "the devil's invention," said a third; "a formula for a solid, consistent, long-term loser," said a fourth. Despite the naysayers, Bogle ultimately persuaded Dean Witter to lead an underwriting of the new fund. It took three months to raise the $12 million that formed the initial base for the fund; by the end of 1976, the fund had grown to only $14 million. It was not going to be easy to convince investors to put their money into a fund that would merely match the market; investors wanted to *beat* the market.

Even though he was deeply commited to indexing, Bogle was willing to admit that some active investment managers could add value to the fund management process. In most cases, he argued, these managers either were lucky or were among a tiny group of true investment geniuses—market wizards such as Warren Buffett, Peter Lynch, Michael Price, and Vanguard's own John Neff. In general, though, Bogle maintained that trying to outperform the market was a futile exercise. "Index funds," he said, "are a result of skepticism that any given financial manager can outperform the market. How can anyone possibly pick which stock funds are going to excel over the next 10 years?" In this context, the best strategy was to try simply to match the market in gross return and count on indexing's low costs to earn a higher net return than most competitors.

All of this, of course, was heresy to traditional active fund managers, who argued that the only reason to invest in mutual funds in the first place was to try to maximize returns. Richard Fentin, for example, head of the $14 billion Fidelity Puritan Fund, objected: "We've beaten the market for 5-year and 10-year periods. Does this mean you can't beat the market? Obviously, I'd reject the idea . . . We've beaten the market regularly." (As it happened, Fentin's fund was to underperform the Standard & Poor's 500 index by a wide margin in 1995, bringing its 10-year rate of return to +13 percent versus +15 percent for the index.)

Bogle, undaunted, countered with an army of statistics that showed the dangers of such an approach. In 7 of the 10 years from 1984 to 1994, the S&P 500 index outperformed more than one-half of all fund managers; for the entire 10-year period, it outperformed 78 percent of all general equity funds, a figure that rose to 80 percent for the 10 years ending in 1995. The fact is, when sales charges are factored in, only about one in five mutual funds has beaten the market over time. Unlike the children of Lake Wobegon, not all fund managers can be above average.

Eventually, despite the ridicule of active fund managers, indexing began to catch on. Vanguard Index Trust enjoyed positive net cash flow in each year of its existence, and had grown to $500 million by the end of 1986—a decade after Vanguard's pioneering vision. That same year, the Colonial Group introduced an index fund, the industry's second. (It would be out of business by 1990, however, because it carried a punitive load and a high expense ratio, eliminating any ability to match the index.) By 1988, Fidelity and Dreyfus had followed suit with their own index fund offerings. From 1984 through 1994, Vanguard Index Trust—modeled on the S&P 500 Index—earned a return of 290 percent, compared to 224 percent for the average general equity fund. Even so, Bogle noted that, despite their early successes, index funds had not become a phenomenon. He called Vanguard's indexing strategy "an artistic, if not a commercial, success."

That changed during the 1990s, when indexing really took off. The 500 Portfolio of Vanguard Index Trust, which topped the $1 billion mark in 1988 and began the 1990s with assets of $1.8 billion, grew to $15.6 billion by mid-1995, making it the fourth largest equity mutual fund in the United States.

For Vanguard, an index fund modeled on the S&P 500 was only the beginning. As the 500 Portfolio grew in market acceptance and in successfully operating at minimal cost, Bogle's confidence in the concept increased. The Standard & Poor's 500 represented roughly 70 percent of the market. What about a portfolio that tracked the remaining 30 percent? Vanguard's Extended Market Portfolio, formed in 1987, enabled investors to do exactly that, tracking the Wilshire 4500 Index. Later, to simplify the process of holding both the 500 Portfolio and the Extended Market Portfolio, Vanguard offered the Total Stock Market Portfolio, essentially owning the entire stock market by tracking the Wilshire 5000 Index, the most comprehensive market index available. In 1989, the Small Capitalization Portfolio was introduced, using the Russell 2000 Index of small stocks as a benchmark, and a lower-cost 500 portfolio was designed for institutional investors with at least $10 million to invest.

In a speech before the Financial Analysts of Philadelphia in 1990, Bogle said, "The introduction of index funds focusing on growth stocks and value stocks awaits only the development of a Growth Index and a Value Index." Standard & Poor's introduced these two new indexes in May 1992, and just two months later Vanguard launched portfolios with like objectives. In all, Vanguard's U.S. equity index funds boomed, with aggregate assets reaching $24 billion in mid-1995.

Bogle was confident that the principles of indexing would also work in world markets—perhaps work even better, since the expense ratios and portfolio transaction costs of international mutual funds were far higher than for U.S. funds. Vanguard International Equity Index Fund was introduced in 1990, with European and Pacific portfolios; an Emerging Markets Portfolio was added in mid-1994. Each of these portfolios found its place among the largest international funds, with aggregate assets in mid-1995 totaling almost $2 billion.

Nearly a decade after introducing the first equity index fund, Vanguard applied the indexing theory to the bond market, using the Lehman Aggregate Bond Index as a benchmark. The Total Bond Market Portfolio of Vanguard Bond Index Fund (then named Vanguard Bond Market Fund), reflecting the market value of all taxable U.S. bonds, was founded in late 1986 to provide the same advantages of low cost, high quality, and broad diversification to bond fund investors that Vanguard Index Trust provided to equity fund investors. Early in 1994, without much enthusiasm from his associates, Bogle inaugurated three additional bond portfolios—short-term, intermediate-term, and long-term—based on the appropriate Lehman indexes. The three new portfolios, like the original all-market bond portfolio, met with modest early acceptance, but by June 1995 the aggregate assets of the four portfolios of Vanguard Bond Index Fund had grown to $2.5 billion.

Late in 1994, Vanguard Tax-Managed Fund and Vanguard LifeStrategy Funds were introduced. The Tax-Managed Fund, which comprised three portfolios designed to minimize realization of taxable capital gains and income distributions, managed the portfolios as index funds and quickly reached $250 million in assets. The LifeStrategy Funds included four portfolios with varying allocations to Vanguard stock and bond funds, and relied on an index strategy to assemble each of its asset allocation components. Its assets totaled $380 million in mid-1995. All of the stock index portfolios were managed by Vanguard's core management group, the bond portfolios by its fixed-income group.

VANGUARD INDEX PORTFOLIOS

Vanguard expanded the concept of indexing from a narrow base limited to the Standard & Poor's 500 index to a full "product line" of 19 index portfolios, with aggregate assets totaling $26 billion by mid-1995.

INDEX PORTFOLIOS
Assets at June 1995
(Millions of Dollars)

Portfolio (Number)	
S&P 500 (2)	$17,415
Extended Market (1)	1,197
Total Stock Market (1)	1,152
International Equity (3)	1,699
SmallCap Stock (1)	747
Balanced (1)	484
Value (1)	361
Growth (1)	158
Bond (4)	2,485
Tax managed (4)	486
Total (19)	$26,184
Percentage of Vanguard Total Assets	17%

Compared to Vanguard's $26 billion total, aggregate index assets managed by Fidelity, Dreyfus and T. Rowe Price—all of which limited their gambit almost entirely to Standard & Poor's 500 portfolios offered largely to investors in employer-sponsored 401(k) thrift plans—totaled just $5 billion. Even taking into account all competitors in the industry combined, Vanguard's index funds, with the field left open to them, commanded a market share in 1995 of nearly 60 percent of total index mutual fund assets.

The scope and magnitude of the Vanguard index funds has so far been ignored by most competitors, and not nearly matched by those who have entered the fray. The reasons, Bogle suggested, must include their lack of missionary zeal for the indexing concept, born of professional pride and confidence that their own organizations will provide superior market returns, and their recognition that there is not much profit to be made in matching indexes. What is more, all of the index competitors have thus far refused to meet the low-cost standard for index funds set by Vanguard. They were, in Bogle's words, "dragged kicking and screaming into indexing, praying that investors would accept the handicap that high cost imposes." While the expense ratios for index funds run by Vanguard's competitors averaged 0.65 percent annually, Vanguard's was usually 0.20 percent or less, representing 0.01 percent for portfolio supervision and 0.19 percent for administration and shareholder record-keeping costs. In all, Vanguard's success was based on the fact that, as *Morningstar Mutual Funds* asserted, "Nobody indexes better than Vanguard."

■ ■ ■

Vanguard, by 1995, had staked much of its reputation and a major portion of its asset base on the concept it had pioneered nearly two decades earlier. With highly predictable short-term relative returns and odds that strongly favored more-than-competitive long-term returns, this no-thrills-or-chills strategy in equity management, like Vanguard's fixed-income strategy, seemed to Bogle to carry little, if any, risk of failure. Nonetheless, he constantly challenged his own confidence level, often asking his associates, "What can go wrong?" No answer was forthcoming. Bogle, ever the contrarian, said this response worried him.

In the face of growing acceptance by investors of the index concept, Vanguard continued to warn index fund investors that, in the uncertain world of investing, index funds might face unexpected challenges. In "The

Triumph of Indexing," a booklet written by Bogle early in 1995, he went to great pains to underscore this uncertainty:

> During the first quarter of 1995, the Index outpaced fully 90% of all actively managed mutual funds. This remarkable ranking should under no circumstances be regarded either as repeatable or sustainable. It arose from unusually favorable returns for the large capitalization blue-chip stocks that dominate the Index relative to small capitalization and speculative stocks, which play an important role in the portfolios of many higher-risk equity funds.

George U. "Gus" Sauter, Vanguard principal and head of its core management group, has run the firm's equity index funds since 1987. When an investor puts money into a Vanguard index fund, Sauter noted, he and his team invest it immediately. If the fund is sitting on any excess cash while the market goes up, the performance of the portfolio will lag behind that of the market. Sauter also discussed the theory behind maintaining the appropriate weighting for each stock in the index: "Conceivably, we could buy a small slice of each one of the 500 stocks in precisely their proportions in the index; we actually don't do that. Instead, we might buy a smaller sample of the entire index in order to keep costs down. What's more, we can minimize our transaction costs, our brokerage fees, and our custody fees by buying slightly larger share lots—at least 1,000 shares of a stock." For more broadly diversified indexes, Vanguard developed its own set of computer programs called optimizers. These programs perform millions of calculations to generate a selected list of recommended stocks, which as a group parallel the target index and whose returns should track the index with a high degree of precision. So far, in fact, "tracking error" has been minimal.

Sauter counsels patience for investors in index funds: "In the longer term, the advantage of index funds comes through. It is like the story of the tortoise and the hare. The tortoise just plods along slowly and steadily, and finally wins the race. That's what we're doing."

Not surprisingly, even after demonstrating superior performance, indexing has had its critics. One is A. Michael Lipper, president of Lipper Analytical Services, which tracks mutual fund performance. Lipper observed that many investors might not have the gumption to stick with an index fund when it dipped in value along with the stock market. Moreover, he added, if large numbers of shareholders bailed out of an index fund in a down market, it could be disastrous, leading to substantial liquidations of portfolio securities. Bogle countered by citing two reasons that an index fund based on the Standard & Poor's 500 Index could well lose less value in a down market than nonindexed funds: (1) the Standard & Poor's 500 comprises high-quality, highly liquid stocks; and (2) most nonindexed funds today seem to hold riskier, less-liquid stocks.

Another critic has been Arnold Kaufman, editor of Standard & Poor's newsletter, the *Outlook,* who said that, in a lengthy bear market, "The passive investment strategy of typical index funds might produce greater losses than equity funds that build cash reserves, focus on high-yielding stocks, or employ hedging techniques." Fidelity's Richard Fentin joined the critics: "We aggressively manage the money because our shareholders expect us to be aggressive. Even in a conservative fund like my own, we're aggressive. Why would anyone not want to be aggressive with your money? If you didn't want to be aggressive, why go into mutual funds? Don't you want to beat the market? Do people want to achieve only average returns?"

Despite the critics, Bogle's concept attracted supporters. In a 1990 interview with *Barron's,* Peter Lynch, Fidelity Magellan Fund's superstar manager, observed that most investors would be better off in index funds than in actively managed funds:

> You've had eight years of an up market and the public is out of it. They think of the so-called professionals, with all their computers and all their power, as having all the advantages. That is total crap . . .
>
> It's getting worse, the deterioration by professionals is getting worse. But the public thinks they are doing great because the average fund is up 283% in 10 years (compared to 344% for the S&P). They have made over four times on their money. But they'd be better off in an index fund.

An article in the *New York Times* on August 13, 1995, entitled "How to Squeeze Blood from a Benchmark" began, "Call it Bogle's revenge. For years, John C. Bogle, chairman of the Vanguard Group, has been lecturing that it is folly to try to beat the market. This year, he looks like the wise man." The article noted that, based on total returns, the average domestic equity fund was trailing the S&P 500 Index. In fact, the index had outpaced 82 percent of all actively managed funds in 1994 and 78 percent during 1995. Partly in response to this success, investors were rushing to index funds.

That same month, *Money* magazine focused on index funds, beginning with a strong editorial endorsement headlined: "Bogle Wins: Index Funds

Should Be the Core of Most Portfolios Today." The editorial, written by Executive Editor Tyler Mathisen, embraced the index concept, calling on *Money*'s readers to make "a complete reorientation of your expectations as an investor." He described the three principal index fund advantages of low operating cost, low transaction cost, and low exposure to capital gains taxes as "a trio as impressive as Domingo, Pavarotti, and Carreras." Mathisen concluded with personal congratulations to Bogle: "So here's to you, Jack, you have a right to call it, as you recently did in a Vanguard sales booklet you wrote, 'The Triumph of Indexing.' "

Money's cover story was entitled "The New Way to Make Money in Funds Today: Start with Index Funds and Add the Market Beaters." Gus Sauter was among the portfolio managers pictured on the cover, and the article gave special attention to the 500 Portfolio of Vanguard Index Trust. Its performance put the fund in the top 25 percent of all 369 diversified equity funds with 10-year records. Moreover, the 500 Portfolio—earlier recommended by *Money* in its November 1994 cover story on the nation's 25 largest mutual funds—had 14 percent less volatility than the average equity fund. *Money*'s observation that the index funds that charged the lowest fees came closest to matching the performance of their indexes must have been gratifying to Bogle. He was particularly delighted with the skills of Sauter and his staff in meeting the increasingly tough standards of matching the multiple target indexes that Vanguard had established as benchmarks. "Gus has done all that we have asked of him, and done it in a first-rate manner," Bogle said appreciatively.

The concept of indexing had equal support from learned economists. Nobel laureate Paul Samuelson of the Massachusetts Institute of Technology said, "Indexing is like watching paint dry or like kissing your sister. It's Dullsville. It just happens, and it's been demonstrated in the last four decades that the best and the brightest do not deliver to their customers or to their own private portfolios as good a return over any extended period as the broadest indexing does." And another Nobel laureate, William F. Sharpe of Stanford University, placed Bogle in his "pantheon of heroes" for, among other things, Bogle's pioneering forays into indexing.

UNDER ONE ROOF

Bogle is often asked how Vanguard's actively managed equity funds can exist compatibly under one roof with its passively managed index funds. His response is that he sees no conflict or problem whatsoever: "First, the value of indexing lies largely in its exceptionally low cost structure. Since the Vanguard managed ·

equity funds generally have expense ratios no higher than the 40 to 50 basis points range—due to our organization's focus on minimizing costs and vigorous negotiating of fees paid to our external advisers—they are quite competitive with the costs of indexing, and thus have much less 'headwind' than a competitor with, say, a 200 basis point (2.0 percent) aggregate cost structure." So, he emphasizes, "a Vanguard managed equity fund should have almost an even chance of beating the indexes."

Second, he says, "if we do our job of selecting, monitoring, and, if necessary, replacing our external advisers, we should, with our experience and judgment—and patience—be able to retain advisers with above-average chances of success over time. It is a tough job, but whether by dint of luck or skill, so far we've had reasonable success in doing so."

Finally, he concedes the obvious: "In this business, as it has existed in the past and as it exists today, you cannot escape the reality that it is built on traditional active management. No matter what history has taught us, it is unclear if, when, and how, index investing will become the rule rather than the exception."

Even as the media and others threw their support to indexing, most of the mutual fund industry did not feel obligated to fall into place. Indexing was counterintuitive; many refused to believe that passive management could outpace active management, and investors still hoped to identify the best managers and take advantage of their skills. (Bogle called this factor "Hope springs eternal," from Alexander Pope's *Essay on Criticism*.) Although the future for indexing seemed bright, it had barely scratched the surface of the mutual fund industry. Stock index funds in 1995 still represented less than 4 percent of the $1 trillion invested in equity mutual funds; bond index funds represented even less—about 0.6 percent of the $700 billion invested in bond mutual funds.

Indexing had been part of Jack Bogle's vision ever since he broached the subject in his Princeton thesis in 1951. He introduced the idea in 1976 when others in the mutual fund industry thought it was unwise—perhaps even unpatriotic. Yet in two decades he had promoted "the devil's invention" deftly and aggressively, and the theory of indexing had been borne out in practice. As 1995 came to a close, indexing was on its way to becoming a major force in the mutual fund business.

THE MAN
WHO WALKED
ON WATER

ESPITE HIS FIRMLY HELD BELIEF that investors *as a group* would benefit by holding a core investment in index funds, Bogle also embraced the traditional managed approach to investing. Doubtless one reason was the success of the early flagship of the Vanguard fleet, Windsor Fund, which over a long period had earned returns well in excess of those of the Standard & Poor's 500 Index. Ironically, it was this actively managed equity fund— and not Vanguard's hallmark index funds—that was the engine that drove Vanguard's growth in the 1980s. Adding to the irony was the fact that the more venturesome investment style of John Neff, Windsor Fund's veteran manager, was what helped catapult Vanguard into the big leagues.

Neff is a straight-speaking Midwesterner whose mother thought he should have become a lawyer because he was always ready to engage others in debate. "You'd argue with a signpost," she told him. Neff was born on September 19, 1931, in Wauseon, Ohio. When he was four, his parents divorced. His mother remarried when he was 10, and his stepfather, who was working in the oil business, moved the family to Texas. In the years that followed, the family's day-to-day, paycheck-to-paycheck lifestyle challenged Neff, who later said, "I decided then that I was going to manage money well."

After graduating from high school, Neff moved to Michigan, where he worked in factory jobs before joining his father's thriving automotive and industrial equipment supply business in Toledo, Ohio. After a two-year stint in the navy, he enrolled at the University of Toledo and two years later graduated summa cum laude in industrial marketing, discovering investment management along the way. Studying under Sidney Robbins, head of Toledo's finance department, Neff grew interested in the value investing approach of Benjamin Graham and David Dodd, the strategy he would adopt in managing Windsor Fund. Neff went on to earn a master's degree in banking and finance at Case Western Reserve University.

Upon graduation in 1955, Neff considered entering a brokerage firm's training program in New York City but instead took a research job in the trust department of National City Bank in Cleveland, Ohio. His job was to recommend investments for the trust department in eight industries. But he grew somewhat frustrated with his job, as he and the other trust department personnel differed widely in their investment approaches. Preferring equities, Neff thought taking a more aggressive approach to investing, sticking one's neck out a bit, would be more rewarding. The trust investment committee, however, wanted "comfortable things," reflecting the bond background of the head of the committee. Nevertheless, Neff gained an excellent background in equity investing, staying at the Cleveland bank until 1963.

Shopping around for a new job, Neff interviewed with numerous mutual fund firms in New York and Philadelphia, including Wellington Management Company. Though Bogle was not among the executives who interviewed him, Neff recalls meeting Bogle by chance in the corridor: "We had an immediate kinship because there was something about me that he liked that later he couldn't quite put his finger on. I know exactly what it was, though. We both had crew cuts then." Wellington's executives hired Neff with the challenge to figure out a way to make himself valuable to the company. He began working for Wellington Management Company in the summer of 1963—in his words, as a jack of all trades.

In 1963, Wellington managed just two funds, the $1.6 billion Wellington Fund and the Windsor Fund, with a mere $75 million in assets. Windsor had fared poorly in its first five years, especially from 1961 to 1963, and Robert Kenmore, who had been the principal portfolio manager, left Wellington Management just before Neff's arrival. "I sensed that the fund was a waif," said Neff, "a derelict that needed a strong rudder and good leadership." He wrote a white paper on what was wrong with the fund and what could be done to improve it. Someone must have liked what he suggested, for within a year he was appointed Windsor's portfolio manager.

Now Neff had a chance to prove himself. A six-member investment committee supervised the fund, and Neff, at first not a committee member, ostensibly reported to them. From the beginning, though, he didn't consult the committee before deciding what to do; rather, he approached committee members individually, feeling they would be "outmanned" by his expertise, his logic, and his command of even the smallest details about the companies whose stocks he would acquire for the fund. Within a year he became a member of the investment committee.

At first, investor purchases of Windsor Fund shares were modest, averaging $600,000 a month. While the fund did well after Neff took over, other funds in the industry were doing even better. "They were speculative and risky, and paid the piper later on," Neff observed, adding that one of those funds was Wellington's own Ivest Fund, acquired as part of the 1967 merger with TDP&L. By the fall of 1967, Bogle was beginning to sense that Wellington Management was focused on improving the performance of Wellington Fund—leaving Windsor alone in Neff's hands—and had not portrayed Windsor Fund's investment objectives and policies with sufficient clarity to the public. "We must ask whether the Windsor 'image' is clear," he wrote in a confidential report. "Have we gotten our story across to dealers? How can we give this Fund the support it deserves?"

The fact was that Windsor, under Neff's aegis, had become at once conservative and aggressive: conservative in the sense of his "prudent man" approach to value investing, emphasizing carefully analyzed stocks with depressed market prices and usually generous yields, an approach designed to limit downside risk; aggressive in the sense that the portfolio was highly concentrated in Neff's favorite issues, meaning that the fund's returns over the short term would be less predictable relative to the returns of far-more-broadly diversified competitors. However difficult it was to articulate, the Windsor story did finally get across.

By 1969, the performance of Windsor was turning around. Of the 174 funds whose performance was tracked by veteran analyst Arthur Lipper, Windsor was 24th during the five-year period from 1967 to 1972. This record was good enough to carry Windsor's assets at the end of 1972 to $550 million. It also helped to win Neff, now managing the $50 million closed-end Gemini fund as well as Windsor, a seat on the Wellington Management Company board. The fund's performance, though, was poor in the early 1970s, as large growth stocks dominated the marketplace. Neff called these years frustrating and perplexing. In 1972, Windsor ranked 172 out of 296 funds tracked by Lipper, and even in the bear market of 1973, declined considerably more than the market. Still, *The Wall Street Journal* wrote that Neff was "well regarded among some of Wall Street's savviest professionals," and quoted one senior partner of a brokerage firm as saying, "If anything happened to me, I'd like John to run my family's money. He's a sound guy, he'll do well over the long run, and he'll be ahead of the game in a bear market because of his soundness."

Such confidence would be rewarded in the years to come, and Windsor's longer-term performance record has indeed made it one of Vanguard's stars. Windsor had $225 million in assets in 1968, when Wellington Management Company's total assets were $2.6 billion; by 1974, when Windsor Fund became part of the Vanguard Group, its assets had climbed to $300 million, even as Vanguard's total assets had declined to $1.4 billion. In 1975, when the stock market was up 37 percent, Windsor rose an astonishing 54 percent, its best annual return ever. By 1981, Windsor had crossed the $1 billion mark in assets and constituted 25 percent of Vanguard's total fund assets of $4 billion; the only Vanguard fund with more assets was the $1.1 billion Vanguard Money Market Trust–Prime Portfolio. By the end of 1984, Windsor was the largest equity mutual fund in the country, with more than $2.5 billion in assets. As the fund's assets approached the $3 billion mark early in 1985, the decision was made to close the fund to new investors, largely because Neff was beginning to see Windsor's burgeoning size as a liability, compromising his ability to manage the fund in a manner consistent with the best interests of its shareholders.

WINDSOR II

Bogle and Neff had always agreed that a mutual fund's performance success could lead to an asset base so large that the fund would be difficult to manage effectively. In other words, they both believed that good fund performance could be jeopardized over the long term by asset growth that made it impossible to pursue the strategies and tactics that had led to the fund's success in the first place. They agreed that closing Windsor Fund to new investors before its asset size became a liability was not a question of *if* but *when*.

Early in 1985, Neff came to Bogle to say that he believed the time had arrived, and the decision to close Windsor was made.

The fund had assets of $3 billion, and the torrential cash inflow from investors was coming at an accelerating pace. Yet Vanguard needed a "growth and income" fund to fully pursue its marketing strategy. Clearly the new fund could not be managed by Neff, who already felt he had more than sufficient assets to say grace over. So Bogle and his staff made a diligent study of other advisers, and selected Barrow, Hanley, Mewhinney & Strauss of Dallas, Texas, to run what would be dubbed Windsor II. Vanguard made it crystal clear that the name was chosen to relate the new fund with Windsor's objective but not its strategies, and that Neff—and indeed Wellington Management Company—would in no way be associated with it.

The closing of Windsor Fund was both announced and implemented on May 15, 1985 (in Bogle's view, an earlier announcement would simply have promoted the flow of additional investments into the fund), a decision almost without precedent in an industry in which gathering the largest possible amount of assets was traditionally the name of the game. The offering of Windsor II began on June 24, 1985, amid fears at Vanguard that the company would be criticized for misleading the public by using the Windsor name, as well as virtual unanimous opinion outside Vanguard that the new fund could not possibly live up to Windsor Fund's performance success.

A decade later, however, in mid-1995, it was clear that Barrow Hanley had measured up to Vanguard's high expectations. The 10-year record of Windsor II paralleled Windsor's, and in fact provided a slightly higher rate of return with somewhat less volatility. Today, each of the Windsor Funds stands independent of the other. In mid-1995, Windsor Fund's assets stood at $12.5 billion; Windsor II's at $9.3 billion. They ranked, respectively, as the 6th and 12th largest of all U.S. equity funds.

■ ■ ■

John Neff's approach to investment management is called value investing, and he is arguably the best at it in the business. He adopted the strategy in the early 1960s, long before it became fashionable, and he has stuck with it despite the year-to-year variability of its success. He has never been bothered by the perception that some of his stock picks are bland—banks and utilities, for example. Nor has he been bothered when others question why he buys stocks that are in disrepute, for this is the essence of value investing: buying cheap, out-of-favor stocks—the "misunderstood and woebegone," Neff calls them—and selling them later when the market embraces them.

Neff contends that investors often overpay for the prospects of growth in a stock—"overpay" because, in his view, the "growth" in growth stocks may not last very long after it has been recognized. He has more interest in income, contending that an investor can realize a better return from a slow-growth company that can pay a high dividend. "Everything," he said, "gets back to total return versus price paid."

Neff's strategy, then, is to search for overlooked companies with low price/earnings ratios and above-average yields. "The trick is to buy the stocks when they are being overlooked and before the price-to-earnings ratio gets upgraded," he said. "What you're really doing is buying decent goods at a discount. If you're right on the fundamentals, you've got to make out . . . And if you're wrong, well, you didn't pay an arm and a leg for the stock, and the yield . . . gives you some downside protection."

The hardest part of stock picking, said Neff, is to know when to get out of a segment of the market. Neff has taken Windsor Fund in and out of a number of industries. At one point in 1986, for example, 24 percent of Windsor's assets were in oil stocks; at other times in the 1980s, the fund has held no oil stocks. As much as 15 percent of the Windsor portfolio has been invested in auto stocks at various points in Neff's tenure, but there have also been periods when the fund held no auto stocks. Sometimes Neff favors telephone stocks, other times bank stocks; he has been in and out of Atlantic Richfield six times in 31 years. In 1994, he loaded up on commodity cyclicals, including chemicals, papers, and metals; he then scaled back the fund's cyclical weighting from 15 percent to 7 percent in the same year as they became market favorites, but was back at 13 percent of the fund's portfolio by the end of the year. Always, the basis for the formula that determines what he buys (or sells) is total returns relative to price/earnings ratio.

One area of the stock market for which Neff has always had a soft spot is the auto industry, an area that is often scorned by many investment professionals. In the late 1980s, Neff held large positions in General Motors (GM) and Ford, but he began selling GM in 1988 and withdrew from both GM and Ford entirely in 1991. Then, in the summer and fall of 1994, he loaded up on out-of-favor auto stocks, including investments of $500 million in both Chrysler (the largest position of any mutual fund) and Ford. In the case of Chrysler, he believed that the minivan and Jeep Cherokee would return the company to good profitability; he was rewarded in April 1995, when a takeover bid sent Chrysler's stock up $9.50 per share in one day.

By the mid-1980s, it was clear that Windsor Fund was on its way to becoming one of the most successful funds ever. *Institutional Investor* put Neff on its May 1985 cover, with the title "How John Neff Does It." The lead for the article was: "His record of the past two decades is the stuff of which money management legends are made. What does the Windsor Fund's manager do that others don't?" Neff's secret was to get to know the fundamentals of a company down to the smallest detail. He not only read annual reports and trade journals but also reread them over the weekend—along with a stack of *Wall Street Journal*s from the previous week—to search for some nuance he had missed. On Mondays he grilled his staff with tough questions, seeking more and more information on companies that had caught his interest, particularly those that the Street was neglecting.

Under Neff's direction, Windsor Fund produced a remarkable record of performance and its shareholders prospered. An initial investment of $10,000 in Windsor Fund on June 30, 1964, would have grown to $550,000 by June 30, 1995. The fund ranked in the top 5 percent of all funds in the Lipper rankings during that period. "I'm only kidding slightly," said A. Michael Lipper, president of Lipper Analytical Services, "when I say a lot of people think John walks on water."

VANGUARD'S MANAGED EQUITY PORTFOLIOS

Neff's formidable name, reputation, and success made Windsor Fund the capstone of Vanguard's position as a leader in performance results among equity and balanced funds. The success of Windsor II enhanced this leadership position. And the records of Vanguard's other actively managed funds reaffirmed that leadership. After Vanguard made a change in the investment adviser to the U.S. Growth Portfolio in 1987, the Portfolio came into its own; the International Growth Portfolio also provided returns well above competitive norms. Primecap Fund was so popular as a top performer that in 1995 it had to be closed to new shareholder accounts, like Windsor a decade earlier.

Perhaps most satisfying to Bogle was what he described as the renaissance of Wellington Fund, which had been hurt by poor performance after the merger. The turnaround began in 1978, when Vanguard directed a change in the fund's equity portfolio from a growth to a value orientation. The timing was fortuitous. It emerged to become a performance leader among balanced funds. Its assets, which had plummeted from $2 billion in 1966 to less than $500 million in 1982, soared to almost $11 billion by mid-1995. In all, June 1995 assets of the firm's managed equity portfolios (including balanced portfolios) totaled $58 billion.

MANAGED EQUITY PORTFOLIOS
Assets at June 1995
(Millions of Dollars)

Windsor	$12,474
Wellington	10,623
Windsor II	9,349
Wellesley	6,489
International Growth	3,176
U.S. Growth	2,881
Primecap	2,708
Asset Allocation	1,396
Explorer	1,350
Morgan Growth	1,246
Equity Income	901
Other (13)	5,723
Total (24)	$58,316
Percentage of Vanguard Total Assets	37%

As Bogle looked back over the years, he couldn't help but marvel that managed equity portfolios had accounted for 95 percent of Vanguard's asset base when it began operations two decades earlier, compared to 37 percent currently. With 63 percent of assets now in defined asset class and index portfolios, the firm's asset base had become far more diversified and less prone to risk.

Neff's reputation reached such heights that when *Institutional Investor* polled 50 top investment managers and asked whom they would select to manage their personal assets if they could not do it themselves, 7 chose Neff; no one else came close to receiving that many votes. He was being called a guru, a legend, terms he was not comfortable with. "I'm just a simple stock picker," he liked to say. Yet on January 27, 1992, *Business Week* noted, "If Peter Lynch was the fund industry's Babe Ruth, Neff is its Lou Gehrig," implying that Neff was a rare blend of high performance and endurance. In March 1995, *Money* magazine called Neff one of the smartest investors ever and one of investing's all-time all-stars. Agreeing with these appraisals was Duncan M. McFarland, Wellington Management's president and CEO and Neff's longtime colleague: "Neff's a different breed of cat. The word is unique . . . He just has a focus and dedication that we may see again, but I doubt it. He works harder than most . . . He sees where things are going. Neff's a giant, make no mistake about it."

Although Neff was part of Wellington Management Company, he worked out of the Philadelphia office. After Vanguard was founded, he kept his office at Wellington Management Company, which was located physically within the Vanguard headquarters. Though their paths did not cross frequently, Bogle and Neff had a mutual respect that manifested itself at crucial times. Neff had cast the only vote in favor of Bogle on January 23, 1974, when the Boston partners ousted him as president and CEO of Wellington Management Company. In the early 1980s, when Bogle was looking for investment management talent that would help Vanguard become fully independent, he sought (in vain) to have Neff come to work for him at Vanguard. He wanted Neff not only because of his personal loyalty but because of the role that Windsor Fund had played in Vanguard's success, particularly in attracting countless new investors to other Vanguard funds. "Bogle mentioned it once, suggesting we form a new company that I would run, which would become an investment adviser to Windsor and Gemini. It took five minutes of talk. I said no," Neff said tersely. "Bogle did not come back with a formal offer."

For his part, Bogle wanted Neff because it seemed logical for the two to work together, and hiring Neff would have saved Vanguard some investment advisory fees. "John felt a loyalty to Wellington Management Company," Bogle said with disappointment, "and I respect him greatly for that." Yet in the spring of 1995, Neff was still occupying an office in the Vanguard complex, and still talking warmly about Bogle: "I don't think I would have imagined, or even he would have, that from that $1 billion base, Vanguard would become a $150 billion company. If you do a good job . . . the world does beat a path to your door. Jack was street smart and mutual fund wise."

Bogle, in turn, freely expressed in his high regard and appreciation for Neff. Noted Bogle, "It would be impossible to underestimate John's importance to Vanguard's survival in the early years. His well-earned reputation enhanced Vanguard's credibility and created acceptance in the investment community as we struggled to establish our own identity.

What's more, as the performance of Windsor Fund improved, it began to attract significant cash flow, in many years accounting for 50 percent or more of the total net cash flow invested in Vanguard's equity funds. In one year, 1978, Windsor's net cash flow totaled something like $70 million, compared to a net *outflow* of $150 million for all of Vanguard's other equity-oriented mutual funds combined. Vanguard—and I—will be indebted to John for a long time."

■ ■ ■

October 19, 1987, Wall Street's blackest day since 1929, gave Neff ample opportunity to demonstrate that he had street smarts of his own. On that day, he had been in Detroit calling on Ford and GM executives. When he returned to Philadelphia at the end of the day, he stopped by the office before going home. Only a mail clerk was around.

"So, is the world coming to an end?" the clerk asked Neff.

Neff laughed—and with good reason. That day he had put $118 million to work buying stocks; he planned to double that amount the next morning. While other investors were panicking, discarding stocks they had placed their faith in for years, Neff was busy buying them up at bargain-basement prices—some at one-third the price they had sold for a week earlier. To his credit, he had the cash to do it. Long before October 19, Neff had concluded that the stock market was overvalued, so he sold millions of dollars' worth of stock, parking the cash in short-term securities. When prices plunged to where he thought they should be, Neff went on a buying spree. The result was that in the teeth of the 1987 crash, the 166,000 investors who had turned $5.5 billion of their money over to Neff reaped large profits in 1988.

In 1989, after being closed for four years, Windsor opened its doors to new investors. Perhaps a telling tribute to Neff is that the fund had to close again just five months later under the weight of a new $1.1 billion. Neff, though, met with another rough patch in 1989 and 1990, when the fund took a hit on bank and savings and loan stocks. In the 1990 annual report to Windsor shareholders, Bogle addressed the problems in the very first sentence of his chairman's letter: "This is my 21st chairman's letter, and it is by all odds the most difficult I have ever had to write." Later, Bogle noted in a speech that "Windsor Fund—the flagship of our fleet for so many years—has, for its second consecutive fiscal year, turned in an investment performance that is disappointing in the extreme." With the market down 7.5 percent, Windsor was down 28 percent, a performance that Bogle said verged on appalling.

Although those two years were a letdown for Neff, his overall reputation remained undamaged: His average annual return over the previous
20 years was 13.2 percent. He recovered from the down years of 1989
and 1990, and by May 1994 Windsor had total assets of $11 billion. By
May 1995, Neff had earned an average annual return for shareholders over
his 30 years as portfolio manager of 13.5 percent, compared to 10.2 percent
for the bellwether Standard & Poor's 500 Index.

In the fall of 1994, Neff announced his retirement at a press conference—an unusual step for Vanguard but one it took because of the wide-
spread interest in Neff's career. He indicated that he would leave Windsor
Fund at the end of 1995 but that he would be available for consultation
should the new manager need it. Succeeding Neff was 51-year-old Charles
Townsend Freeman, who joined the Windsor team out of Wharton in 1969,
serving as assistant portfolio manager since 1975.

C H A P T E R

SWISS ARMY
TO THE RESCUE

BY 1987, JACK BOGLE WAS GROWING WARY. He began to fear that Vanguard was getting too big and that outside events could bring its rapid growth to an abrupt halt. Over the previous 12 years, Vanguard's assets had grown at a supersonic annual rate of 27 percent—42 percent between 1980 and 1987. In April 1986, the company's assets passed the $20 billion mark; just nine months later, $25 billion; by May 1987, assets approached $30 billion. Investors who in 1979 had been putting $5 million a month into Vanguard funds were now investing at the rate of $5 million an *hour*. The company now had 1.5 million investors in 44 funds, compared to the 11 funds it had at the start of 1975.

During the long-running bull market in stocks that began in 1982, most investment firms looked good; as discussed in Chapter 15, Bogle liked to say that it took no genius to do well when the markets were on your side. During the five years beginning in 1982 and ending in 1986, the annual rate of return on common stocks was 20 percent, one of the best five-year periods in the 70-year modern history of the stock market. Bonds, too, were showing hefty profits. From 1982 through 1986, the annual rate of return on long-term U.S. Treasury bonds had averaged a whopping 22 percent, by far the best five-year period ever for long-term Treasuries. As

1987 began, rates on certificates of deposit had fallen to 6 percent, so investors were closing their savings accounts and switching to stocks and bonds—and to mutual funds. The rising tides of the financial markets were lifting all the boats in the industry. But Vanguard was determined to be successful on its own terms, not the industry's.

Vanguard was beginning to break away from the rest of the industry pack. The business press began to take notice of the company, and sympathetic stories about it were appearing in newspapers and magazines with increasing frequency. Typical of these was an article called "Out of the Ashes," in the September 25, 1985, edition of *Forbes,* whose lead read, "Ten years ago, John Bogle presided over a mutual fund complex in disarray. Today The Vanguard Group is one of the country's most successful fund operators." In March 1988, an article appeared in *Institutional Investor* entitled "Doing It Jack Bogle's Way: Vanguard's Maverick Chairman Has Some Very Definite Ideas about What Mutual Funds Should—and Shouldn't—Do." Bogle's core philosophy—no thrills or chills, stay the course, avoid fads—was now beginning to resonate with the press.

Even as Vanguard reveled in its success, the exponential growth was taking its toll. Assets were pouring in at such a clip that the firm was caught somewhat off guard. Record-keeping errors were increasing; customers were getting busy signals when they called; equipment was faulty; personnel were in short supply. In response to these challenges, Bogle hired Vincent S. McCormack, formerly executive vice president of the Philadelphia Stock Exchange, to the position of senior vice president of operations. McCormack proved to be a master of the processing area and immediately began to bring the problems confronting Vanguard's operating division under control. Indeed, the changes that McCormack instituted would prove to be critical when, less than two years later, Vanguard would be hit by huge transaction volumes generated by the stock market crash of October 19, 1987. When McCormack retired in 1995, Bogle felt deeply indebted to him for his service "above and beyond the call of duty." He referred to him as "invincible Vince," and described him as "one of the unsung heroes of Vanguard's success."

McCormack was among the first at Vanguard to recognize the growing role that information and communication technology would come to play in the burgeoning mutual fund industry, and he pushed for Vanguard to "tool up" with state-of-the-art computer systems. While Bogle approved the move, ever the man of the slide rule, he remained a reluctant warrior on the technological battlefield: "Technology leadership is too expensive," Bogle said at the time.

■ ■ ■

Bogle's wariness about Vanguard's size was well motivated. He began to notice that Vanguard—in 1987 the number three firm in the industry behind Fidelity and Merrill Lynch—was paying a price for growth, evidenced by the letters that flowed into his office. Most voiced similar complaints: Getting someone on the phone was difficult; documents arrived with errors; phone calls were not returned. One frustrated client wrote to Bogle asking why Vanguard was open 168 hours a week for marketing information but only 40 hours a week for client service. The Bogle Barometer, as he called these letters, was registering stormy weather.

The crew, too, was churning the seas. With Vanguard's dizzying success in the mid-1980s, its employees started to feel increasingly excluded from the rewards that soaring assets and huge cash inflows might have generated for employees of other fund complexes. Morale sagged, and Vanguard executives realized that more attention had to be paid to the firm's 1,000 crew members. Surveys of the Vanguard crew showed that while Vanguard was doing a good job at providing job security and establishing a strong corporate image, it was doing less well when it came to job training and employee compensation. Changes were instituted, some of which included improved compensation programs, the start-up of a house organ called *Crew's News* to improve communication, and subsidized off-site day care for children of the crew. At first, Vanguard executives believed that only minor changes were needed to correct personnel problems. That belief was an illusion, for simmering beneath the surface were broader problems that needed to be identified and corrected—quickly.

Bogle's other fear—that external events could shock the industry—was about to be realized. The crisis that shook Vanguard and the nation at large proved to be a blessing in disguise, for it warned the company of major changes it had to make. The problems began in April 1987. Surging interest rates had created a turbulent bond market, as the yield on the benchmark 30-year Treasury bond rose from 7.5 percent to 8.7 percent and its market price dropped 12 percent—all in a few weeks. The result was that industrywide net investments in bond mutual funds went from a positive $20 billion in January to a negative $13 billion just 10 months later. Vanguard witnessed a massive exchange of cash from its long-term bond funds into its money market funds; in two months, cash redemptions and net exchanges out of Vanguard's bond funds approached $1 billion.

Bogle darkly worried about what he called the 202 Scenario, in which car after car turned off Route 202 into Vanguard's parking lot, and investors stormed the building to redeem their assets. The scenario worsened as a news network sent a helicopter to film the traffic jam, which was then televised on the evening news. In its turn, the press would publish sensational articles, and a redemption panic would result. The prospect of such a redemption panic was new and frightening to Vanguard, prompting senior executives to worry that they might be about to witness the company's demise. Recalled Jack Brennan, "It felt like we were going to slowly liquidate into oblivion."

During the previous 10 years, with money flying in the door rather than out, Vanguard executives had given little thought to the issue of liquidity. It seemed unlikely that a crisis of this proportion would ever take place, so Vanguard never thought much about the consequences of managing its funds with very small liquidity reserves, in some cases as little as 1 percent of assets. Now, suddenly, the question was asked aloud: Did Vanguard have enough cash to meet all the redemptions it was experiencing in its fixed-income funds?

In order to raise cash during periods when redemptions and net exchanges exceed purchases, mutual funds must liquidate large amounts of securities. In April 1987, as more and more securities were being sold in the marketplace during the bond market crash, dealers were lowering their "bids"—the prices they were prepared to pay for the securities. These lower bids forced bond fund prices even lower, prompting more investors to redeem their fund shares, requiring the Vanguard bond funds to sell more securities, driving bond fund prices down even further, and so on. Brennan asserted gloomily, "It felt like it was never going to end."

At times of crisis, it is enough for some investors to know that someone is at the other end of the phone. But in that near-disastrous spring of 1987, there simply were not enough Vanguard staffers on board to handle the increased phone volumes—somewhere between 8,000 and 16,000 calls per day. Every hour, investors were calling into Vanguard and no one was answering the phone. Said Brennan, "Not getting an answer from a mutual fund company is the equivalent of a line of people waiting outside the bank to retrieve their money and not being able to get it."

As investors deluged Vanguard with requests to switch from bond portfolios to money market portfolios, Vanguard realized that it had no backup system for dealing with increased phone volumes in a crisis. Something needed to be done, and fast. Vanguard responded by instituting a program that would enable the company to instantly double its phone-answering capacity should the need occur. The program put into place by the fall of 1987, called the Swiss Army, was modeled after the Swiss system for calling up well-trained reserves for emergency duty. It required everyone, from Bogle and Brennan down to the frontline crew, to put in four hours of phone service twice a year, and to be available on demand when the phone volumes warranted it. No exceptions. As a result of the Swiss Army system, by 1995 Vanguard was able to put 1,500 employees into emergency phone service on a few hours' notice. The Swiss army system would come in handy even for minor crises such as icy-weather days.

THE SWISS ARMY

Bogle explained the origin of the Swiss Army name in a speech he gave on June 23, 1987, in which he compared Vanguard's independent strategy to stay out of the war to gather mutual fund assets with Switzerland's strategy to remain neutral as a nation. "Since 1515, Switzerland has been content to let the great powers of Europe fight their own wars and pay the terrible price in-volved," said Bogle. "It has maintained its neutrality not by *having* an army, but by *being* an army, a strategy that has kept Switzerland peaceful and prosperous—with its own distinctive culture, values, and ethics—while others have fought the same wars over and over again." It was a harbinger of how Vanguard would have to prepare for a stock market crash, which was to come quite soon enough, in mid-October of that same year.

Also as a result of the bond market crisis, Vanguard took another step that calmed investors' nerves: establishing a permanent liquidity reserve of 8 percent of assets for each of its municipal bond fund portfolios, a policy designed to have cash on hand to meet redemptions that came during periods in which bonds could be sold only at fire sale prices. Vanguard's reaction to the bond market crisis in April would help the company through an even larger trauma that shook the financial markets in October.

Before the stock market began heating up in the summer of 1987, Bogle had been saying that it was only a matter of time before the stock market dropped 100 points in a single day. On Friday, October 16, his prediction came true when the Dow Jones Industrial Average dropped 110 points. Then came Black Monday, October 19. The market opened weakly on that day, with the Dow falling 50 points, but then the market unraveled and was down 300 points by three o'clock. An hour later it closed in chaos, down 508 points, wiping out almost 25 percent of the market value of all U.S. equity securities (and 35 percent below their value at the late-August market high).

During that week, 114,000 calls came in to Vanguard, nearly three times the normal volume. Many were from investors who wanted urgently to switch from equity funds into money market funds; others were from people who simply wanted guidance. To help handle the calls, the newly established Swiss Army was called into action and the size of the investor information staff doubled overnight.

On Tuesday, October 20, Bogle himself went on the client service phones and took 110 calls from investors in seven hours. Although Vanguard's assets had dropped $2.1 billion the day before, he knew from these calls that the company would weather the storm, for he sensed equanimity in the investors' voices. It was soothing just to hear the chairman's voice on the other end of the line, urging them to stay the course. (He gave the same advice the next day on national television in an NBC interview.) One caller, however, almost rattled him. A woman from Hawaii told him that she was so scared that she was going to jump out the window. Feeling more like a psychiatrist than a business executive, Bogle tried to calm her. "Don't worry," she said, laughingly, "I only have a one-story house."

Vanguard employees smiled when they heard that Fidelity, which surveys had shown was the only mutual fund firm that outranked Vanguard in customer service, had to apply a seven-day settlement provision in meeting redemption requirements. Vanguard, meanwhile, was able to meet every redemption. Because of the chaos on October 19, Fidelity turned away 150,000 calls, and the next day its fund prices were not listed in the business press. Vanguard's were. Journalists were able to reach Bogle on the phone as late as 10:00 PM, and, in contrast to executives at other mutual fund firms, Bogle chatted away: "Sure, it's close enough to a disaster," he would say, "but we're here. What do you want to know?" In an industry where reputations are built on trust, Vanguard's preparedness paid off. Its handling of the crisis enhanced its image immeasurably.

Bogle called Vanguard's response to the 1987 crash one of the most rewarding experiences of his career. "We proved to our clients—and, far more importantly, to ourselves—that Vanguard could take the hardest imaginable punishment that the financial markets could hurl at us and remain steadfast, proud, resilient, even cheerful. There is no question in my mind that on that dark day . . . we were the best performing company in this beleaguered industry." Brennan agreed: "I have very fond memories of the 1987 crash. I have never been more proud and enthused about Vanguard than at that time."

As 1987 came to a close, it was clear that Vanguard was, in Brennan's words, "better, stronger, and more confident." The firm's fund assets were actually up for the full year, from $25 billion to $27 billion. The high interest income earned on bonds during the year had been largely sufficient to offset the price declines of April and September. Taking into account dividend income, the investments of the Vanguard bond fund shareholders were, by and large, at about the same level at year end as at the year's outset, before the crisis in the bond market. Despite the stock market crisis, the investments of Vanguard's equity fund shareholders were also largely intact; among the firm's 23 equity funds, all but 5 met or exceeded their peer performance standards, and the 500 Portfolio of Vanguard Index Trust actually enjoyed a modest positive return (4.7 percent) for the full year. Meanwhile, the returns on Vanguard's money market funds continued at industry-leading levels—and all five Vanguard funds outpaced industry norms. Vanguard's client base rose to 1.8 million investor accounts, and the company handled some 4.5 million purchases, redemptions, and exchange transactions during the year.

Although the first four months of 1988 were slow, Vanguard rebounded from the 1987 crash reasonably well. With equity, balanced, and long-term bond fund purchase volume down 65 percent year over year and cash flow into these funds dropping from $2.1 billion to $144 million, Vanguard's money market and short-term bond funds were a source of solace, growing from $5 billion in March 1987 to $10 billion in June 1988. At the same time, assets of Vanguard's bond funds fell from $10 billion to a total of $8 billion.

It was beginning to dawn on Bogle just how successful the Vanguard experiment could be. The company's assets under management had grown 25-fold in the 15 years from 1974 to 1988, from a little more than $1 billion to $34 billion. In 1975, the company had 59 employees; it now had 1,700. Of the 2,653 mutual funds in the United States, only 3 had lasted more than 60 years in their original form: Massachusetts Investors Trust, State Street Investment Trust, and Wellington Fund. While the total assets of the mutual fund industry grew 13 percent in the two years following the stock and bond market crashes, Vanguard's shot up an astonishing 32 percent.

Contributing to Vanguard's ability to withstand the crash, says Bogle, was the Vanguard philosophy. Of particular importance was the firm's tradition of encouraging balanced investing, with a portfolio that included stocks, bonds, and cash reserves—a philosophy that the company's own asset base reflected. Also important was the firm's overall conservative investment philosophy. Said Bogle, "We have tried to avoid short-term fads and fashions, emphasizing conservative funds with predictable investment characteristics rather than high-turnover funds with narrow or speculative objectives that are unlikely to endure."

Vanguard had always jumped out of the way of any fad that hit the market. When many of Vanguard's competitors were bringing out adjustable-rate mortgage funds, Vanguard held back, its senior executives convinced that they were too complicated to allow the typical investor to understand their special risks. Other investment fads that Vanguard eschewed included "government plus" bond funds, short-term international bond funds, prime-rate trust funds, and many sector funds. (Vanguard did, however, introduce a few sector funds; its health care fund turned out to be its top performer from 1980 to 1995.) Vanguard also steered clear of exotic "derivative" fixed-income securities that magnified price volatility, sometimes by large multiples.

One of the most important steps forward the company took was its decision to aggressively pursue the institutional business, which represented just 25 percent of Vanguard's assets. According to Vanguard executives, one reason the institutional side remained "the little sister" to the individual side of the business was that institutions were never one of Bogle's strong interests. His focus had always been on the little guy. Vanguard could woo individual investors one by one, through word of mouth. But "on the institutional side," said one staffer, "you had to use the S word, you had to sell . . . The business doesn't walk in the door. And that's sort of anathema to Jack Bogle. He doesn't think investments should be sold."

Nonetheless, Bogle enthusiastically endorsed the decision in 1984 to reach out for a larger piece of the institutional business. Vanguard's focus was on 401(k) thrift plans, already burgeoning in importance, and the firm began to put into place the complex systems required to administer them. One of the most important decisions in the institutional effort was the 1988 hiring of James H. Gately, one of the few "big hitters" the company had brought in from the outside. At the same time that Gately was hired, Vanguard reorganized its institutional business, which had been fragmented throughout the company. Rather than pursuing every company with a 401(k) plan, it decided to focus instead on the larger companies. As the 401(k) business exploded in later years, Vanguard was well positioned to take advantage of the growth, and was to become the second largest provider of these plans.

The final years of the 1980s and the first few years of the 1990s were a period of skyrocketing growth for Vanguard. From the close of 1987 to the beginning of 1990, Vanguard's assets increased 32 percent, the highest growth rate among the "big five" direct-marketing mutual fund companies. (Fidelity was second at 18 percent, followed by Dreyfus, 15 percent; T. Rowe Price, 14 percent; and Scudder, 7 percent.) Vanguard offered 56 funds; its staff had grown to over 2,000; it had 3 million shareholder accounts and was establishing 3,000 new accounts every day; and its assets totaled $55 billion, a figure that would *triple* over the next five years. In 1991 the company's assets grew 38 percent, aided by a strong rebound in the stock market following 1990's market decline. Vanguard also gathered enormous assets in 1991 from its bond funds, particularly the short-term bond portfolios, the GNMA portfolio, the U.S. Treasury bond portfolio, and the municipal bond fund portfolios. Vanguard's net cash flow of $2 billion in January 1992 was more than the company's entire asset base when the company was founded in 1974.

Of course, the entire mutual fund industry was growing at a rapid clip. A decade earlier, only about 600 mutual funds existed; now the number was over 3,000. In 1990 mutual fund assets passed the $1 trillion mark, representing 60 million shareholder accounts—five times the number just a decade earlier.

Despite its rapid growth and its increasing clout in the mutual fund industry, Vanguard was still acting like a small company. While others in the industry were implementing new technology, Vanguard was not; securities trades, for example, were still settled on paper. There was no human resources policy manual, no trading guidelines, no formal code of ethics. (Bogle's code was: "Do what's right; if you're not sure, ask your boss.") The company was growing, and that was all that really mattered. There seemed to be no reason to change what was clearly working just fine the way it was.

THE GREAT
SACRED COW
SWEEP

Y 1990, JACK BOGLE WAS ABLE TO PROCLAIM, "Vanguard has emerged as a leader in the mutual fund industry." He and the other senior Vanguard executives were pleased that the company was meeting the needs of so many investors. While Bogle conceded that Vanguard did not yet lead the industry in investment returns—that is, it could not claim to be the across-the-board leader in each mutual fund category—it was near the top in every major industry segment. It was the leader in money markets, among the leaders in the bond sector, and not far behind Fidelity in the equity sector. In another vital category—the quality of service to shareholders—Vanguard dominated industry surveys. *Financial World* magazine ranked the company number one in 1990 in an independent survey of mutual fund investors, tabbing the company as the elite service provider in the industry. Vanguard would continue to take top honors in all subsequent *Financial World* surveys. The company was able to provide this high level of service even while it was lowering its funds' expense ratios. In 1980, its average fund expense ratio was 0.59 percent of average fund assets. By 1990, that figure had declined 40 percent, to 0.35 percent of assets. During the same period, the expense ratios of Vanguard's chief rivals had risen from 0.62 percent of assets to 0.85 percent, an *increase* of nearly 40 percent.

Best of all, the media loved Vanguard. "The Best in the Business" was what *Financial World* called Vanguard in a February 1991 cover story in which it rated 17 Vanguard funds among the "100 best mutual funds." That June, *Fortune* magazine named Vanguard a "clear winner" in mutual fund performance, as the company swept the magazine's three fixed-income categories and placed second in the growth-and-income category. The following month, *Forbes* chimed in by naming among its "best buys" 24 Vanguard funds—more than any other fund family. Then in an extensive article in its December 30, 1991, issue, *Fortune* called Vanguard "A Fund Family for the 1990s." The article pointed out that, since 1985, Vanguard's assets had grown 333 percent, compared to 267 percent for Fidelity, 148 percent for Dreyfus, and 93 percent for T. Rowe Price. By the end of 1991, Vanguard's assets totaled $77 billion, a phenomenal $21 billion increase in a single year; 12 months later, its assets were poised to cross the $100 billion mark.

■ ■ ■

Unquestionably, Vanguard in the early 1990s was a different company from the one Bogle had founded in 1975. Yet during the company's 15 years of explosive growth, Bogle had managed to preserve the bedrock principles on which the company was founded. Conservative investment strategies had worked, and Bogle had no reason to change his thinking now.

Bogle was shrewd enough, however, to understand that one measure of a company's strength is its ability to adapt to new realities. He recognized that the industry was changing and that some tinkering with Vanguard's tactics was needed. Other mutual fund companies, for example, were exploiting advances in computer technology faster than Vanguard was. More important, Vanguard's rivals were beginning to respond to the company's competitive cost advantage, especially in the bond, money market, and index fund segments. To attract some of Vanguard's potential customer base, these rivals were introducing new lower-cost funds and new services, such as investment advice. In this climate of competitive pressure, Bogle and the senior executives of Vanguard needed to rethink some of the tactics that had driven the company's growth in the past. On June 6, 1992, as he made his way to Skytop, a resort in the Poconos, for Vanguard's annual off-site strategy

session, Bogle mulled over the strategic changes he intended to propose
to the company's executives.

At the main meeting opening the two-day session, traditionally high-
lighted by his sort of state-of-the-union message, Bogle quickly turned to
a competitive overview of the industry, referring to a collection of charts
he had prepared. "We're going to kill some sacred cows today," he
announced. Bogle then proceeded to make his way through a series of
charts, each headed by the word SACRED, followed by a picture of a cow,
followed by the notation #1, #2, and so on through to #12. Beneath each
headline appeared a single statement—sometimes brief, sometimes
lengthy—reflecting a widely held "sacred" tenet of Vanguard's strategy:

1. We shalt [sic] not manage (active) equity assets. (Nor active
    fixed-income assets.)
2. We shalt not be a technology leader.
3. We shalt not (cannot) provide custom-made investment advice
    and asset allocation guidance.
4. We shalt not match the fee waiverers.
5. We shalt not engage in distribution through banks.
6. We shalt not engage in the institutional money market
    business.
7. We shalt not engage in "wrap accounts."
8. We shalt not engage in major advertising expenditures.
9. We shalt not engage in major international activities.
10. We shalt not engage in a retail "bricks and mortar" network.
11. We shalt not engage in "low load" distribution.
12. We shalt not engage in unrelated (tenuously related?)
    businesses.

As Bogle made his way from chart to chart, the group could scarcely
believe what it was hearing. Was Bogle really proposing that each of these
founding Vanguard principles be struck down? After all, nearly all of them
were *his* sacred cows. The answer, it turns out, was no, not all—but four
of the most important cows were in fact about to perish. Bogle was
suggesting that many of the beliefs that the people at Vanguard—particularly himself—took for granted could no longer be treated as such if
Vanguard were to remain competitive in the years ahead.

Some of the sacred cows, including #1, were already in the process
of change. He noted that six months earlier, Vanguard's core management

group had been allocated 6 percent of the assets of Windsor II (about $200 million) on a test-case basis to demonstrate its skill. If it was successful, he saw no reason that the group couldn't manage small portions of other Vanguard "multimanager" funds, and, again depending on its success, couldn't ultimately manage an entire fund, whose performance record would be subject to public scrutiny. (In fact, in less than a year, the core management group would also be responsible for $100 million of the assets of Morgan Growth Fund, and in mid-1995 would be tapped as the investment adviser for the Aggressive Growth Portfolio of the new Vanguard Horizon Fund. By then, the core management group would be providing active management to nearly $1 billion of Vanguard fund assets.)

Abandoning some of the sacred cows would require a somewhat greater change in course. For example, Vanguard had never emphasized being a leader in what could be described as client-visible technology (sacred cow #2). In fact, it had boasted that it would never spend the huge sums—as Fidelity had—that would be required to become such a leader. Technology of this sort had always been regarded by Bogle as more of a nuisance than a tool. Bogle now admitted, however, that he saw the light.

Under Jack Brennan's direction, the company had already begun to invest heavily in upgraded computers, phone systems, local area networks, and other back-office architecture. Bogle asked that the investment in technology—both client visible and back office—be accelerated. He paraphrased a quotation from a *Forbes* article that appeared on September 23, 1985, in which he had said, "We are not going to be a technology leader. We cannot afford to." He said that his next quote in *Forbes* would be: "We *are* going to be the technology leader; we cannot afford *not* to."

Within months of the Skytop meeting, the company would set off on a new course—intensive and expensive—to win technology leadership. This massive undertaking would be dubbed Vanguard's "Information Technology Voyage," and would be conducted under the leadership of Brennan and Robert A. DiStefano, senior vice president of information technology. A 1969 graduate of Saint Joseph's University, DiStefano joined Vanguard in 1984 with 15 years of hands-on experience in the management and implementation of information technology.

According to Bogle, "I cannot overstate the enormous contribution that Bob has made to Vanguard's success. Of course he had the knowledge and experience in computers and data processing, but he brought much more than that to the table: a breadth of vision, business sense, and a belief in the Vanguard mission. He has emerged as a first-rate leader." In all, he seemed the perfect candidate to sensibly integrate technology into everyday life at Vanguard.

Another sacred cow that seemed easy to discard was #3. Vanguard had never given investment advice, in part because it was not licensed to do so. Personal investment advice had always seemed best handled by an investment counselor. Vanguard's function, on the other hand, was to give potential investors all the information they needed to decide on a course of action for themselves. Bogle told the group that he wanted to drop that sacred cow, because people wanted and expected Vanguard to provide an investment advisory function. (Bogle was not talking about initiating a brokerage business, for the company had already entered the discount brokerage business in the 1980s, a move designed to give its shareholders the opportunity to buy individual stocks and bonds through Vanguard. He had approved the move on the condition that no resources be expended on advertising the new service.) Bogle felt that despite the perennial uncertainty of the financial markets, asset allocations among stocks, bonds, and cash reserves could properly be made "at the margin," and that the mystery of fund selection could be solved by heavy reliance on the Vanguard index funds. What he had in mind was the development of a service providing fund selection and asset allocation advice to clients. Vanguard's formal development of this kind of service would begin two years later.

Sacred cow #4 was also on his discard list. Bogle despised the pervasive industry practice of temporarily waiving a new fund's expense ratio in order to achieve a short-term increase in yield, what he called a teaser rate. But he wanted to deal with what he believed might become an industry trend: the creation of special classes of money market and bond funds with high minimum balance requirements and reduced ongoing expenses. In 1992, Fidelity had begun to develop a product line of such funds, strategically categorized as the Spartan Funds. These funds, which required minimum investments of at least $10,000, were aimed at relatively affluent shareholders. The Spartan Funds' expense ratios (in the area of 0.45 percent, after temporary fee waivers) represented important price cuts by Fidelity, although they remained considerably higher than Vanguard's normal fund expense ratios averaging 0.30 percent.

At Skytop, Bogle proposed the introduction of a new group of funds, which he dubbed the Admiral Funds. They would mimic four of Vanguard's existing U.S. Treasury portfolios—the U.S. Treasury Money Market Portfolio and the Short-Term, Intermediate-Term, and Long-Term U.S. Treasury Bond Portfolios. Like the Spartan Funds, the Admiral Funds

would be targeted for affluent investors, requiring a $50,000 initial invest-
ment. To further undercut Fidelity, Vanguard would reduce the expense
ratios of the Admiral Funds in half, from roughly 0.30 percent to 0.15
percent. The Admiral Funds, Bogle admitted, were "a shot across Fidelity's
bow."

Three years after what came to be known as the Skytop speech, the
first four sacred cows had been killed and Vanguard was engaged in four
critical new initiatives: (1) active equity management, (2) technology
leadership, (3) custom-tailored investment advice, and (4) low-cost funds
for investors with substantial assets. While Vanguard still had not engaged
in major international activities (sacred cow #9), in 1995 it opened a small
exploratory office in Australia to seek a foothold in that country's burgeoning institutional business. Although Vanguard still had not pursued
the regional sales center "bricks and mortar" strategy of its major competitors (sacred cow #10), in 1994 it launched a client service center in
Phoenix, Arizona, to provide phone support to the Valley Forge headquarters. (By the end of 1995, this new satellite campus employed more than
200 crew members.)

The fact that six of the other sacred cows remained alive reflects how
deeply they were ingrained in Vanguard's culture. Bogle indicated a
willingness to reexamine them but ultimately believed they should remain
sacred. That Bogle, ever the archetype of conservatism, was willing even
to discuss the remaining sacred cows raised intriguing questions about the
Vanguard leader. Was this first step merely the opening shot of a campaign
to institute even more changes in the company? Had the leopard changed
his spots? Was Bogle about to launch another revolution? Or would Jack
Brennan, whom Bogle increasingly looked to as Vanguard's next-genera-
tion leader, be the one to challenge the remaining principles?

When the final judgment was in, the lesson at Skytop was that while
Bogle was willing and eager to make necessary changes, no changes would
be made under Bogle's watch that might jeopardize Vanguard's principles
of low-cost operations and no-load distribution, built on the philosophy
of "If you build it, they will come." In short, Bogle was willing to discuss
eliminating some of Vanguard's self-imposed competitive constraints, but
its tactics—exemplified by the 12 sacred cows—would not undermine the
architecture of the company. The most sacred of Vanguard's founding
principles would remain unchanged.

Bogle closed his Skytop remarks with a stern warning about future
challenges. Given Vanguard's growth momentum, he wondered whether
Vanguard couldn't learn a lesson from Icarus, the mythological figure who

soared so high that the sun melted his homemade wings and he plunged into the sea and vanished forever. Citing a then-recent book entitled *The Icarus Paradox,* Bogle noted that the enterprises most likely to fly too close to the sun had three major characteristics: "(1) they were highly successful; (2) they had a strong and clearly defined culture and strategy; and (3) their leader had been in charge for a long time."

Bogle did not have to tell the Skytop group what enterprise he was describing. He simply said: "Forewarned is forearmed."

C H A P T E R

PRESS ON
REGARDLESS

THE YEAR 1993 WAS EVENTFUL for Vanguard. By now, growth had become a given. When Vanguard crew members gathered at the Valley Forge Music Fair for the 1993 Vanguard Business Planning Meeting, Bogle announced that the company's assets had been growing at an annual rate of 27 percent since 1975. On January 18, 1993, assets crossed the $100 billion mark, and each crew member received a Tiffany bowl depicting the Battle of the Nile, with the inscription "Majestic Milestone Day." In March, Vanguard became the second largest mutual fund complex in the world, surpassing the Merrill Lynch Funds. The company added two new portfolios to its Vanguard Variable Annuity Fund—an Equity Income Portfolio and a U.S. Growth Portfolio—and prepared filings for numerous additional funds to be offered in 1994. By June, Vanguard fund assets had climbed to $110 billion, by September, $120 billion; on December 31, assets reached $127 billion, a 30 percent increase for the year.

As its growth accelerated, Vanguard made ongoing efforts to further streamline its operations and improve its capital structure. With regard to its capital structure, Vanguard had approval from fund shareholders to allocate no more than 0.25 percent of fund assets to cover capital expenditures. The company, though, believed it needed to boost its available capital to provide it with greater ongoing flexibility. In 1993 it received approval both from the SEC and from fund shareholders for a capital allocation policy that would create a ceiling equal to 0.40 percent of assets.

At the same time, Vanguard won SEC and shareholder approval for a change in how external investment managers were selected. Until then, a fund had to call a shareholder meeting every time it wanted to change either an adviser or an advisory fee structure. Now Vanguard could add an adviser and negotiate fees simply by going to the board of directors and following up with a notice to shareholders explaining any changes. By not having to call a shareholder meeting every time it needed approval for an adviser, Vanguard would save investors millions of dollars.

The year 1993 also saw the publication of Bogle's investment book, *Bogle on Mutual Funds: New Perspectives for the Intelligent Investor.* Bogle had put considerable personal effort into the text, repeatedly reworking his drafts, never satisfied that he had written something in precisely the right manner. His hope was that the public would treat the book seriously, not just as another primer on mutual funds. The book gave him a chance to show investors that at heart he was an intellectual, and it was written at a sophisticated level he knew would be over the heads of some readers. He was urged by the publisher to simplify some of the language and concepts, but he flatly refused; he wanted the financial community to judge him at what he regarded his best, however complex some of the ideas may have been.

The reviews for *Bogle on Mutual Funds* were mostly warm, and although the book was beyond the grasp of novice investors, many reviewers thought it was the best work ever written on mutual funds. Business columnist Craig Stock of the *Philadelphia Inquirer* wrote: "I'd estimate that there is at least one useful suggestion or important idea for every couple of pages in this 306-page book. That's a darned good return for your reading investment."

BOGLE ON MUTUAL FUNDS

The publication of *Bogle on Mutual Funds* proved to be one of the signal events in Bogle's long career. It received critical acclaim from investors and the media, and spent many months on some best-seller lists. It has already become one of the best-selling financial books of all time, with more than 200,000 copies sold in hardback and 50,000 more sold in softback. Bogle points with pride to the fact that he has received hundreds of letters from Vanguard shareholders who have read the book and bought additional

copies for their children and grandchildren as gifts. He revels in
the comments he has received, and recounts some of his favorites
with ease:

- The dean of the Philadelphia investment community: "A
  real blockbuster that will have long-term benefits to
  investors in general as well as to people who invest
  primarily in mutual funds."

- The head of a major financial services firm: "Bingo!"

- A writer of best-selling nonfiction books: "I have read
  every syllable. Written with marvelous clarity. Spoken
  like every ink-stained wretch who is not self-deluded. It
  is easier to shimmy up a mile-high pole than to complete
  a piece of writing. You got up there, though."

- A major financial consultant: "In my humble opinion, the
  best book about investing ever written."

- A financial analyst and shareholder: "When you suggest
  that you attempted to write a book that would do justice
  to *The Intelligent Investor,* my initial reaction was to call
  you an egoist. I stand corrected. Your book is now
  seated in a place of honor, on the shelf next to Ben
  Graham."

- A reviewer: "An equal to *The Intelligent Investor*? Well,
  no, but it's still pretty darned good. There simply is no
  better book on funds anywhere. It will be definitive for
  years."

- Another reviewer: "An awesome overview of investment
  company products and services . . . Among the minute
  details included, Bogle tells not only how to improve
  your backhand, as it were, but how to get the best grass
  or clay for the tennis court."

- Still another reviewer: "I reluctantly confess that it is the
  best book on mutual funds in years. Reluctantly, because
  everyone from Warren Buffett to *Money* magazine loves
  this book, and because it would be more fun to deflate
  the self-righteous than to encourage them."

Plaudits from the business press continued for Vanguard in 1993. In October, *Fortune* singled out 13 Vanguard funds as top performers in its 1993 Investor's Guide. Its rankings were based on three-year total returns, adjusted for taxes and sales loads, if any. Among the Vanguard funds cited were six internally managed funds—four equity index funds and two municipal bond funds.

The year 1993 came to its conclusion in dramatic fashion: a "call to arms" of the Swiss Army. On the day after Christmas, a snowstorm hit. The roads were so bad that Vanguard president Jack Brennan had to run the eight miles to work. Slowly, the Vanguard crew members trickled in for work. Brennan recalled that when three institutional salespersons arrived, they did not even take off their coats; they grabbed their Swiss Army notebooks and hit the phones. To Brennan, the entire crew's response to the crisis was encouraging: "After all, in California [where a caller might be located] it wasn't icy. It was critical for Vanguard to deliver uninterrupted service to the client and treat the event as business as usual."

■ ■ ■

The growth train screeched to a halt in 1994. Phone volumes were down, transaction volumes were down, the number of new accounts was down, and outgoing IRA transfers were up. Vanguard staffers watched gloomily as the bond market took a sharp downturn and large numbers of bond fund investors abandoned ship.

For the first time in memory, Vanguard's market share slowed its upward course, and even eased fractionally downward. In 1980, the company's assets represented 9 percent of the assets of all direct marketing (usually no-load) funds. That figure climbed to 20.5 percent in 1992 and leveled off in 1993, only to ease back to 20.0 percent by the close of 1993, a seemingly insignificant decline, but a portentous sign for Bogle. Much more significantly, Vanguard's share of industry cash flows—a more sensitive indicator of investor sentiment and the lifeblood of any fund company—dropped from 26 percent in 1991, to 20 percent in 1993, to about 10 percent in the first six months of 1994. The figures suggested that while $26 of every $100 investor dollars were invested in Vanguard in 1991, only $10 of every $100 were three years later. Many of those investors were calling Fidelity, which was having a banner year. Many of its funds were beating their competitive averages by wide margins and 61 percent of the net cash inflow of direct-marketed funds found its way to Fidelity that year. Fidelity became the darling of the media, its advisers thought of as the most gifted in the world. While Vanguard's assets grew 4 percent that year, Fidelity's grew 16 percent.

In Bogle's view, what forced Vanguard to suffer in comparison with many other firms in 1994 was its corporate philosophy. Its loss of market share, he said, resulted because Vanguard, with its eyes on the long term, was in a marketplace in which "short-term results are the name of the game." What kills investors in mutual funds, he said, was volatility. After a fund's net asset value had climbed from $10 to $30, everyone started buying it; thus, when the fund subsequently dropped to $20, the average investor, who bought at $30, lost one-third of his or her money—despite the fact that the fund's asset value was still up 100 percent. Heavily publicizing such volatile funds was not a good long-term marketing strategy, he argued, yet it was done all the time in the mutual fund industry.

In the face of this unfamiliar adversity, Bogle set out to galvanize the crew around the Vanguard philosophy at the 10th annual Partnership Plan picnic on June 4, 1994, giving a speech entitled "The Road Less Traveled By." Bogle's speech was inspired by Robert Frost's conviction that taking the road that diverged "has made all the difference." Bogle had missed the previous Christmas party because of poor health, and many Vanguard crew members were beginning to wonder how long he could continue at the helm. On that brutally hot June day—stifling under the tent that had been erected at Vanguard's headquarters—Bogle did not feel well, and Jim Norris suggested that perhaps he shouldn't deliver his speech. It was part of Bogle's character, though, to "press on regardless," so he spoke to the crew members jammed into the tent set up on the lawn of the Malvern complex.

In his speech, Bogle candidly addressed the company's problems, and made clear that, although the Vanguard philosophy was temporarily out of favor, the firm was not about to change from being "a conservative, disciplined, thrifty enterprise." He went on to say that the crew "must look ahead to more rational stock and bond markets, in which our Funds will shine whether the trends are up or down. Sooner or later the investment pendulum, having swung to the speculative extreme, swings back to the defensive extreme, finally coming to repose in the conservative center, before repeating the cycle again."

He then discussed the competition, noting that other mutual fund giants, like Fidelity, were spending large amounts of money on advertising, giving their funds more exposure and attracting more assets. While Vanguard was still spending about $6 million on advertising each year,

Fidelity was said to be spending something like $100 million. Bogle emphasized that Vanguard had to "add to public awareness of who we are and how we serve investors." If some listeners wondered whether that meant the company was going to increase its advertising, Bogle hinted as much when he said that Vanguard must "reconsider our deliberately timid (both in amount and content) advertising strategy, building—forcefully, tastefully, candidly—on the power of the Vanguard name." It was time, Bogle seemed to be suggesting, to kill another sacred cow.

Bogle also acknowledged that the company's standing was suffering due to the poor performance in 1993 of its two largest growth funds, combined with a lack of aggressive, high-risk funds among the company's fund offerings. Bogle assured the crew that Vanguard was "taking steps to repair the chinks in our equity fund armor." The company would have to improve the investment performance of its equity funds through more rigorous evaluation and selection of advisers, with a continuing emphasis on long-term performance. Bogle stressed: "We must capitalize on the success of our index strategy . . . but we must develop an active equity management group within Vanguard both to manage allocations of assets from existing funds and to manage new, and in some cases, more aggressive funds," making it clear that they must be "targeted to truly long-term investors, not fund speculators." Finally, he warned, "Vanguard must continue our drive to lower costs if we are going to maintain—and even increase—our pricing advantage."

Bogle ended his speech by reaffirming his conviction that Vanguard's conservative and disciplined approach to investing, combined with low cost, was the correct long-term philosophy, and decried the industry's short-term "quick buck" focus. He warned the crew that while "this was the first rough patch we have encountered since 1981. . . it will by no means be the last, nor, in all likelihood, the worst, challenge we will ever face." To honor Vanguard's founding principles, he continued, Vanguard need only "base its business judgments on three standards: One, what is best for our clients? Two, what is best for our crew? Three, what is the best way to manifest the tradition and character symbolized by our flagship?"

"If we meet these three goals," he concluded, "there are no markets, no foes, no internal dissension, no winds, no tides, no circumstance that could ever deter us from ultimately raising our flag and signaling victory."

At these words, the audience immediately rose to its feet and broke into applause. Said Norris, "I thought, 'This is sort of a defining moment for the company. Here was this man who had managed in one single speech to put the whole thing into perspective. He laid it on the line. We were nearly 4,000 strong. A big company. We were having big company growing pains. We were being challenged. Nothing more, nothing less.' "

■ ■ ■

Although 1994 was a year of retrenchment, Vanguard was hardly in trouble. A February *U.S. News & World Report* article ranked the firm among the top 10 mutual fund families in investment performance. In March, Vanguard added three new bond index portfolios to its defined asset class lineup. On April 4, 10,000 people phoned Vanguard, a one-day record. Then, in May, *Forbes* published its annual listing of best buys in the mutual fund industry. Of the 35 funds cited, 16 were Vanguard funds. The next closest fund family received but five citations.

Even with the lull in asset growth, Bogle worried about the disadvantages of Vanguard's huge size, especially bureaucracy and impersonality. (Partly for this reason, Bogle appeared regularly for lunch in the Galley, saying hello to as many people as he could as he passed by.) He wanted to build the company's assets, but he was just as happy to do so by "growing" the assets of existing shareholders. That way Vanguard could save on costs—one telephone call instead of several, he liked to point out. He also recognized that Vanguard's past asset growth rate of 27 percent annually was not sustainable: If it keeps up its present pace, he liked to joke, "we'll be bigger than the federal government eventually." His preference was for "moderate growth"—10 to 15 percent a year—that might be sustainable.

IT'S DIFFERENT TODAY

Ray Klapinsky was there at the birth of Vanguard, and he remembered how little Bogle had authority over in 1975 compared to how much Vanguard's span of activities had increased 20 years later. "It started out with what we called the compromise position, and it looked like Bogle wasn't getting very much, other than being a titular fund CEO. But over the years, there was a whittling away, with Vanguard taking over all administration, then all distribution, then laying on additional investment advisers, then a major portion of investment advice. I never envisioned back in 1975 that we'd be doing all that we are doing today."

Karen West, who also remained part of the Vanguard crew in 1995, echoed Klapinsky's thoughts on the huge increases in the activities Vanguard performed and pointed to a similar increase in the complexities of Vanguard's duties. In the early days of the company, calculating the legions of figures a mutual fund company needed was hard to do under the pressure of daily deadlines, with the help of antiquated machinery. Now, as she sat at her desk looking around at all the computer terminals she and her staff use each day, she realized that life at once had gotten both more complicated and simpler: more complicated because of the proliferation of funds and the kinds of financial instruments they held; simpler, thanks to computers and automation.

"It's fairly daunting," she said. "In the old days, we handled just bonds, stock, and money markets. Now there are all sorts of complex combinations that are being created. Vanguard doesn't get involved in exotic derivatives, but we do deal with some other complicated instruments in currency and index options, for example, meant to minimize risk. Then, about eight years ago we got more involved in international securities. Then there were variable rate instruments. And the tax law got much more complex. It's different today."

Bogle was pleased, however, that Vanguard's immense size had not become a license for senior leadership to reward itself with fancy perquisites. He noted that Putnam in Boston had just built an elegant new dining room for its executives, wine cellar and all. Bogle, of course, opposed such frills. He noted that at senior staff meetings over lunch, each person paid out of his or her own pocket. "We're not talking about money. It's an attitude. We don't need Dover sole flown in from England like Henry Ford II did."

Vanguard ended 1994 still as the second largest mutual fund firm in the industry, behind its major rival Fidelity. Fidelity had $263 billion in assets and a 34 percent share of the direct marketing business, up from a 31 percent share at the end of 1993. Although Vanguard's assets had grown $5 billion to $132 billion, its 20 percent share of the direct marketing assets was virtually unchanged. Jack Bogle was disappointed, not as much as in Vanguard's investment performance during the year, but in the way the public was being romanced by Fidelity. In his view, too many investors were willing to accept Fidelity's implicit claim that its funds posed acceptable levels of risk. In fact, much of Fidelity's 1994 growth seemed to be a carryover from its exceptional investment performance in 1993.

But the tenor of the market seemed to be changing in the latter stages of 1994, shifting from reward seeking (aggressive) to risk aversion (conservative) in a difficult year for stocks and bonds. In this environment, Fidelity's aggressive investment approach stung both its stock funds and its bond funds. (In response, its fixed-income fund investment management group would soon be reorganized and its philosophy would become more disciplined and conservative.) In contrast, Vanguard's conservative approach, as Bogle had predicted in his speech at the Partnership Plan picnic in June, had come front and center. The bull market in 1995 confirmed the trend, as Vanguard's conservative, low-cost funds led the way. Importantly, the Standard & Poor's 500 Index outpaced 85 percent of all actively managed equity mutual funds.

As the market winds turned in its favor, Vanguard recovered from its 1994 troubles, rebounding steadily during the first half of 1995. The news was good on virtually every front. Vanguard's share of cash flow rose to 26 percent, while Fidelity's fell to 36 percent. Compared to 1994, Vanguard's monthly cash flow was up 126 percent, from $500 million to $1.1 billion; Fidelity's, in contrast, had fallen by 41 percent. Among 50 outstanding funds that *Small Business* magazine chose in its March edition, 3 of 35 stock funds and 5 of 15 bond funds were Vanguard's. The company won *Financial World*'s service quality award—again. The number of investor purchase transactions increased 25 percent over 1994. Vanguard's share of the direct marketing business began to rise again, reaching 20.9 percent by mid-1995, while Fidelity's share had slipped to 33 percent. It was also proving to be a stellar year for Vanguard in terms of investment performance: during the 12 months ended June 30, 1995, its bond and money market funds outperformed 90 percent of their peers, its equity funds 84 percent, and its balanced funds 92 percent.

On May 20, 1995, Vanguard fund assets crossed the $150 billion milestone and totaled $155 billion at the end of June, broken down this way:

Fund Portfolios	Number	Assets
Defined asset class	37	$ 71 billion
Index-oriented	19	26 billion
Managed equity and balanced	24	58 billion
Total	80	$155 billion

Of its $155 billion of assets under management, Vanguard was internally managing $85 billion, $59 billion in defined asset class funds and $26 billion in index funds, or 55 percent of the total. The remaining 45 percent—$70 billion—was managed by 18 external advisers. Wellington Management Company managed $33 billion in equity and equity-oriented (balanced) portfolios and $12 billion in fixed-income portfolios, including the high-yield bond, the long-term corporate bond, and the GNMA port- folios. Other external equity advisers managed the remaining $25 billion.

A positive development was the revival of Wellington Fund. By July 1972 its assets had fallen to only $467 million. The fund rebounded, though, with a substantial improvement in investment returns and growing acceptance of its conservative philosophy. By early 1988, it had resumed its place as the largest balanced fund in the industry, surpassing the $1.5 billion asset total of Investors Mutual. By May 1995, Wellington Fund's assets passed the $10 billion mark.

Equally gratifying was the fact that Vanguard's average expense ratio remained by far the lowest in the industry—0.30 percent of assets com- pared to the industry average of 1.05 percent. This low expense ratio helped make Vanguard's bond funds among the best performers in the industry. At the same time, the passively managed Index Trust 500 Port- folio had attracted $13 billion in assets, and its rock bottom expense ratio of 0.20 percent and avoidance of transaction costs helped put it ahead of 77 percent of all U.S. stock funds over the previous 10 years.

In spite of all these positive developments, Vanguard was still getting bad press for its actively managed equity funds. *Forbes* noted on May 8, 1995, that a number of the funds had trailed Vanguard's own index funds by as much as three percentage points over the past decade, failing to note that they were nonetheless outpacing most competitive funds, which also trailed Vanguard's index funds during the period.

That same month, an article written by *Bloomberg* business news correspondent Mary Rowland was critical of Bogle: "As Bogle reluctantly moves toward relinquishing the Vanguard reins, the house that Jack built appears to be in need of repair. Although Bogle remains the guiding force of the company, people at the top of the industry have been whispering that the vision is no longer there." Bogle countered that the story was something of an about-face for Rowland, who earlier had praised Bogle in her book *The Fidelity Guide to Mutual Funds,* for the creation of the first index funds, calling them his brainchild, and in an article in *Lear's* magazine entitled "John Bogle: The Mutual Fund Investor's Best Friend."

The idea that Bogle's vision was slipping seemed questionable, given the sharp rebound the company was to enjoy in 1995. If anything, Bogle seemed to be expanding his vision to adapt to the changing needs of investors. In the summer of 1994, Vanguard set forth in a somewhat different direction when the company began developing four new, more aggressive fund portfolios that eventually debuted in 1995. Bogle named them the Vanguard Horizon Fund—"for investors with long-term investment horizons and a willingness to assume above-average risks." The fund comprised four separate portfolios: Capital Opportunity, Aggressive Growth, Global Equity, and Global Asset Allocation. These portfolios combined what Bogle called more aggressive management with Vanguard's trademark low costs. The Capital Opportunity Portfolio was the riskiest of the lot. The Aggressive Growth Portfolio, with some 75 percent of its assets targeted for medium-sized firms and 25 percent for small firms, was the first "free-standing" actively managed fund run by Vanguard's Core Management Group. The Global Equity Portfolio (which added currency risk to the traditional risks of equity investing) invested in stocks from both the United States and abroad, and the Global Asset Allocation Portfolio would undertake the strategy clearly articulated by its name, a strategy few existing comparable funds had been able to successfully execute.

The launch of these four funds provoked a great deal of talk in the industry and in the financial press. For one thing, Vanguard seemed to be veering from its long-standing views that aggressive growth funds were too risky for investors, and that international funds could carry the large risk of currency volatility. Bogle recognized that the four new portfolios represented a moderate change in Vanguard's course and acknowledged that the time had come for Vanguard to broaden its traditional conservative mandate. Vanguard was getting beaten by rivals with a variety of aggressive strategies, and Vanguard had to do something to strike back. It was time to carve up another sacred cow.

The new funds also raised talk that Vanguard was veering from its long-held diffidence toward active management. Bogle had always said that the chances of any fund like these four outperforming a comparable market index were no better than one in four. Bogle explained Vanguard's apparent course change to Warren Boronson of the *Bergen County Record*: "Up to now, we haven't offered investors an alternative to essentially a very conservative investment program. And we continue to believe that a core portfolio should consist of a stock-index fund, a bond-index fund, along with maybe one of our Windsor Funds, our U.S. Growth Fund, and our U.S. Treasury Funds. But we thought we should make available a few more funds. One of our largest competitors [Fidelity] has 27 domestic growth and aggressive growth funds; we have 5. Well, we're going all the way to seven, so we won't be in that league. That's a good league only if you want hyped short-term performance."

In essence, Bogle was saying to the investor: If you're going to invest actively, at least do it Vanguard Horizon's way, which continues to stress the need for a long-term investment horizon, no loads on investor purchases of shares, exceptionally low expenses, and relatively low portfolio turnover. To discourage short-term speculators from jumping into and out of the new portfolios, raising their investment turnover and the costs borne by the long-term shareholders (and causing them to realize taxable capital gains), Bogle attached a 1 percent redemption fee—payable directly to the portfolio—for investments held for less than five years. (Investors in the 1990s on average were holding mutual funds for about 2.7 years, compared to 12 to 15 years in the 1950s and 1960s.) In all, Bogle had no trouble adding a more aggressive component to Vanguard's overall array of conservative funds—on his terms.

Nonetheless, the press was skeptical about the new funds. *Forbes,* for example, ended its May 8, 1995, article on Vanguard on a sour note: "Our advice: Until these . . . funds have been tested in the performance race, give them a pass. Despite Vanguard's success in bond and index funds, its low-budget philosophy has so far produced mostly disappointing results in stock-picking and market timing." The tepid reception by the media seemed to have little effect on investors' acceptance of the new Horizon Portfolios. By late 1995, the portfolios had accumulated assets of some $250 million. Ironically, the Aggressive Growth Portfolio, managed by Vanguard's Core Management Group, was the largest and most successful of the four portfolios.

■ ■ ■

Without knowing he was doing so, Bogle had defined the theme for Vanguard's mission in 1993–95 in his address at the commencement exercises for the graduates of the Owen Graduate School of Management at Vanderbilt University in May 1992. The title of his remarks was "Press On Regardless," a theme he would use again one month later in his speech to the crew at the Vanguard Partnership celebration. The phrase had been part of Bogle's family background ever since his late uncle Clifton

Armstrong Hipkins acquired an old New England lobster boat with that name. Bogle thought the phrase would be appropriate as a motto for Vanguard.

Bogle had recalled St. Paul's statement "I press toward the mark," and also traced an historical usage of the term *press on* to president Calvin Coolidge, who stated in a speech, "Nothing in the world will take the place of persistence . . . not talent, not genius, not education . . . The slogan 'press on' has solved, and always will solve, the problems of the human race." In his speech to the crew—following an enormously successful year for Vanguard in terms of asset growth, service quality, and fund performance—Bogle noted that adding the word *regardless* was simply "a reminder that the company and the crew had to press on under all imaginable circumstances, including both triumph and disaster." He emphasized his point with an excerpt from Rudyard Kipling's poem "If":

If you can dream, and not make dreams your master,

If you can think, and not make thoughts your aim,

If you can meet both Triumph and Disaster,

And treat those two impostors just the same.

Bogle went on to say, "The challenge is to persevere in times 'thick' and times 'thin' alike. All of us at Vanguard must press on—perhaps even more passionately—with our mission in these seemingly easy, bright days, and despite what can be fairly described as our triumph."

In the three eventful years following that speech—not to mention Bogle's "sacred cow" speech to the senior managers of Vanguard—his company had come a long way. Some of its traditional limitations had been lifted, but its bedrock principles had been reaffirmed and remained intact. Meanwhile, assets had quadrupled. The upward long-term trend in its market share had been interrupted and then resumed. The captain and his ship had pressed on regardless—through some easy breezes and then through some hard seas—and had continued to steer a steady course.

THE FIDELITY WARS

FIDELITY INVESTMENTS OF BOSTON, founded in 1933, became the largest firm in the mutual fund industry in 1987 and has remained so ever since. Vanguard, on the other hand, having begun as a new name in the industry in 1975, ranked a distant 10th in terms of total assets in 1980. It rapidly ascended in the fund standings, however, holding the fourth position in 1990 and moving to its number two ranking in 1993. Even mighty Fidelity, with an annual growth rate of 29 percent, could not quite match the Vanguard experience. Fidelity and Vanguard were increasingly recognized as the "big two," the dominant players in the mutual fund business.

Inevitably, given the stature of these two titans, Fidelity and Vanguard were perceived as being at war with each other. If there was in fact a war it was undeclared, but it was played out in various subtle and not-so-subtle ways. The people at Vanguard had difficulty concealing their sense of outrage at some of the things Fidelity was doing, and Bogle at times talked as if the two firms were in a fight to the finish. In character, Bogle predicted that "the best built ship with the most sensible battle plan and the finest crew will triumph."

Fidelity, for its part, rejected the notion that a war was under way. Said Peter Lynch, the legendary former head of Fidelity's mammoth

Magellan Fund, "I've read all the stories about the [war]. But I don't see people around here wearing T-shirts that say 'Crush Vanguard.' " Richard Fentin, who ran Fidelity's second largest equity fund, the $14 billion Puritan Fund, was surprised to hear a Vanguard staffer's comment that Fidelity does not care about its shareholders the way that Vanguard does. "The fact is," Fentin said, "we do care for the shareholder. We care about the bottom line and good performance, and that's what the shareholder is basically interested in." In the meantime, Fentin had kind things to say about Bogle: "I think of Bogle as the industry's conscience. He always comes down on the side of the shareholder. He's very consistent, very straightforward."

In a February 1995 speech to the Harvard Business School Association of Boston (in Fidelity's backyard, fittingly enough) entitled "Strategy Follows Structure," Bogle used the opportunity to articulate some of the fundamental differences that separated Vanguard from the rest of its major competitors in the industry. Although the comparison was directed toward the industry in general terms, Bogle seemed to have in mind Fidelity in particular. In fact, although he mentioned no specific names in his remarks, he could hardly have been clearer when he referred to a Boston titan as "by far the industry giant in terms of assets, and a very formidable competitor indeed."

Bogle's thesis, in substance, was that Vanguard's unique business strategy flowed directly and inevitably from its mutual corporate structure, in which its mutual funds are internally managed on an at-cost basis. By the same token, the strategy followed by the managers of most mutual fund complexes flowed from *their* structure—funds that are captive to external management companies interested, naturally, in making entrepreneurial profits for themselves. When asked directly whether the reference to "the industry" in his speech was merely a euphemism for Fidelity, Bogle was noncommittal, saying only, "If the shoe fits . . ."

"STRATEGY FOLLOWS STRUCTURE"

The title of Bogle's speech to the Harvard Business School Association—"Strategy Follows Structure"—was a play on "Form follows function," the well-known design principle of architect Louis Sullivan. The first exhibit that Bogle shared with the audience summarized what he regarded as the seven major differences between Vanguard and the industry.

IS THERE A DIFFERENCE?

	Vanguard	Industry
1. Ownership	Fund shareholders	Management company
2. Profit orientation	High (for shareholders)	Very high (for management company)
3. Investor costs	Very low	Very high
4. Service quality	Excellent	Excellent
5. Risk aversion	High	Moderate/low
6. Indexing	"Missionary zeal"	"Kicking and screaming"
7. Marketing strategy	Conservative	Aggressive

Bogle concluded the speech with these words, "Given our Vanguard corporate structure and the strategy it dictates, our basic approach is fundamental. Success, however defined, is the ultimate test of the strategy engendered by our unique structure; indeed, our strategy is virtually compelled by that structure. I believe that success will be—and should be—defined almost entirely by the relative *net* investment returns that we actually earn for our own fund shareholders and the services we provide to them. If we accomplish these two objectives, our asset growth and, for that matter, our market share, will take care of themselves. Time alone will tell whether our strategy will succeed or fail . . . and I can hardly wait to find out!"

In that regard, the overwhelming distinction between Vanguard and Fidelity is their respective corporate structures. Vanguard, because it is operated at cost for the benefit of its owners—the shareholders of its mutual funds—operates exclusively with its fund shareholders' financial interests in mind, and is oriented toward enhancing their returns. Fidelity, while it also strives to serve the financial interests of its fund shareholders, is also oriented toward maximizing the profits earned by its management company. In his speech, Bogle quickly pointed out: "I am not arguing that there is anything wrong, as such, with the assets of fund shareholders being the basis for the creation of scores of centimillionaires among the owners of management companies. Indeed, that's the American way."

Vanguard and Fidelity are also vastly different in their approach to investors. Vanguard offers its funds on a no-load basis and directly to investors, successfully positioning itself as the lowest-cost provider of funds. In contrast, Fidelity is represented in a range of distribution channels: most of its funds are no-load, but some have a low load and others are sold at full load through brokers. In addition to being a financial supermarket, Fidelity is involved in nonfinancial businesses, including a limousine service and a financial magazine, *Worth*. Fidelity has taken on all comers, from discount brokerage firm Charles Schwab to Wall Street giant Merrill Lynch. When asked about Vanguard's no-load strategy, Peter Lynch remarked, "No-load wasn't a success. You didn't hear it spoken about at cocktail parties."

The two giants differ markedly in their investment strategies as well. Vanguard is conservative, Fidelity aggressive. Under Fidelity Chairman Edward C. "Ned" Johnson III, Fidelity has long emphasized higher-risk funds, intensive securities research, quantitative investing technology, and giving young portfolio managers—of both equity and bond funds—wide latitude and discretionary authority. Under Bogle, Vanguard has focused on index funds, on conservative fixed-income funds with clearly defined quality and maturity standards, and on prudent equity funds for the long haul. At Fidelity—at least in Vanguard's view—the focus is on the short term, and on taking large risks, often invisible to shareholders until they come home to roost. For their part, Fidelity executives could not figure out why an investor would want to get into a mutual fund just to preserve his or her money: "That's what banks do."

The two firms also follow disparate approaches to the marketing of their mutual funds. In a speech to the Vanguard crew in 1992, Bogle said, "The industry strategy—including, but in no way limited to, Fidelity— of hyping past performance or number one rankings might be 'our bag' if only past returns or rankings had anything to do with the future. Unequivocally, they have no predictive value. The creators of these ads must know it, so what is the point, really, of implying that they do? In the short term, it may pay off; in the long term, that approach is more likely to cause dissatisfaction when expectations aren't met."

Bogle also contrasted the industry's free-spending attitude toward advertising and promotion with Vanguard's penny-pinching ways. "The financial benefits of growth in this industry," he said, "go to management companies, not to fund shareholders." The industry's very structure, he further argued, makes competitors into aggressive asset gatherers. "We spend about $6 million a year on advertising and promotion, while our large competitors may spend more than 10 times that amount," Bogle said, offering another obvious reference to Fidelity.

Vanguard's approach to marketing might have been best illustrated by its handling of Vanguard Primecap Fund in the spring of 1995. This aggressive large-cap growth fund was one of the five top-performing funds of the previous decade. Vanguard had kept a low profile for the fund, and had spent virtually nothing to advertise it, although the media began to acclaim its performance. Reporting on an outstanding year of performance in the fund's 1994 annual report, though, Bogle was very cautionary; he warned investors about the risks involved in the fund's high concentration of technology stocks and told investors that it was unlikely Primecap would perform as well in the future. Still, a surge in investor purchases during 1994 turned into a cascade early in 1995, and the Fund's assets rose to $2 billion. So, Vanguard closed Primecap Fund to new investors on March 7, 1995. In its press release announcing the closing, Vanguard said that, after consulting with Primecap Management Company, it made the decision because it believed that the growing cash inflow could be difficult to put to work effectively and promptly, and that much of the cash entering the fund was from short-term speculators "who perenially look to jump on the latest 'hot fund' bandwagon" only to drop it immediately when the fund hits an inevitable rough patch. Since this kind of activity was, in Vanguard's view, "detrimental to long-term shareholders who remained in the fund 'through thick and thin,' " it felt its first responsibility was to existing shareholders.

One notable distinction between the two firms that did not make it into Bogle's Harvard Business School Association speech was the differing style of the firm's leaders. If Bogle was available to answer questions from the press, Fidelity's Johnson generally was not. It hardly seemed possible that anyone could feel more possessive about his firm than Bogle, even though under Vanguard's mutualized structure he did not own a single share of it. Johnson, in contrast, owned a controlling interest in Fidelity Investments, manager of the Fidelity funds; *Forbes* estimated Johnson's personal and family net worth at $5.1 billion. He had taken over Fidelity from his father and maintained a reclusive posture, for years not letting anyone learn the smallest detail about the company if he could help it. He rarely appeared in the press, preferring to let his multimillion-dollar advertising budget speak for the company. In contrast, here is typical Bogle, letting his views about his rivals be known in a speech whose language was strong, even for him: "Our rivals are doing what too many consumer products businesses have been doing since time immemorial:

come as close to the edge of proper conduct as you think you can get away with. What I am doing is disputing their implicit philosophy that providing advisory services to mutual funds is just another business. Surely they want to serve their fund investors, just as we do. But they *also* want to serve their private owners, who control their funds and in essence set their own fees. I believe, however, that no man can serve two masters."

Whatever the motivation for the competition between the two firms, it grew throughout the 1980s. At the beginning of 1980, Fidelity had $6 billion in assets compared to Vanguard's $2 billion. More than 15 years later, on June 30, 1995, the Fidelity funds had $310 billion of assets (of which $260 billion were no-load or low-load funds considered to be in the direct marketing category), compared to $155 billion for the Vanguard funds (all directly marketed on a no-load basis). Of the 10 largest fund companies in 1984, only Vanguard and Fidelity had increased their market share by June 1995. Indeed, during he period from 1980 to June 1995, Fidelity's fund assets grew by 5,000 percent; Vanguard's grew by 6,500 percent.

In the competition for assets, Fidelity enjoyed a major advantage in the equity fund field, while Vanguard had achieved an edge in the fixed-income fund arena. Many new investors were turning to money market funds and bond funds—Vanguard's strength—to replace low-yielding bank accounts. Although Fidelity had significant assets in bond funds, its strength was in stock funds, especially the spectacularly successful $50 billion Magellan Fund, by far the nation's largest fund. Given the success of both companies, the financial press and the investing public took great interest in the tactics and countertactics that marked their struggle.

■ ■ ■

As Vanguard grew, Bogle made a determined effort to treat that growth as only marginally important, saying that it was not a significant measure of success. Most Vanguard crew members could recite Bogle's famous two rules of market share:

1.   Market share must be earned, not bought.
2.   Market share is a measure, not an objective.

Not only did such a philosophy take the pressure off the Vanguard staff, it had the related effect of taking some of the wind out of Fidelity's sails. If size was not crucial, there was no need to stand in awe of Fidelity. If Fidelity had won the race to be the biggest, well, Vanguard would win the race to be the best.

At least this was the impression Bogle liked to convey in public. In reality, though, Bogle was an intense competitor with an admittedly large ego, and being number two lacked the cachet of being number one—bringing to mind Bogle's efforts as a teenager to get his teachers to reconsider his grades so that he could graduate at the top of his class rather than second. To have beaten out hundreds of fund families might have been good enough for a less competitive person, but no matter how much he disclaimed it, being second to Fidelity in assets managed must have bothered Jack Bogle.

Bogle therefore savored those times when Vanguard seemed to be triumphing. An example was on May 3, 1995, when he was greeting some visitors in his office. No sooner had they taken their seats than he thrust a copy of that day's *New York Times* in front of them, asking, "Did you see the great article about Vanguard?" Actually, the story, which was spread across the top of the first page of the business section, mentioned Vanguard only in passing. It was about Fidelity. Its headline read: "A Bond Fund Strategy Too Clever by Half: Fidelity Stumbles in an Attempt to Repeat Its Success with Stock Funds." The year before, Fidelity had announced that it was on its way to becoming as big a force in bond funds as it was in stock funds. "A year later," the *Times* reported, "that plan has ended in disaster." Many of its managers, along with their bosses, had been forced out or reassigned.

As interest rates rose in 1994, thousands of investors suffered huge losses, making the year a difficult one under any circumstances for bond funds. But compounding the problem for Fidelity were its heavy bets on Mexican debt instruments and on derivatives. "Fidelity," the *Times* wrote, "has always wanted to be the biggest and the best and make more money at the same time. So, unlike many of its competitors, the company was willing to scour the most obscure corners of the bond market and take big bets in the hopes of making big hits, the same way it did with stocks." It is easy to imagine how much Bogle, always the conservative, must have been gratified by this assessment.

The battlefields on which Vanguard and Fidelity met most often were the conference rooms of large corporations, competing head-to-head in the institutional business, especially the 401(k) business. Often, a Vanguard official would meet his counterpart from Fidelity on the way in or out of a sales meeting. This competition for institutional dollars intensified the struggle between the two giants. "When investment performance is not going well here," said Jim Gately, a senior vice president who had run the institutional division until mid-1994, "it is likely to be going well there, and the reverse. If they have a rough patch, we can see the phone calls flowing here."

■ ■ ■

Although the business press increasingly shaped its stories to suggest that Vanguard and Fidelity were in a state of open war, Jack Brennan sought to dismiss that perception. "We don't run our business around Fidelity," he said. When *Smart Money* wrote an article about the rivalry in October 1993, entitled "The Clash of the Titans," it personalized the struggle, describing "two vain men (Bogle and Johnson) looking to outwit each other." The article seemed to delight in suggesting that the two hated one another. (Johnson was depicted as "struggling to contain his irritation" and, "in a voice filled with sarcasm," asking, "Say, has [Bogle] written his own obituary yet?") Brennan thought the magazine missed the point by focusing on personalities, and on whether Vanguard or Fidelity was somehow right in its strategy: "They had a great chance to write about Jack and Ned [Johnson] and two very different ways to pursue the same business, each of which has been incredibly successful."

At times, though, Vanguard's ambivalence about the Fidelity wars showed through. Its corporate communications department seemed to relish a November 29, 1992, *Boston Globe* article entitled "In Your Face, Fidelity," which discussed Vanguard's success. According to the newspaper, Vanguard had purposely held its first invitation-only seminar for wealthy investors that month on Fidelity's home turf in Boston. That decision, the *Globe* suggested, was part of Vanguard's aggressive strategy of trying to increase its business at Fidelity's expense.

To Vanguard officials, Fidelity enjoyed an edge in the "war" in part because of its enormous size, which allowed it to heavily outspend Vanguard in advertising. The sales commissions and advisory fees generated by Fidelity's Magellan Fund alone were more than Vanguard's entire budget in 1995. The Boston giant also emphasized a more exciting part of the business. "There's a lot of glamour to equity performance," said Jack Brennan. "There's no glamour to bond funds. Nobody seems to want to write about bonds, even though it's where people have half their money."

Friction between the two firms reached a peak in 1992, when Vanguard's management asked the SEC to grant it the right, if ratified by fund shareholders, to manage the company's capital needs more flexibly by increasing the amount of shareholder equity available to Vanguard as a financing mechanism. Of immediate concern was the best way for Vanguard to finance its new $200 million office complex already under construction in Malvern, Pennsylvania. In November, Fidelity made the extraordinary move of asking the SEC for a hearing on the Vanguard application. It wanted, its executives said, simply to find out whether Vanguard's financing technique could apply to investment advisory firms whose ownership structure differed from Vanguard's.

Bogle was livid, and he pulled no punches in responding to press inquiries about the Fidelity hearing request. In a story headlined "Fidelity Takes a Swipe at Rival Vanguard," *The Wall Street Journal* quoted Bogle: "To me, it's inconceivable for the Commission to hold a hearing on this mean-spirited, half-baked, arrogant interference in our internal affairs." Buying none of Fidelity's arguments and worried that the hearing could delay the construction project and limit Vanguard's financing options, he added, "It's hard to see whether [Fidelity's behavior] is venal or stupid. It's got to be one or the other. If it's venal, it's an unwarranted interference in our internal affairs. If it's stupid, it's because they didn't read our application and realize that this is not something new and creative. This structure of financing has been in place for 17 years, ever since Vanguard was founded."

As the public learned about the issue, many wrote letters of support to Vanguard. Some investors who owned funds in both groups wrote to Fidelity's Johnson, and sent a copy to Bogle. One of these letters in particular gratified Bogle, and he occasionally read excerpts from it to visitors. In it, the writer assailed Fidelity's general approach to the mutual fund business: "Fidelity has become, in my view, a conglomeration of low-load, high-expense, 12b-1 junk funds, many with little reason for being other than huckster marketing. And you squander shareholders' money on junk ads, junk mail, and junk publications. Moreover, I have yet to see a word in the general financial press from Fidelity regarding its concern for its investors' interests; John Bogle goes to bat for us publicly all the time."

Eager to end the squabbling, the SEC persuaded Fidelity to withdraw its request for a hearing. In an ironic footnote to the whole episode, interest rates fell far enough that Vanguard finally borrowed the money and thus did not use shareholder assets to build the new campus.

"THE MAN BEHIND THE VANGUARD CAMPUS"
In speaking about the sprawling 200-acre Vanguard campus, Bogle could scarcely contain his pride at the job that Ralph K. Packard, senior vice president and chief financial officer, and his team had done in bringing the project to fruition. Packard, a former

lieutenant in the U.S. Navy with an undergraduate degree from Holy Cross College and an MBA from Cornell University, had joined Vanguard in 1986 as vice president and controller following a stint as senior vice president and controller of Society for Savings in Hartford, Connecticut.

"We had every expectation when we hired Ralph that he had the ability to manage our Fund Financial Group and our Corporate Accounting activities, and to develop and implement the kind of sophisticated financial controls that were necessary for an organization like Vanguard that was growing at breakneck speed," Bogle noted. "And he did those jobs expertly." Given Packard's strong background in financial operations, it was not surprising that, when Bogle and Brennan first began discussions about the new Vanguard campus, they immediately tapped Packard to lead the effort. "He'd done an outstanding job for us over the years," said Bogle, "and he was a natural fit for a project of this enormity."

Despite this obvious example of the heated competition between Vanguard and Fidelity, Bogle, like Brennan, continued to publicly disclaim the notion that a state of war existed between the two firms, emphasizing that the firms' objectives and strategies were starkly different. Bogle went so far as to state categorically that he had "absolutely no interest in being another Fidelity." While that may be true, the tenor of the competition between the two firms suggests that there is ample reason to be skeptical.

At the time of the widely publicized spat over Fidelity's hearing request, Bogle delivered a speech to the Vanguard crew entitled "A Willing Foe and Sea Room," the name of which was taken from an old British Navy toast. Bogle's remarks suggested that he clearly relished the competition with Fidelity for dominance in the mutual fund industry, using terms such as *battle* or *fight* more than 30 times. He concluded his remarks with a quotation from Gutzon Borglum, the sculptor of Mount Rushmore: "Life is a kind of campaign. People have no idea what strength comes to one's soul and spirit through a good fight."

Whether the war really exists or not, there seems little doubt that Vanguard is prepared for battle.

C   H   A   P   T   E   R

A CROSS BETWEEN DON QUIXOTE, RALPH NADER, AND HENRY FORD

THE ORIGINAL MANDATE of the Vanguard experiment was to give shareholders the best possible deal by redirecting "profits" from the management company to the shareholders' pockets (in the form of lower expenses). Over the company's 20-year existence, it had succeeded in this mandate, returning $5 billion in profits to investors; in 1994 alone, total profits returned to Vanguard shareholders totaled $969 million. Other evidence pointed to the success of the Vanguard experiment—the company's asset size, its service leadership; and, perhaps most important of all, its reputation as an industry benchmark for everything from expense ratios to disclosure of risks in investing.

Most business leaders would have been satisfied with that kind of performance record, but Bogle had a broader vision. Not content with building a mutual fund giant, he wanted to transform the industry, in the process turning his own company into a beacon that would light the way. He saw much that, in his view, was wrong with the industry: excessive fees; heavy sales charges; management company greed; lack of candor with investors; aggressive money managers who went for the fast buck, the short-term killing; misleading advertisements touting the latest "hot funds" despite minuscule odds that the fund would stay hot. "Somewhere along the road," Bogle said, "the industry has lost its way. In my view, too many fund complexes have put the business need for asset gathering (and the attendant enhancement of profits earned by fund managers) ahead of the fiduciary duty to provide efficient asset management at the lowest reasonable prices, the better to enhance the returns earned by fund shareholders."

Despite his strongly held beliefs, Bogle insisted he was not so naive as to imagine that the leaders of the lucrative, fast-growing mutual fund industry were going to sacrifice the money pouring into their pockets because Jack Bogle said it would be good for their souls. He knew that he had attracted the attention of numerous critics, some of them deeply angry at him, who argued that he had no business erecting a mutual fund company that put so much power in the hands of fund shareholders; that he had eviscerated the strength and authority of some of the most success-ful management companies in the industry; that he had done the industry a disservice by rejecting the traditional way of running a mutual fund company.

In public, Bogle was called a maverick, an iconoclast; The *Washington Post* affectionately described him as "the bad boy of the mutual fund business . . . a man with an attitude." Before a large audience in open session at a general membership meeting of the Investment Company Institute, Bogle heard himself described as a Communist and a Marxist. (When the speech was over, Bogle approached the speaker and, tongue-in-cheek, thanked him for his generous characterization. "In the office," Bogle said, "I am often called a Fascist.") None of these kinds of com-ments deterred Bogle. "I don't think I would win any popularity contest," he said with an almost fierce pride.

In essence, Bogle carried on a monologue with the industry, urging reforms that had as their goal the creation of Vanguard clones. The irony is that the more he succeeded in transforming the industry, the more competition he would create for Vanguard; as other firms became more shareholder-oriented and cost conscious, they would begin to appeal to the same customers that Vanguard was trying to attract. If it seemed as though

Bogle was intent on shooting himself in the foot, he simply could not be bothered. He was out to transform, and he would not be deterred.

■ ■ ■

Bogle had little chance of succeeding in his efforts to persuade the industry to restructure along Vanguard lines. Said George Putnam, head of the Putnam mutual fund organization, "The Vanguard structure is an option many of us could follow if we had difficulty with our corporate owners, but the larger you are, the more established you are in your own way of doing business, and the more difficult it is to change." Howard Stein, the head of Dreyfus, had misgivings about Vanguard's structure, contending, for one thing, that it deprived Bogle of emergency capital. He asked a *Fortune* reporter, "What if Vanguard had a problem with one of its money market funds? Where would the capital come from to shore it up?" (In typical fashion, Bogle retorted, "If Dreyfus guarantees to shore up its own money funds, why doesn't it say so in its prospectuses?")

When it came to promoting lower expenses, Bogle enjoyed considerably more success. Indeed, the mutual fund industry looked at least slightly different in 1995 because of his efforts. Two decades ago, the industry's sole emphasis was on getting the best possible performance out of its funds; today, a growing number of Vanguard competitors stress the role of low expenses in doing so. The press, too, began to accept the argument that lower expenses meant higher returns to shareholders. For instance, in arriving at its annual "best buys" mutual fund list, *Forbes* magazine bases its analysis partly on past performance and partly on costs.

Bogle began his cost-cutting campaign in 1975, when the funds set off on the road to complete independence. The campaign was strengthened with the decision to go no-load in 1977. Overnight, Vanguard, with $1.5 billion in assets, became the second largest no-load company in the industry (behind T. Rowe Price, with $2 billion in assets). The industry watched carefully, for Vanguard was the first major mutual fund firm to convert from load to no-load distribution. Apparently, the rest of the industry saw some advantage to Vanguard's shift in strategy: within a few years, Fidelity went partially no-load, and Dreyfus, which had run derisive ads debunking Vanguard's no-load decision, converted some of its funds to no-load. Later, even Merrill Lynch would create a new marketing arm to teach brokers how to sell no-load funds, a concept that was scorned by the firm in earlier days. Ever since Vanguard made the decision to go no-load, the concept has permeated both bond fund and equity fund segments of the industry. Of the mutual funds introduced in 1995, for example, fully 45 percent were no-load funds. Until Jack Bogle began to champion it, this was a concept that was anathema to most of the industry.

Going no-load, however, was only part of the campaign to give investors a fairer shake. Equally important was keeping operating expenses low. "In 1981," said Bogle in a 1991 speech to the North American Securities Administrators Association, Inc., that helped launch an industrywide debate, "assets of equity funds totaled $40 billion, and the average expense ratio was 1.04 percent; in 1991, with equity fund assets totaling $250 billion, the ratio has risen to 1.45 percent. Thus, industry expenses are up nearly eight-fold, from $470 million to $3.5 billion, with industry assets up only five-fold. The real issue is *not* why expense ratios are up by so much, or even at all [in the face of our industry's staggering rate of growth]. The issue is why they have not declined. For believe me, there *are* substantial economies of scale in this business."

Vanguard set an example for the industry by becoming the most efficient, lowest-cost provider of mutual funds in the United States. "Investors," said Bogle, "are figuring out that costs are exceptionally critical in money market funds, very critical in bond funds, and somewhat critical in stock funds." Vanguard's money market funds had established a new, far lower expense ratio standard for the entire money market arena. Index funds, too, can be run at low cost, and Bogle was the first to introduce this kind of fund to the industry. While the original reception for index funds was chilly, investors have been warming up to them, investing substantial dollars through the mid-1990s. Bogle has been given full credit for the growing success of index funds.

Not surprisingly, the industry was slow to respond to Bogle's efforts to lower costs. Eventually, though, some firms did, often lowering costs temporarily. Bogle was skeptical that this strategy constituted imitation. In the early 1990s, Fidelity introduced its Spartan Funds, a line of predominantly money market and fixed-income funds for more affluent investors. With no loads and temporary annual management fee waivers, they became, incredibly, cheaper than Vanguard's funds, at least until the fee waivers ceased, as soon they did. In response to this challenge to its low-cost supremacy, Vanguard introduced its Admiral Funds lineup. The result was a fascinating competition, as some of the major mutual fund players engaged in a series of price-cutting moves and countermoves. Dreyfus joined the fray when it introduced a line of money market funds aimed at providing the highest possible yields by waiving all management fees and subsidizing other fund expenses. In time, however, the fees returned to higher levels—after numerous shareholders had joined the fund because of its higher yield. Bogle considered this strategy—which he described as the "teaser rate strategy"—to be unconscionable: "Companies heavily advertise these funds when expenses are being waived and yields are relatively higher, but there is never a similar campaign when the fee waiver is rescinded and yields become relatively lower."

There was no clear-cut winner of what some dubbed the money market wars. Dreyfus temporarily gained some market share but appeared to suffer cuts in profits; the market share gains evaporated when fees were reinstated, yields fell, and shareholders redeemed their shares. Fidelity brought in billions of dollars in new assets, but it was not about to transform all of its investment strategies. For Vanguard, the wars were a double-edged sword. The company was flattered that some of its giant competitors were emulating it, but for the first time it felt pressured by these giants and began to reexamine some of its long-held views.

The level of fund costs was not the only industry practice that Bogle wanted to transform. He also stood alone in arguing in favor of candor and full disclosure of all costs in annual reports and advertising. In particular, he wanted to see accurate information about how much it cost the individual to invest in a fund. In part because of Bogle's complaints, beginning in the 1980s each mutual fund prospectus has contained in its introductory material a simple explanation of precisely what it costs an investor to join the fund. Such disclosure had always been required, but it had been difficult to locate in a lengthy and detailed prospectus.

Bogle was also the motivating force behind more open discussion and analysis of fund performance. Until the early 1990s, annual reports of many funds often contained no direct indication from the fund manager of how the fund had performed in the past relative to a market index. In a 1989 speech, Bogle challenged the Securities and Exchange Commission to require that "a fund's total return be presented at the beginning of its annual report, along with any relevant standards of comparison," as well as an annual "mandatory 'Management Discussion and Analysis' of the year's results, including the fund's goals and objectives, and its success (or lack of the same) in achieving them, including an analysis of the major causative factors in its performance." In 1992, the Securities and Exchange Commission adopted just such a rule, requiring that annual reports (or prospectuses) of all funds include all of the items that Bogle noted in his speech. Bogle's own candid letters to shareholders in Vanguard's annual reports have become a benchmark for the industry, nudging other firms to adopt a more open attitude to investors when informing them of how their funds have performed.

Although Bogle has been the main voice urging reforms like these over the past 15 years, the SEC's current focus on disclosure is hardly owing to him alone. Yet the staff of the commission always seems to look to Vanguard for leadership, and in 1994 Vanguard was one of eight mutual fund organizations asked by the Securities and Exchange Commission to lead an effort to simplify fund prospectuses. Each of the firms has prepared its own version of a new "profile prospectus." This one-page document, meant to replace the typical 40-page, legalese-laden prospectus, highlights briefly the fund's risks, fees, expenses, and investment strategy, and includes a 10-year performance chart. The SEC has also solicited comment on its proposal to improve disclosure regarding money market funds, and is proposing as well a requirement that such funds disclose their holdings on a monthly basis.

Apart from urging candor, Bogle has also confronted the issue of director compensation. Long before the press became interested in directors' fees, Bogle was critical of independent directors who collected huge fees for doing little work, at the same time ignoring the needs of shareholders. When *The Wall Street Journal* revealed that some independent fund directors were being paid $200,000 to $450,000 per year for doing very little, Bogle responded, "It's unconscionable. Why pay anyone that kind of money to sit in on four meetings a year? The only reason, tacit and not explicit, is if you thought the director would vote the right way— to approve high fees and not to reduce them, and to perfunctorily extend the management company's contract."

■ ■ ■

While Bogle has his share of critics, he has also won some grudging respect in the industry. When pressed, mutual fund leaders have acknowledged that the reforms Bogle has backed have improved the industry. Merrill Lynch's Arthur Zeikel, whom Bogle considers a good friend, called Bogle "a combination of Don Quixote and Ralph Nader."

"I don't think people are angry at what he's done," said Zeikel. "I don't think people are disturbed that Jack has taken bread from their table. He's forced us to demonstrate that we can bring value to the table in a different way than Vanguard brings value to the table. I hate to use the word, but to some extent, he's the conscience of the industry."

Jon S. Fossel, chairman and CEO of Oppenheimer Management Corporation, offered similar respect, though grudgingly: "Jack loves to get up on the platform and remind the rest of us that we could follow in his footsteps and deliver a lower-cost product . . . The industry sometimes gets a little irritated by Jack Bogle's zealous defense of his own business strategy. Jack doesn't want to deal with all the facts, but that's fine. That doesn't mean the industry doesn't respect him, because I think we do."

"A LICENSE TO STEAL"

Being a maverick may be in the Bogle genes. Bogle's maternal great-grandfather, Philander B. Armstrong, brought mutual property insurance to the fore in 1875. He founded several insurance companies, including Phoenix Mutual and "The Armstrong."

When Bogle first saw a summary of Armstrong's background, he was stunned to read phrases like the following: "He conceived the idea of mutual insurance . . . Armstrong's methods are original and diametrically opposed to almost every recognized underwriter in the country . . . His theory, which his own success has practically demonstrated . . . is to deal directly with the insured without the intervention of agents, brokers, or middlemen . . . His methods have invariably been approved by the public, [but] have been severely criticized by his opponents, but by his boldness, often amounting to audacity, he has invariably achieved success." Bogle also located a copy of a speech Armstrong had given in St. Louis, Missouri, in 1886, which concluded with: "To save our business from ruin, we must at once undertake a vigorous reform. To do this, the first step must be to *reduce expenses.*" (Italics in original.)

Armstrong's crusade for reform was articulated in his book, published in 1917, entitled *A License to Steal: Life Insurance, the Swindle of Swindles. How Our Laws Rob Our Own People of Billions.* It was, like *Bogle on Mutual Funds,* an insider's view of an industry. The Armstrong book railed against the incestuous relationship between insurance companies and state regulators; the Bogle book rails against the incestuous relationship between mutual funds and investment advisers.

Bogle said he may yet write another book pursuing this conflict in greater depth, but disavowed the use of such a strident title. "Grandpa Armstrong must have been a less diplomatic man than I am," Bogle said with a smile.

Bogle has always known that there were important economic interests at play and that the industry was not going to conform to his views simply because he voiced them in an articulate manner: "You can't expect somebody in the real world to say, 'Well, I've got a $5 billion mutual fund complex and, by owning its investment adviser, I personally am worth $150 million. (Currently, management companies are valued on average at about 3 percent of fund assets under management.) Now all of a sudden I'm going to go to the directors and say, I want my $150 million of value to go to the funds' shareholders.'" Nonetheless, Bogle believed that in time the industry would change.

While Bogle attracted respect in many quarters, his peers in the industry could be sharp and pointed in their dissent from his views. Fidelity's Ned Johnson asserted: "We offer many services that Vanguard doesn't. I think Jack Bogle forgets there is more than one way to run an investment company." Johnson took aim at the Vanguard practice of using external investment advisers for some of its funds. He told *Forbes,* "We bring our people along from the day they start here as junior analysts. We don't rely on contracted money managers we have no control over." It was an ironic stab at Bogle, whose main theme for the past two decades has been the need for the complete independence of funds and their shareholders from the management company.

To cynics, Bogle's reformist campaign was nothing more than a confidence game. They were convinced that Bogle's pronouncements were part of a preconceived marketing strategy aimed at getting Vanguard free publicity. Bogle's love affair with controversy, they argued, was nothing more than an attention-getting device. And to be fair, it is probably true that no one in the industry had the same flair for wielding pungent, hard-hitting language than did Bogle. Even Ian MacKinnon, a senior vice president at Vanguard, noted, "He gives good sound bites." For his efforts, Bogle was rewarded with considerable media attention. In a feature article titled "The Power of Mutual Funds," *Business Week* named him a "superstar of the mutual fund industry." Wrote *Money* magazine: "John Bogle bestrides mutual funds like the leader of no other industry. He is not only its Henry Ford, the price-cutting apostle of prudence. He is its Ralph Nader, the inveterate scourge."

Despite its ambivalence about Bogle, the industry could not ignore him, for he had become a force with the media, and what he had to say often made sense. During the growth years of the 1980s, there was not much incentive for firms to follow him. The 1990s, though, have been leaner, and penny-pinching has become more common. In this environment, Bogle's message has become more persuasive, and his name comes up more often: "I suppose Bogle will have something to say about this."

All in all, Bogle's quest to transform the mutual fund industry has remained just that—a quest. He has succeeded in some areas, failed in others. But what makes him unique is that he undertook the quest in the first place. If he had been less iconoclastic, few would have paid attention to him. If he had been less successful in business, fewer still would have listened to what he had to say. By staking out the moral high ground and by practicing what he preached in creating the second largest mutual fund company in the world, Bogle guaranteed that he would be heard and that Vanguard would become a benchmark for the industry.

C H A P T E R

THE SUCCESSION

I N THE SPRING OF 1995, when Jack Bogle turned 66, he began to think about reducing his work load. He had wanted to leave Vanguard in good condition and, after a record year, it seemed like an opportune time to do step down without disrupting the company. All around the place was the smell of success. Investors were picking up the phone to turn their money over to Vanguard as fast as they could.

If the timing was right financially, it was also right for assuring a smooth transition in leadership. Bogle's successor originally was to have been Jim Riepe, who left Vanguard in 1982 rather than wait for the uncertain future chance to run the firm. Though he never really got over losing Riepe, Bogle knew he had to develop an heir apparent. In September 1982 he hired as Vanguard's president a former associate, Jerald L. Stevens, whom he hoped to groom as his replacement as chief executive officer. Stevens, who had proceeded from Yale to Harvard Business School, worked for Wellington Management Company after his graduation in 1967. He left Wellington Management Company in 1973, ultimately becoming vice president for finance and administration at Yale University from 1977 until 1982, when he joined Vanguard. Bogle described Stevens as "brilliant," but the chemistry was bad between Stevens on the one hand and Bogle and the board of directors on the other, and Stevens left in January 1984.

With Stevens's departure, Bogle turned to his newly hired assistant, John J. Brennan. Like Riepe before him, Jack Brennan seemed ideal; he was young, smart, articulate, energetic, ambitious, and endowed with a sense of complete integrity—all attributes that Bogle admired. More important, Brennan shared Bogle's fundamental business philosophy: an intense focus on the interests of shareholders.

While Bogle came to regard Brennan as his successor not long after he was hired in 1982, there was never any public announcement within the company that Brennan would someday take over for Bogle. While he quickly rose to chief financial officer in 1985, and to executive vice president in 1986, the first clear indication that he would be Bogle's successor came in 1987, when Brennan was elected to serve on the Vanguard board of directors. Then, in 1989, he was elected president.

If Bogle was reasonably sure about Brennan, the decision was never chiseled in stone. The closest Bogle ever came to a formal announcement was in a 1990 brochure called "The Vanguard Advantage," which described the virtues of the company. Included in the booklet was a photograph of Walter Morgan, Bogle, and Brennan; the caption read, "To clarify the line of succession, in mid-1989 John J. Brennan was elected President of The Vanguard Group and each of our investment companies." The picture told the entire story: here were Vanguard's leaders, past, present, and future. Nonetheless, in a December 1991 *Fortune* story, Bogle said, "Jack Brennan could still use a bit more seasoning."

■ ■ ■

In early 1995, before Bogle made the decision to relinquish the position of CEO, an associate mentioned to him that Vanguard's policy was that no one could serve on the board beyond age 70, suggesting that Bogle would have only four more years of eligibility to serve on the board. Bogle's reply appeared to suggest that he had no plans to step down voluntarily, and that only his health would determine his future: "I don't know if I will make 66. If I make 70, I'm sure that the Vanguard directors will consider making an exception for the company's founder."

Bogle had always taken a matter-of-fact attitude about his health problems; he was famous for leaving the office each night with the words "See you tomorrow, Lord willing." For most of the board members, raising the subject of Bogle's health, even in the privacy of a board meeting, bordered on the insensitive. There clearly existed a significant risk that Bogle's health could deteriorate suddenly and rapidly, and some wondered privately how long Bogle could continue to defy the odds in his ability to triumph over his health problems. Some even believed that Bogle should slow down not so much for business reasons but for the sake of his own well-being.

Given the precarious nature of Bogle's health, the transition issue was a delicate one for the board of directors. As early as the late 1980s, the board had complete confidence in Brennan's ability to assume the reins of the company should something happen to Bogle. However, they were concerned that not enough was being done to make sure that the shareholders of the funds got to know Jack Brennan and gain confidence in him as a leader. They knew that as long as Bogle was around, the chances of anyone else sharing center stage were slim. But they urged him nonetheless to give Brennan more responsibility, to make him more visible as a leader. "We didn't want shareholders to think the organization was dependent on one man, because it isn't," said Barbara Hauptfuhrer. "I think Brennan believes in what Bogle does. He's strong, but . . . it would have been hard for anybody to demonstrate that kind of strength while Bogle was around."

Bogle apparently agreed. He knew that he had to make way for the next generation of leaders, but he wanted the transition to be handled in an orderly process. Brennan gradually took on more direct responsibility for the operations of the company. He gave more speeches, his name appeared in print more often, he toured the country talking to groups of shareholders, and he began meeting with many of Vanguard's large institutional clients. Bogle made a point of consulting with Brennan on key strategic decisions, and Brennan began to place his mark on the company. This was both a gratifying and a frustrating time in his Vanguard career—gratifying because he knew that he would one day be captain of the ship; frustrating because he had to play a delicate game, remaining deferential to Bogle. Nonetheless, with the rest of the company and the entire industry watching, he was trying on the captain's uniform, occasionally even wearing it in public.

While Brennan would also face the difficult task of rallying the crew behind him, most staffers seemed to have the highest respect for him and thought that there would be some things to look forward to about the transition. Bogle had been so dominant and hard-driving that any of his personal weaknesses were dismissed as irrelevant. Some of his associates believed that, as the years went by, those weaknesses—some real, some perceived—were serving as an anchor that slowed the ship: Bogle had little interest in information technology; he was too inflexible in his disdain for riskier funds; he had no love for international funds, or international marketing of U.S. funds, or even for highly speculative funds. Brennan, in contrast, was a technophile, and he took a less rigid line toward international expansion and more aggressive funds. To many staffers, he would be the ideal leader in the post-Bogle era.

What's more, while they admired Bogle and recognized that he was one of the giants in the field, Vanguard staffers knew that the company—indeed the entire industry—was changing and they were dubious that Bogle would be able to change with it. Said Jim Norris, "I don't believe Jack Bogle is capable of being a facilitator, of doing 'the management thing.' He would probably say so himself. In fact, I remember him saying once, off the cuff, 'I've never managed someone in my life.' Jack Brennan, on the other hand is the consummate manager; he runs the day-to-day activities of this company. Jack Bogle's primary involvement has really been as the leader . . . his has been the vision."

Of course, everyone in the company accepted that Vanguard would maintain the fundamental principles of the past: low-cost operations, disciplined investment policies, high-quality service, no-load distribution, candid communications—in all, putting shareholder interests first. There might be some tinkering with tactics in the post-Bogle era, but the underlying mutual corporate structure, the heart and soul of the Vanguard experiment, was sacred. Said one Vanguard insider, "There is no one sitting around here saying, 'Wait till Bogle leaves and we'll bring the company public; we'll all be filthy rich.' None of us is naive enough to deny that our success is built on our mutual structure. That's the most fundamental part of the equation."

■ ■ ■

Although retirement clearly was on his mind, Bogle was not acting like someone who was ready to relinquish power. In December 1994, Bogle and six other senior executives were gathered at the American College in suburban Philadelphia, an executive education center, for a two-day strategy session. Attending the meeting, besides Bogle and Brennan, were Jeremy Duffield, Ian MacKinnon, Bob DiStefano, Bill McNabb, Gus Sauter, Jim Norris, and John Heywood. Bogle seemed especially combative during the course of the two-day session, and some who were in attendance later expressed disappointment that there was not more give-and-take about issues they wanted to discuss. Then, early in May 1995, Bogle learned from a story in *The Wall Street Journal* that Vanguard had signed a letter sent by several mutual fund firms to California governor Pete Wilson urging him to turn up the pressure on Orange County, which was maneuvering in bankruptcy court to default on $1.3 billion in municipal bonds. Bogle was upset when he read the story for the first time in the paper, believing that a letter expressing Vanguard's policy position should have been submitted to him for approval. Again, not the posture of a man with one foot out the door.

Yet shortly thereafter, when Bogle made the decision to retire, he did so quickly and without fretting about it. The only Vanguard person he told about the decision was Brennan; otherwise, he kept his decision a secret until the May 19 Vanguard board meeting. In the end, what tipped the scales for Bogle was his health. He knew that he faced an uncertain future because of his heart ailment. Further, he did not want to cling to power past retirement age. Most important, he wanted to leave while Vanguard was at the top. By mid-1995, Vanguard had emerged as one of the most successful firms in the industry, its reputation was at an all-time high, and the Bogle Barometer—the letters that streamed into his office—expressed little but praise and respect for Bogle and the company he had founded.

At the May 19 board meeting, Bogle announced that he planned to step down as CEO effective January 31, 1996, but that he would, if the board approved, remain as chairman of the board. Bogle was ambiguous about what would change once the transition had taken effect. He told associates that he planned to come in to work four days a week, so little would change there, except he would take more vacation time. He indicated that he planned to continue to watch over the interests of the shareholders and the crew, to write, to give speeches, and to try to keep the mutual fund industry moving in what he saw as the right direction. In short, he would continue to be Jack Bogle.

A May 25 press release confirmed these details. While the release appeared to convey the message that Bogle was stepping down, toward the end it quoted him as promising, "I will still be around." The press release also announced that he planned to nominate Brennan, his heir apparent, as his successor as CEO. In the release, Bogle called Brennan "the best person I could possibly have found . . . a man of extraordinary character, intelligence, diligence, and judgment." It should be noted that Bogle recommended, and the board agreed, to make Brennan's appointment effective seven months later because Bogle felt that Vanguard should give shareholders plenty of notice before the change actually occurred.

When the news became public, rumors began to fly that Bogle had resigned because he was nearing a heart transplant operation, rumors that Bogle would not talk about other than to say that the near future seemed "very scary." He continued to receive letters from shareholders wishing him well and offering him advice. One writer proposed that he read a book about a cayenne pepper therapy as a cure for his deteriorating heart. Bogle responded, "Believe me, I am at the point where I'd try just about anything!" Dr. Lown, too, expressed respect for his patient: "I haven't seen anyone live as long with such a complex heart ailment. His life is an important lesson for me as a doctor and for others who are much less afflicted than Jack Bogle has been. It has been a lesson for others who have yielded to their disease totally and let the ailment dominate their lives."

The press gave Bogle's announcement considerable coverage and reacted favorably to Brennan's accession. There were also accolades about the succession plan. *Mutual Fund Market News* reported, "Analysts, industry watchers and management experts are all applauding the move, while lamenting the industry's loss of a true leader. Said Jeffrey Sonnenfeld, a management professor who runs the Center for Leadership and Career Studies at Emory University, and the author of *Hero's Farewell,* a book on CEO succession, 'It's a win-win situation. An internally groomed John Brennan shows great continuity of command. This has really reduced a lot of anxiety. There is no period of bewilderment and confusion. No horse race. No playing of individuals off of each other.' "

Bogle had long worried about Vanguard's future, expressing concern that, for all of its success, it could fall abruptly from its heights. That future was now in the hands of Jack Brennan, and all eyes were focused on him. While most were confident that he would hew to the basic Vanguard values, no one expected that he would be a carbon copy of Bogle, and few thought that would be a good idea. "There will never be another Jack Bogle," said Gerald Perritt, editor of the *Mutual Fund Letter,* "but Brennan is more polished, more of a diplomat, and that's what Vanguard will need in the years ahead." Said Ken Martin, managing director of Hay Management Consultants, "Jack Brennan is the perfect complement to Bogle partly because there's a clear generational split between them, mentor-student, rather than a peer filling Bogle's shoes. Brennan is a very bright, aggressive guy who's been able to adapt . . . to working for a very dominating, opinionated, entrepreneurial kind of a guy, a mythic figure."

The transition raised a number of questions about the shape that Brennan's leadership would take. First, would Brennan maintain Bogle's focus on the shareholder? Noted economist and Nobel laureate Paul Samuelson believed that Vanguard's shareholder focus was "the primary thing that differentiates Vanguard from the rest. I'm interested to see under

Brennan if it will have this focus. Vanguard is essentially run for the interest of the investors. It's not true of the 20 biggest companies in the mutual fund industry. Not one of them other than Vanguard is, by my way of keeping the score, focused on the net interests of investors." Many of Vanguard's supporters, though, recognized that it was relatively easy to stand on principle while riding the bull market of the 1980s and 1990s. They were worried about how Brennan would react if the marketplace became less accommodating.

A second question concerned Brennan's attitude toward the rest of the mutual fund industry. Brennan was not cut from the same cloth as Bogle, so it seemed unlikely that he would suddenly turn preacher or that the competition with Fidelity would be the good-guys-versus-bad-guys morality play that it had seemed to be in the past. Some Vanguard executives worried that Brennan had spent too many years (13) under Bogle's tutelage to take advantage of his newfound powers and responsibilities. Their concern was that even with Bogle abandoning the center stage, the new leadership would have to continue to explain and justify Bogle's views.

A third question concerned Brennan's willingness to take Vanguard down new paths. While most Vanguard executives seemed to want someone who, like Bogle, was able to enunciate basic values, they also wanted someone with more of a pragmatic outlook. In the three years since the 1992 Skytop speech, Bogle had desanctified five of the most important of his sacred cows: Vanguard was itself managing the Aggressive Growth Portfolio of the new Horizon Fund; the Information Technology Voyage was proceeding with remarkable success; the implementation of Vanguard's investment advisory program had almost reached fruition (although many were disappointed that it had taken far longer than anyone had anticipated); the super-low-cost Admiral Funds were introduced; an office was opened in Phoenix. Yet some of the executives who had heard the Skytop speech had hoped that more changes would have taken place.

A final question, related to the third, was whether Vanguard would remain strictly a mutual fund organization or whether it would evolve into a fully diversified financial services organization. Bogle had always resisted the idea of Vanguard itself being involved in other financial services; in support of his view, he pointed to an unsuccessful attempt on the part of Fidelity to enter the credit card business. Some Vanguard insiders, however, wanted to rethink that resistance. Said one, "There's no doubt it may add to our expense ratio to get into CDs or the insurance business, but we could do it with higher quality, and we already have a strong fixed-income management business, so that would be a perfect match for us." Others wanted to see Vanguard expand its still small brokerage business. Yet another area ripe for expansion was the international arena. Said one Vanguard official: "We'll be offering funds in Europe someday. I don't think we'll be doing it while Jack Bogle's alive."

In one of the few public comments Brennan has made about how he would put his stamp on Vanguard, he told *Money* magazine in May 1995, "The home computer is becoming a new version of the 800 telephone number. Within a few years, people will be able to transfer money from their bank to buy a Vanguard fund through their home computers. I want to be sure we make the investment to stay competitive in the new technology." Brennan also said he would stress index funds in the future, as Bogle had: "It is becoming more and more clear that indexing works, that it is not just theoretical. I think competitors will find it hard to match us on indexing because it must be done so cheaply to be effective. And we're the best at low-cost management. Jack Bogle made sure of that."

Brennan offered more detail on his views regarding the transition in an interview with the author, although he spoke with a slight edge to his voice, as though uncomfortable with the subject. He addressed the subject of his leadership versus Bogle's: "I will not be Jack Bogle, I cannot be Jack Bogle, and I should not try to be Jack Bogle. However, I can, must, and should be an articulate spokesman for Vanguard, for shareholders, and for fund investors as a whole. Will I do it the same way as Jack? No. Will I be as fervent as Jack about it? I hope so."

Brennan then went on to discuss how the company is likely to change: "The company is dramatically different today than it was even 10 years ago. Our resources to make positive changes for the shareholders are dramatically improved. To facilitate the way we serve our clients, we'll spend $20 million this year on experimental technology; that kind of an investment would have been 20 percent of our budget a decade ago. I think we'll see the most change in the way we interact with our clients. But what will change is less important than what will not change, and that is the underlying philosophy and values of the organization."

When asked precisely what he will change, Brennan concluded: "I'm not a change-for-the-sake-of-change person. I don't see any reason to immediately put my stamp on the organization. The questions I want to answer are: Will we still be the most respected organization in the business when I leave? Will the value we provide to shareholders be substantially greater? And will the core values be unchanged in the face of continued growth? That's how I'll measure my success."

Brennan revealed much about the kind of leader he is likely to be when asked to reflect on his 13 years with the company. He noted that what struck him most was the way the company had remained true to its principles. "I don't think we've compromised a nickel on our fundamental values as we've gotten bigger," he said. "We don't have big shot executives. No one has company cars, parking spaces, or club memberships. I even feel a little bit guilty having an office with a window. We travel coach on planes, we eat in the company cafeteria, we don't play golf, we don't boondoggle." Referring to the enormous assets that Vanguard has accumulated, Brennan noted with pride, "I still look at every dollar that we spend as if it were coming out of my own pocket."

Brennan also addressed the issue of compensation: "Many of our competitors sneer at us, because we're not worth the $10 million or $100 million—or even $1 billion or more—that they may be worth personally. The wealth we've created goes back to our shareholders . . . I think there is an element of jealousy about the cleanliness of our existence [and] our sharply focused approach to this business . . . Most industries need a Vanguard, an oddball who allows you to calibrate yourself. We're the proverbial open book."

■ ■ ■

It pleased Bogle that, when he announced he was stepping down from active duty, he received warm praise from many friends—and some former foes. Robert Doran, now chairman and managing partner of Wellington Management Company, had by 1995 left behind much of the bitterness of the early 1970s. "I have no difficulty saying with sincerity that Jack is a very brilliant person," he said. "His concept of Vanguard, while not the only way that a mutual fund company can thrive and prosper, was a unique way. He really carved out an important place in the business. Vanguard's structure has . . . served the shareholders well." Doran conceded that his struggles with Bogle had been difficult, but, as he pointed out, "There has to have been something in the spirit or personality of the individuals that allowed them to overcome some period of awkwardness and then serve the shareholders, do the job, move on." Indeed, in 1995 Wellington Management Company still managed $45 billion of assets for Vanguard.

Arthur Zeikel of Merrill Lynch led the chorus of praise: "He treats people with a high degree of integrity. He won't lie, he won't steal, he won't cheat. He stands for goodness and virtue. When he sees things are wrong, he's a standard-bearer protecting the industry from falling into ill repute . . . Jack Bogle is the only one in the industry who could bring together the intellectual understanding of the process, the willingness to do it, and the stick-to-it-iveness that allowed him to build a business around his theories. This guy is America's evangelist."

Peter L. Bernstein, a well-known economic analyst and author of *Capital Ideas,* offered this assessment of Bogle: "You get the sense that at Fidelity they must hate him plenty. Fidelity came reluctantly to no-load and it was the competition of Vanguard that did it. Jack Bogle has done everything possible to solicit that dislike; he differentiates his product and that gives him more ego satisfaction. The more they hate him, the more he thinks that what he's doing is right. He's a very unusual man. You don't encounter people with that level of integrity in any business."

Recognition of the unique strategy that Bogle had established for Vanguard also came from outside the industry. Harvard Business School professor Michael E. Porter—generally considered America's preeminent academic expert on corporate strategy—singled out Vanguard in a keynote speech at the 1993 general membership meeting of the Investment Company Institute. With Bogle seated in the audience, he told the gathering of mutual fund executives that the industry had grown fat and lazy and was in danger of losing its competitive edge. It had become a "me-too" industry, with most companies undifferentiated from one another and stuck in the middle. Bogle's rivals were aghast to hear Porter say that only one firm in the entire industry had differentiated itself from the pack— Vanguard, the only firm he mentioned in his one-and-a-half-hour lecture. He cited Vanguard as having "a genuine, unique, sustainable competitive advantage" and told Vanguard's rivals that they would soon learn from the Vanguard challenge what rivalry was all about. Porter went on to warn that "if Vanguard abandons its posture as a measured, careful, gentlemanly competitor, the industry hasn't seen anything, yet." Praise like this for the company he gave birth to must have gratified Bogle more than any personal praise he could have received.

■ ■ ■

On October 18, 1995, Bogle entered a Philadelphia hospital. For some time he had been on a list of candidates for a heart transplant. His cardiologists decided his heart had deteriorated so much that he should have the operation. He was expected to remain in the hospital for at least three months awaiting a suitable heart, so he turned the hospital room into an office.

He saw Brennan once a week, spoke on the phone with Vanguard executives, continued to write annual reports, and spoke with the author a number of times. His spirits were high, and although he never said so, he seemed to look forward to surgery so that he could carry on with his life.

Though he had done more than anyone else to transform the mutual fund industry, Bogle still wished for more change. He wanted the industry to do more for fund shareholders, and he still hoped that his conservative approach to investing, especially indexing, would attract more imitators. He wished that fund directors would be more accountable and that advisory fees would come down more. (Brennan was not so sure that was such a good thing to wish for: "Bogle would like them to come down because he's a missionary. I'm just a business guy. I like being in the real low-cost position relative to the industry.") He also wished that some of Vanguard's equity funds were performing better.

Bogle could take comfort, though, in the knowledge that the mutual fund industry appeared to be moving in the direction he wanted. A conviction seemed to be growing in the mid-1990s that fund costs were too high, that service could be better, that staying the course was more practical than seeking short-term gains, that it was not possible to predict how investments would fare based strictly on past performance. The mutual fund industry had not yet come around entirely to Bogle's way of thinking, but it did seem to be acknowledging that his ways had merit. While his quest to transform the industry had not yet been fulfilled, the Vanguard experiment had proved the worth and durability of the philosophy adopted by Bogle at the company's founding. And that, as Jack Bogle liked to say, was a good start.

EPILOGUE

JANUARY 1996

Early in January, from his hospital room, John Bogle penned his traditional New Year's message to the Vanguard crew, his final message as Vanguard's chief executive officer. He had gained increasing confidence that the seeds of transformation sown by Vanguard were beginning to sprout—that the quest to transform the mutual fund industry was no longer an impossible dream.

As he saw it, Vanguard was beginning to have an impact on the industry's high costs, lack of candor, and investment techniques. In his message, entitled "Patience, Persistence, and Courage," he said:

> Few observers have yet discerned the full extent to which our persistence has already changed this industry. But the outlines are beginning to come into focus.
>
> - In the money market fund segment our low expense ratios have set the standard, with these clear consequences: (1) the virtual inability of funds with *grossly* excessive costs to extract significant amounts of assets from investors; (2) the formation by two of our major competitors of new "lines" of funds for smart (and substantial) investors, priced well below their mainstream funds, if still far above ours; and (3) the tawdry practice of "teaser yields," in which a fund's yield is temporarily subsidized by its adviser in order to overstate the yield that can be expected in the future. The first two trends

clearly suggest that intelligent investors are aware of costs; the third is an industry "black eye" that, sadly, goes mostly ignored by the press.

- In the bond fund segment, Vanguard has become the largest presence among direct marketing firms, with investor assets now exceeding $40 billion. What is more, our bond fund assets are now 8% above the level reached at the close of 1993 (near the market peak that preceded "the troubles" of 1994). During this same period, Fidelity's bond fund assets dropped by –16%, T. Rowe Price's by –6%, and Scudder's by –24%(!). A *New York Times* headline several months ago graphically illustrated Vanguard's performance leadership using a "horse-race" illustration. The *Times* headline told the story: "Taking a Shine to Bonds? Some Fund Groups Have an Edge: Costs Make a Big Difference over the Long Haul." The text of the article focused directly on Vanguard. Repeated over and over again, this message about the impact of costs is finally getting across to the public.

- In the equity fund field, it is probably fair to say that we have made lesser inroads. But *major* differences in costs *are* becoming more important, contributing to significant favorable performance margins over time. (No matter that they count little in *annual* returns.) Clear definitions of fund policies are becoming more important, as are clear statements of past returns and future risks. Both of these are Vanguard trademarks. And, of course, indexing has "come into its own" as a factor in the marketplace.

- As the leading "pure no-load" fund organization, our startling 1977 decision to go no load has developed into an industry blockbuster. No-load funds are becoming more and more commonplace, sales loads are declining, and "hidden loads" (via 12b-1 distribution charges) are becoming anathema to fund investors. Despite these positive changes, hefty "advisory fees" will result in shareholders saving few, if any, dollars. I am confident that in the long run the intelligent investor will not be deceived.

- Finally, other fund complexes are starting to emulate Vanguard in the completeness and candor of their reports to shareholders. Our suggestion that mutual fund annual reports provide a mandatory "management disclosure and analysis" section and a chart showing ten-year returns compared to an appropriate market index have been adopted by the Securities

and Exchange Commission. If only fund shareholders will
now read—and carefully evaluate—these records, Vanguard
will be the beneficiary.

In all, persistence is carrying the day for Vanguard.

Bogle believed that in the enormous profits made by those who had
formed mutual fund firms lay a thesis that was building its own antithesis.
Once the founders had sold control of their management companies to the
public—or to banks or other financial services firms eagerly seeking quick
and easy access to the booming field of mutual funds—would not the
purchase of management companies by their funds become more accept-
able? In an industry downturn, could not such purchases be made by the
funds at arm's length and on a self-financing basis? This concept, of
course, is what Bogle had proposed to the directors of Wellington Fund
and the other funds in the Wellington Group as in mid-1974. The directors,
however, found this course of action too radical and fraught with regulatory constraints, and followed a more deliberate, one-step-at-a-time course
that, while quite different, would finally lead to the same destination. "But
who can say," Bogle asked, "that, in this era of rapid change, 'another
Vanguard'—or even the Vanguard structure as an industry standard—is
not on the horizon?"

■ ■ ■

"If a man from Mars were to alight on the U.S. financial world today, he
would surely think," says Bogle, "that the present structure of the mutual
fund industry was out of tune with reality. Why are the fund shareholders
treated as second class citizens, subject to the domination of investment
advisors? What is it that compels a $10 billion fund complex—there are
50 complexes that have surpassed that asset level—generating, say, $100
million of revenues, to be operated under a management contract that may
result in costs of $60 million and before-tax profits of $40 million?" The
answers, Bogle asserts, are not self-evident.

Even if a major restructuring of mutual fund management companies
does not come to pass, Bogle believes that there are at least two other
courses of action that would help give fund shareholders a fairer shake.
One is corporate responsibility, with fund independent directors doing
what they are enjoined to do under the preamble to the Investment Company Act: to put the interests of fund shareholders ahead of the interests
of the funds' investment advisers. "The time has come," Bogle asserts,

"for directors to stand up and be counted, and to turn down the advisers' requests for fee increases, the reasons for which are inevitably 'documented' by statistics culled by industry analysts—who, like executive compensation consultants, constantly ratchet up the expense ratio hurdle rate." As Bogle cynically notes, "God forbid that the fees we pay to our advisers should be in the lamentable bottom quartile."

Indeed, Bogle urges, it is the fund directors who should demand lower advisory fees, who should demand information on how these fees are actually spent. How much for advice? For administration? For advertising and promotion? And for whose benefit? "After a certain point," Bogle queries, "does a mutual fund's growth have *any* benefit to fund shareholders, or is it in fact a detriment to the fund's performance? Or is it simply a way of generating still higher profits to the adviser, part of the business of asset gathering that so preoccupies investment advisers?"

In short, Bogle believes that directors need to act with greater independence, knowledge, and vigor. And he believes that the leaders of the Securities and Exchange Commission could make that happen, "if only they would mount a 'bully pulpit' and call for a higher level of diligence and responsibility for fund directors." There is a point, he believes, at which that would happen.

Even if the bully pulpit remains silent, there is a second course of action that would serve fund shareholders in a similar fashion: competition. At present, Bogle observed, fund investors have abundant, even infinite, statistical information ("Too much?" he asked) on costs, past returns, and even some concept of riskiness. Increasingly, they will use that information to develop a sound base of knowledge. And, with time (and experience, probably hard-earned), that knowledge will develop into the wisdom that will make them more successful investors. Said Bogle, "With fund performance known only in the past, and with risk becoming manifest only in the future, price competition—the impact of costs on investment returns—will become a beacon." Adam Smith, he believed, would be applauding.

Are Bogle's thoughts simply idle musings? Or are they the result of missionary zeal? Or of a winning business formula? Or even the vestiges of a power struggle that took place two decades earlier? Only time will tell. But as 1996 began, it delighted Bogle that, as the focus of evaluating performance seemed to shift from the individual fund to the fund family, Vanguard received the number one rating among fund families of every major publication tackling the complex issue: *U.S. News & World Report;*

Barron's; Forbes, based on its list of best buys; and even (albeit in a four-way tie) *Worth* magazine, published by a wholly owned subsidiary of Fidelity. ("The ultimate proof of editorial independence," Bogle added.)

And so, the Vanguard experiment had not only come to successful fruition in a governance sense but also blossomed to become a major force in a competitive marketplace, having earned the most important accolade of all: first in the returns earned for fund shareholders. It was on this gratifying note that Bogle relinquished his leadership of Vanguard, knowing that his quest to transform the mutual fund industry had already made an impact. As Paul Samuelson said in his foreword to *Bogle on Mutual Funds,* "John Bogle has changed a basic industry in the optimal direction. Of few can this be said."

■ ■ ■

NOTE: Jack Bogle received his heart transplant on February 21, 1996, and was released from Philadelphia's Hahnemann University Hospital to return home on March 2. On April 17, he was back in his office. On April 22, he traveled to New York to receive the 1995 Fund Leader of the Year award from *Fund Action* newsletter. On May 8, his 67th birthday, he gave a speech titled "The Case for Index Funds," before a national conference of financial analysts (the Association for Investment Management and Research) in Atlanta. His son John gave him a squash racquet for his birthday. Three days later he was hitting the ball around with son Andrew, Bogle's first taste of a squash court since 1989.

On May 10, 1996, just one year after reaching the $150 billion mark, total assets of the Vanguard funds crossed the $200 billion mark. Bogle was thrilled by Vanguard's milestone, and by his own recovery. He described his second chance at life as "miraculous."

APPENDICES

A P P E N D I X   I

The Vanguard Group: Calendar Year-End Net Assets
(in Millions)

Traditionally Managed Portfolios	1975	1980	1985	1990	1995
Windsor	$438	$828	$4,043	$6,377	$13,072
Wellington	776	612	813	2,449	12,656
Windsor II			212	1,926	9,298
Wellesley	125	100	224	1,022	7,181
STAR			112	1,038	4,842
International Growth			137	734	3,676
U.S. Growth	195	165	149	356	3,361
Primecap			54	305	3,074
Asset Allocation				179	1,595
Explorer	10	28	348	210	1,502
Specialized Health Care			18	164	1,473
Morgan Growth	90	259	665	633	1,314
Equity Income				399	1,103
Other (16)	44	166	1,609	1,838	6,455
29 Portfolios* Class Total	**$1,678**	**$2,158**	**$8,384**	**$17,630**	**$70,602**

Defined Asset Class Portfolios	1975	1980	1985	1990	1995
Money Market - Prime	$5	$405	$1,678	$13,464	$18,876
GNMA		25	1,115	2,469	6,247
Tax-Exempt - Intermediate-Term		21	510	1,411	5,770
Tax-Exempt - Money Market		17	661	2,536	4,076
Short-Term Corporate			193	796	3,621
High-Yield Corporate		9	592	694	2,900
Long-Term Corporate	37	37	297	1,063	2,688
Money Market - Federal			493	1,964	2,619
Money Market - U.S. Treasury			51	1,720	2,553
Tax-Exempt - Insured Long-Term			472	1,251	2,017
Tax-Exempt - High-Yield		24	580	1,017	1,988
Money Market - Admiral U.S. Treasury					1,751
Tax-Exempt - Limited-Term				270	1,683
Tax-Exempt - Pennsylvania Insured				567	1,583
Tax-Exempt - Short-Term		182	561	752	1,410
Short-Term Federal				457	1,404
Tax-Exempt - California Tax-Free MM				729	1,224
Tax-Exempt - Pennsylvania Tax-Free MM				764	1,216
Inter.-Term U.S. Treasury					1,195
Tax-Exempt - Long-Term		49	494	712	1,114
Other (17)				2,238	8,256
37 Portfolios* Class Total	**$42**	**$769**	**$7,697**	**$34,874**	**$74,191**

Index Portfolios	1975	1980	1985	1990	1995
Stock - 500 Portfolio		$99	$394	$2,173	$17,372
Stock - Institutional 500 Index				511	6,674
Bond - Total Bond Market				277	2,821
Stock - Extended Market				179	1,523
Stock - Total Stock Market					1,332
Other (14)			36	173	5,621
19 Portfolios* Class Total	**$0**	**$99**	**$430**	**$3,313**	**$35,343**
85 Portfolios* Grand Total	**$1,720**	**$3,026**	**$16,511**	**$55,817**	**$180,136**

* As of December 31, 1995

A P P E N D I X   II

Vanguard Fund Expense Ratios and Value Added
versus the Mutual Fund Industry

	Vanguard Average Assets (in Millions)	Expense Ratios*			Value Added** (in Millions)
		Vanguard	Industry	Spread	
1974	$1,674	0.71%	1.08%	0.37%	$6
1975	1,759	0.68	1,08	0.40	7
1976	1,967	0.61	1.04	0.43	8
1977	1,933	0.61	0.99	0.38	7
1978	1,919	0.62	1.00	0.38	7
1979	2,197	0.58	0.99	0.41	9
1980	2,658	0.59	0.99	0.40	11
1981	3,460	0.59	0.97	0.38	13
1982	4,544	0.61	0.99	0.38	17
1983	6,419	0.60	0.94	0.34	22
1984	8,233	0.54	0.95	0.41	34
1985	13,018	0.51	0.96	0.45	59
1986	20,489	0.46	0.99	0.53	109
1987	28,188	0.40	1.01	0.61	172
1988	30,639	0.40	1.09	0.69	211
1989	40,695	0.35	1.09	0.74	301
1990	50,916	0.35	1.09	0.74	376
1991	64,841	0.32	1.07	0.75	484
1992	84,549	0.31	1.03	0.72	611
1993	109,501	0.30	1.02	0.72	788
1994	129,427	0.30	1.05	0.75	969
1995	153,754	0.31	1.10	0.79	1,219

* Value Added = Spread x Average Assets

** Average funds expenses as a percentage of average net assets.

Note: The mutual fund industry comprised 270 stock-based funds and 45 bond funds at the end of 1974 and 3,899 stock-based funds, 3337 bond funds, and 1,268 money market funds at the end of 1995. Expense ratios of stock-based funds rose from 1.02% (est.) to 1.44% during this period.

Notes

CHAPTER 1

"I wouldn't slacken . . .," Jack Bogle, interview, August 14, 1995.

"The more competitive, determined, egocentric . . .," from Jack Bogle's eulogy of David Bogle, January 4, 1995.

"It opened my eyes . . .," Jack Bogle, interview, August 14, 1994.

"Not just to tell . . .," Jack Bogle, interview, August 14, 1995.

"I thought I was in heaven . . .," Jack Bogle, interview, May 3, 1995.

"The investment company can realize . . .," "The Economic Role of the Investment Company," a thesis submitted by John C. Bogle to the Princeton University Department of Economics, April 10, 1951, p. 123.

"The investment company has grown up . . .," ibid., p. 122.

"The expectation of miracles . . .," ibid.

"The principal function . . .," Warren Motley, "Regulation of Investment Companies Since 1940," *Harvard Law Review,* July 1950.

CHAPTER 2

"I knew we could . . .," "A Mutual Fund Pioneer Looks Ahead," *Investment Dealers' Digest,* February 29, 1960, unpaged.

CHAPTER 3

"He knows more about . . .," Walter Morgan, interview, May 4, 1995.

"The best thing I ever did . . .," Walter Morgan, letter to the author, November 13, 1995.

"A loyal Princetonian . . .," speech given by Jack Bogle on June 13, 1988.

"Over in the corner . . .," Walter Morgan, interview, May 4, 1995.

"I was clearly . . .," Jack Bogle, interview, February 28, 1995.

CHAPTER 4

"Normal heart," information obtained from records at Blair Academy.

"I was in a decent . . .," Jack Bogle, interview, July 13, 1995.

"It's something that has made . . .," Jack Bogle, interview, May 8, 1995.

"If you're stupid . . .," ibid.

"I liked him . . .," Robert Doran, interview, June 26, 1995.

"You both have to be . . .," John "Jay" Sherrerd, interview, May 17, 1995.

"We're both pretty reasonable . . .," Paul Miller, interview, May 17, 1995.

"Everyone likes a deal . . .," Jack Bogle, interview, May 8, 1995.

"I had this naive idea . . .," ibid.

"Putting together Wellington's . . .," "The Whiz Kids Take Over at Wellington," *Institutional Investor,* January 1968, pp. 24–65.

CHAPTER 5

"They put the pacemaker . . .," Jack Bogle, interview, May 8, 1995.

"It was clear that his survival . . .," Bernard Lown, interview, October 2, 1995.

"Even though I was very skeptical . . .," Jack Bogle, interview, August 14, 1995.

"People who didn't work . . .," John Jackson, interview, July 11, 1995.

"Bogle was right on top . . .," Charles Root, interview, May 9, 1995.

"While the Boston group's . . .," Raymond J. Klapinsky, interview, May 8, 1995.

"Jack's way is *the* way . . .," Barbara Hauptfuhrer, interview, August 3, 1995.

"I knew I wasn't tactful . . .," Jack Bogle, interview, June 21, 1995.

"I don't mind knowing . . .," Jack Bogle, interview, May 8, 1995.

"Private independent . . .," Robert Doran, interview, June 27, 1995.

"At the time, the investment . . .," Jim Riepe, interview, July 24, 1995.

"I taught Jack . . .," Walter Morgan, quoted in "John C. Bogle: Wellington Whiz Kid Grows Older," *Institutional Investor,* June 1972, pp. 63–100.

"Wellington Management's board and I . . .," "Vanguard: A Fund Family for the 1990s," *Fortune,* December 31, 1991, pp. 80–88.

"The elephants were fighting . . .," Jan Twardowski, interview, July 26, 1995.

CHAPTER 6

"Through the wringer . . .," memo written by Charles Root, August 20, 1970.

"Jack has decided . . .," ibid.

"JCB apparently finds . . .," memo written by Charles Root, September 16, 1970.

"CEO out of touch . . .," ibid.

"Serious enough to blow . . .," memo written by Charles Root, October 16, 1970.

"Bogle acknowledged . . .," memo written by Charles Root, December 4, 1970.

"I in effect threw down . . .," Charles Root, interview, May 9, 1995.

"JCB, WNT and RWD all agreed . . .," memo written by Charles Root, December 14, 1970.

Who was "thunderstruck . . .," Charles Root, interview, May 9, 1995.

CHAPTER 7

"I am concerned about . . .," letter written by Barbara Hauptfuhrer to Charles Root, January 3, 1974.

"It would be consistent with . . .," "Mutualizing" Wellington Management Company, a memo submitted by Jack Bogle on January 12, 1974 to the independent directors of the funds.

"We knew that the dismissal . . .,"
Robert Doran, interview, November 20,
1995.

"We are sitting here today . . .,"
statement by Jack Bogle to Wellington
Management Board, January 23, 1974.

"The measure of a man . . .," John
Neff, interview, June 21, 1995.

CHAPTER 8

"I deplored the whole . . .," John
Jackson, interview, July 11, 1995.

CHAPTER 9

"These guys were at each other's . . .,"
Jan Twardowski, interview, July 26,
1995.

"A popularity contest . . .," "Wellington
Meeting: No Waterloo This Time,"
Philadelphia Bulletin, May 1, 1974.

"Everyone must have known . . .," Jack
Bogle, interview, June 21, 1995.

"Substantial corporate self-
sufficiency . . .," quoted in *Philadelphia
Inquirer,* July 30, 1974.

"Bogle wanted mutualization . . ."
Boston Globe, August 5, 1974.

"The biggest risk was that . . .," Ray
Klapinsky, interview, May 4, 1995.

"At the time, there really wasn't
much . . .," ibid.

CHAPTER 10

"A little too much . . .," Jack Bogle,
interview, May 8, 1995.

"The name Vanguard was almost too
good . . .," ibid.

"Don't interpret [the Wellington
Compromise] . . .," "Bogle's Do-It-
Yourself Mutual Funds," *The Sunday
Bulletin Business,* February 9, 1975.

"We all thought it was . . .," Karen
West, interview, May 4, 1995.

"I didn't realize until a year . . .," Ian
MacKinnon, interview, May 3, 1995.

CHAPTER 11

"To confront that issue directly . . .,"
Jack Bogle, interview, May 18, 1995.

"The big competition in the . . .," from
a speech given by Jack Bogle to an
investment group, Boston,
Massachusetts, September 9, 1971.

"I might have . . .," Robert Doran,
interview, November 20, 1995.

"Doran stated that the . . .," Robert
Doran, interview, November 20, 1995.

"You'd come into a meeting . . .," Ray
Klapinsky, interview, May 4, 1995.

"He was properly concerned . . .," John
Jackson, interview, July 11, 1995.

"I was opposed to it . . .," Walter
Morgan, interview, May 4, 1995.

"He went ballistic." Jan Twardowski,
interview, July 26, 1995.

"That decision was significant . . .,"
Phil Fina, interview, May 15, 1995.

"It is simply impossible . . .," Jack
Bogle, interview, August 17, 1995.

CHAPTER 12

"Jack likes the 18th century . . .," Chad
Hardwick, interview, July 10, 1995.

"Vanguard by the year 2020 . . .," Jack
Bogle, interview, February 28, 1995.

"It's fair to say . . .," Jack Bogle,
interview, February 28, 1995.

"Bully pulpit, like Teddy
Roosevelt . . .," Warren Boroson, "Hug
an Index Fund Today," *The Record*
(Bergen County, New Jersey), July 29,
1995.

"Vanguard stands alone . . .," speech
given by Jack Bogle, December 14,
1990.

"There are two ways . . .," Jim Norris, interview, May 10, 1995.

". . . miffed . . .," Jack Bogle, interview, May 18, 1995.

"Jack is in many ways . . .," George Putnam, interview, May 15, 1995.

"There is no question . . .," Jim Norris, interview, May 10, 1995.

"The worst argument you . . .," William McNabb, interview, July 11, 1995.

"most of the people . . .," Ken Martin, interview, May 8, 1995.

"impetuous . . ." Jim Norris, interview, May 10, 1995.

"I don't think any institution . . .," Jack Bogle, interview, July 13, 1995.

"Ego is not a weakness . . .," ibid.

"Everyone here feels . . .," Jeremy Duffield, interview, May 4, 1995.

"When I think of Jack's . . .," Ken Martin, interview, May 8, 1995.

"I wouldn't want on my . . .," Jack Bogle, quoted in "Doing It Jack Bogle's Way," *Institutional Investor,* March 1988, pp. 125–133.

"I'd walk by thousands . . .," John Bogle, Jr., interview, May 16, 1995.

"I've accumulated a decent . . .," Jack Bogle, interview, July 11, 1995.

"For him it was a big . . ." Jim Riepe, interview, July 24, 1995.

"You would think that he . . .," John "Jay" Sherrerd, interview, May 17, 1995.

"I learned to expect . . .," Jan Twardowski, interview, July 26, 1995.

The Lexington Avenue line anecdote was told to the author by Duncan McFarland in an interview on May 15, 1995.

"Jack really has a researcher's . . .," Burton Malkiel, interview, July 24, 1995.

"I wanted to write . . .," Jack Bogle quoted in the *West Palm Beach Post,* August 22, 1993.

CHAPTER 13

"What the financial objective . . .," memo, Jack Bogle, December 1987.

"Wellington Fund's rank . . .," memo to Walter L. Morgan from JCB, 1959.

"We started with the structure . . .," Jack Bogle, interview, August 14, 1995.

"Clearly, given their risks . . .," from Vanguard's Plain Talk about High Yield Bonds.

"I again caution you . . .," Chairman's letter in 1995 Annual Report for Vanguard Index Trust.

"Makes a big difference . . .," Bill McNabb, interview, July 11, 1995.

CHAPTER 14

"Sometimes we thought . . .," Charles Root, interview, May 9, 1995.

"I *love* crisis . . .," speech given by Jack Bogle at the Vanguard officers dinner, November 2, 1989.

"Over the years . . .," letter from Jeremy Duffield to the author, December 4, 1995.

"Caring is a mutual affair." John Bogle, speech to the Vanguard crew, 1988.

"It is really incredible . . .," John Bogle, speech to the Vanguard crew, 1988.

"Bringing out new funds . . .," "The Best in the Business," *Financial World,* February 5, 1991, pp. 32–36.

"Most advertising takes the thrust . . .," ibid.

"Bogle's relationship with the press . . .," Jack Brennan, interview, May 3, 1995.

"When the story came out . . .," Daniel F. Wiener, interview, July 10, 1995.

"In today's boom in this . . .," "In the Vanguard Except in Pay," *Forbes Magazine,* Date 1992.

"Publicity seeker . . .," Jack Bogle, interview, February 28, 1995.

"I hardly know where to begin . . ." Bogle letter to James W. Michaels, April 25, 1975.

CHAPTER **15**

"It was a helluva shock . . .," Jeremy Duffield, interview, May 4, 1995.

"If people want thrills . . .," quoted in the *Philadelphia Inquirer,* April 27, 1981.

"It started out . . .," Bill McNabb, interview, July 11, 1995.

"Never underestimate . . .," Jack Bogle, speech to the Vanguard crew, June 7, 1995.

CHAPTER **16**

"You kind of mentally . . .," Ian MacKinnon, interview, May 3, 1995.

"One of the best . . .," Morningstar Mutual Funds.

"I was only a half-generation . . .," Jim Riepe, interview, July 24, 1995.

"I didn't understand the mechanics . . .," Jack Brennan, interview, May 18, 1995.

"Arguably the most exciting . . .," ibid.

CHAPTER **17**

"There is only so much return . . .," Jack Bogle, interview, August 14, 1995.

"Index funds are a result . . .," "Professional Profile: John C. Bogle: No Frills and No-load at Vanguard," *Financial World,* 1978.

"We've beaten the market . . .," Richard Fentin, interview, June 26, 1995.

"an artistic if not . . .," Jack Bogle, "The Triumph of Indexing," The Vanguard Group, 1995.

"During the first quarter . . .," "The Triumph of Indexing," written by Jack Bogle, January 1995.

"Conceivably . . .," Gus Sauter, interview, May 18, 1995.

"The passive investment strategy . . .," Arnold Kaufman quoted in *Atlanta Constitution,* August 30, 1993.

"We aggressively manage . . .," Richard Fentin, interview, June 26, 1995.

Peter Lynch's remarks about indexing come from "Peter Lynch Talks about Why He's Quitting Magellan," *Barron's,* April 2, 1990.

"Call It Bogle's Revenge . . .," "How to Squeeze Blood from a Benchmark," *New York Times,* August 13, 1995.

"Bogle Wins," commentary from Tyler Mathisen, editor of *Money* magazine, August 1995.

"Indexing is like watching . . .," Paul Samuelson, interview, June 27, 1995.

"pantheon of heroes," William F. Sharpe.

CHAPTER **18**

"I decided then that I . . .," quoted in *Philadelphia Inquirer,* October 2, 1988.

"We had an immediate kinship . . .," ibid.

"We must ask whether . . .," "Wellington Management Company— Planning for Progress," confidential report written by Jack Bogle to the directors, officers, and staff of the Wellington Management Company, September 9, 1996, p. 13.

"Frustrating and perplexing . . .," quoted in *The Wall Street Journal,* January 25, 1972.

"well regarded among . . .," *The Wall Street Journal,* "Heard on the Street," by Dan Dorfman, January 25, 1972.

"Misunderstood and woebegone," John Train, *The New Money Masters* (New York: Harper Collins, 1989), p. 139.

"Everything gets back to total . . .," "How John Neff Does It," *Institutional Investor,* May 22, 1985, pp. 87–102.

"John felt a loyalty . . .," Jack Bogle, interview, October 24, 1995.

"I don't think I would have imagined . . ." John Neff, interview, May 4, 1995.

"Bogle mentioned it once . . .," John Neff, interview, October 23, 1995.

"His record of the past two decades . . .," *Institutional Investor,* May 1995.

"I'm only kidding slightly . . .," ibid.

"Neff's a different breed . . .," Duncan McFarland, interview, May 15, 1995.

CHAPTER 19

"It felt like we were . . .," Jack Brennan, interview, May 3, 1995.

"Not getting an answer . . .," ibid.

"We proved to our clients . . ." Jack Bogle's remarks on the first anniversary of the 1987 crash, October 19, 1988.

"I have very fond memories . . .," Jack Brennan, interview, June 28, 1995.

"better, stronger," Jack Brennan, interview, June 28, 1995.

"We have tried to avoid . . .," speech by Jack Bogle, June 13, 1988.

"Technology leadership . . .," *Forbes,* September 23, 1985.

CHAPTER 20

"The Sacred Cows" are excerpted from a speech Bogle delivered to Vanguard's senior officers on June 6, 1992.

CHAPTER 21

"We must capitalize . . .," Jack Bogle, speech, June 14, 1994.

"This is sort of a . . .," Jim Norris, interview, June 25, 1995.

"It started out with . . .," Ray Klapinsky, interview, May 4, 1995.

"It's fairly daunting . . .," Karen West, interview, May 4, 1995.

"As Bogle reluctantly . . .," "Is Vanguard Veering?" *Bloomberg Personal,* May 1995.

"Up to now . . .," Warren Boroson, "A Few Words of Wisdom," *Bergen Record.*

CHAPTER 22

"I've read all the stories . . .," Peter Lynch, interview, July 20, 1995.

"the best built ship . . .," Jack Bogle speech, December 11, 1992

"The fact is we do care . . .," Richard Fentin, interview, June 26, 1995.

"No load wasn't . . .," Peter Lynch, interview, July 20, 1995.

"our rivals are doing . . .," speech by Jack Bogle, December 14, 1990.

"When investment performance is not . . .," Jim Gately, interview, June 20, 1995.

"We don't run . . .," Jack Brennan, interview, June 28, 1995.

"There's a lot of glamour . . .," ibid.

"To me, it's inconceivable . . .," *The Wall Street Journal,* December 1, 1992.

CHAPTER **23**

"the bad boy . . .," *Washington Post,* August 18, 1993.

"The Vanguard Structure . . .," George Putnam, interview, May 15, 1995.

"What if Vanguard . . .," "Vanguard: A Fund Family for the 1990s," *Fortune,* December 31, 1991, pp. 80–88.

"Since 1981 industry expenses . . .," 1991 speech by Bogle quoted in the *Los Angeles Times,* March 7, 1993.

"Investors are figuring out . . .," Jack Bogle, interview, November 2, 1995.

"It's unconscionable. Why pay anyone . . .," *Bergen Record,* Warren Boroson, July 29, 1995.

"a combination of . . .," Arthur Zeikel, interview, May 19, 1995.

"Jack loves to get up . . .," Jon S. Fossel, interview, July 17, 1995.

"You can't expect . . .," Jack Bogle, interview, February 28, 1995.

"We offer many services . . .," quoted in "Vanguard: A Fund Family for the 1990s."

"He gives good sound . . .," Ian McKinnon, interview, May 3, 1995.

"John Bogle bestrides . . .," "The 12 Commandments of Saint Jack," *Money,* October 1993, pp. 94–98.

CHAPTER **24**

"We didn't want shareholders . . .," Barbara Hauptfuhrer, interview, August 3, 1995.

"I don't believe . . .," interview, Jim Norris, May 10, 1995.

"very scary," Jack Bogle, interview, May 8, 1995.

"I haven't seen anyone . . .," Bernard Lown, interview, October 2, 1995.

"It's a win-win situation . . .," Jeffrey Sonnenfeld, professor, Emory University.

"There will never be another . . .," Gerald Perritt, editor of the Mutual Fund Letter, quoted in "Vanguard: A Fund Family for the 1990s."

"Jack Brennan is the perfect . . .," Kenneth Martin, interview, May 8, 1995.

"the primary thing . . .," Paul Samuelson, interview, June 27, 1995.

"The home computer is becoming . . .," Jack Brennan quoted in *Money,* May 1995.

"I will not be Jack Bogle . . .," Jack Brennan, interview, October 20, 1995.

"I have no difficulty . . .," Robert Doran, interview, May 19, 1995.

"He treats people . . .," Arthur Zeikel, interview, May 19, 1995.

"You get the sense . . .," Peter Bernstein, interview, August 4, 1995.

"me too," Porter speech reported in Jack Bogle speech, June 14, 1993.

"Bogle would like . . .," Jack Brennan, interview, May 3, 1995.

Index

Scudder, 189, 246
Sears Roebuck Acceptance Corporation,
    50
Securities and Exchange Commission,
    48, 57, 101–105, 142, 149, 200,
    222, 227–228, 248
Shanahan, E., 49
Sharpe, W. F., 167
Sherrerd (Bogle), E., 20, 24
Sherrerd, J., 19–20, 24, 29, 30, 115
Sigma Funds, 71
Silberman, J., 102, 104
Small Business magazine, 207
Smart Money, 220
Smith, R., 53, 73, 76, 78, 84, 95
Society for Savings, 221
Sonnenfeld, J., 238
Standard & Poor's 500, 28, 80, 158,
    160, 161, 162, 165, 207
Stanford University, 167
State Street Investment Trust, 10, 11,
    188
Stein, H., 225
Stevens, J. L., 233
Stock, C., 200
Stradley, Ronon, Stevens & Young, 73
Swiss Army program, 185

T

Technivest Fund, 38, 43, 80
Thomson, B., 18
Thorndike, Doran, Paine & Lewis
    (TDP&L), 28, 29, 30, 31, 43, 47,
    58, 120, 144
Thorndike, W. N., 28, 33, 35, 37, 41,
    42, 46, 47, 49, 51, 52, 53, 55, 60,
    61, 66, 67, 68, 69, 88, 95
T. Rowe Price, 17, 40, 116, 146, 147,
    154, 163, 189, 192, 225, 246
Trustees' Commingled Equity Fund,
    150
Trustees's Equity Fund, 38, 43, 85
Tsai, G., 37
Twardowski, J. M., 44, 73, 98, 112,
    116, 129

U

U.S. News & World Report, 136, 05,
    248
University of Delaware, 81
University of Pennsylvania, 37
University of Virginia, 129

V

Vanderbilt University, 210
Vanguard Admiral Funds, 195–196,
    226, 239
"Vanguard Advantage, The," 234
Vanguard Advisor, The, 136
Vanguard Award for Excellence, 133
Vanguard Bond Index Fund, 162, 163
Vanguard Bond Market Fund, 162
Vanguard defined asset class portfolios,
    152–153, 157
Vanguard Emerging Markets Portfolio,
    162
Vanguard Extended Market Portfolio,
    162
Vanguard Group, 7, 26, 40, 63, 73, 81
    Brennan succeeds Bogle, 233–243
    competition with Fidelity, 195–196,
        213–222, 226, 227, 230, 242
    conservative philosophy, 119–125,
        188
    crisis with ship financing bonds,
        154–155
    culture of loyalty and respect, 127–
        137
    develops Swiss Army program, 185–
        187
    expense ratios and value added, 253
    formation, 83–89
    growth during 1980s and 1990s,
        139–147
    impact of growth on operations, 181–
        185, 190
    important role played by Neff, 169–
        179
    index funds, 157–168
    institutional business, 189

Other books of interest to you from Irwin Professional Publishing . . .

BOGLE ON MUTUAL FUNDS
New Perspectives for the Intelligent Investor
John C. Bogle

> "This is the definitive book of mutual funds—comprehensive, insightful, and—most important—honest. Any investor who owns or is thinking of owning shares in a fund should read this book from cover to cover."
>
> —Warren E. Buffett, Chairman, Berkshire Hathaway Inc.

Bogle on Mutual Funds is a straightforward assessment of the industry written for the investor who wants a true and unflinching portrayal. Bogle not only explains the basic principles of canny mutual fund investing, but *Bogle on Mutual Funds* also explores its subtle nuances and exposes the hype and fads that often lure investors into making unwise decisions. This conscientious guide offers strategies for developing a diversified portfolio that will weather the market's short-term variations. Ideal for investors at every level of expertise.
ISBN: 1-55623-860-6

THE VANGUARD RETIREMENT INVESTING GUIDE, REVISED EDITION
Includes The Vanguard Retirement Planner Software
The Vanguard Group of Investment Companies
Spotlights the major issues individuals will face as retirement nears and offers a step-by-step program for making important decisions about the future, today. The Guide will help readers analyze their goals and discover how to save, save, save—it's the prerequisite for a financially secure retirement; choose appropriate investment vehicles that will help them maximize their retirement savings; allocate their investments and savings toward specific goals and objectives. The user friendly software offers colorful graphics, informative tutorials, and clear instructions to help individuals build a retirement plan quickly and easily using two interactive modules, The Savings Planner and The Portfolio Planner.
275 pp. (Paperback)
ISBN: 0-7863-0502-9

(Continued)

SOROS

The Life, Times, and Trading Secrets of the World's Greatest Investor

Robert Slater

Since 1969, the financial world has been charting the meteoric rise of master investor and hedge fund king George Soros. The methods and tactics he has used to reach the zenith of an industry more often littered with catastrophic loss than paved with golden success have for years been Soros' most carefully guarded secret. Now, renowned biographer and *Time* reporter Robert Slater uncovers the brilliant techniques and remarkable insights that have led to the phenomenal success of this Hungarian-born investment titan—and separates the truth from the mystery and exaggerations that surround him.

ISBN: 0-7863-0361-1

INVESTING DURING RETIREMENT

The Vanguard Guide to Managing Your Retirement Assets

The Vanguard Group of Investment Companies

The only book that provides the answers to the questions retirees are faced with daily. It shows retirees and those planning to retire how to: devise a plan of action for managing their retirement dollars that addresses lifestyle issues, leaving an estate, planning for long-term health care, selling a home, and relocating; manage spending and investments to ensure future security; and grow investment assets to stretch throughout the retirement years.

ISBN: 0-7863-0522-3